Theatre, Performance and Technology

The Development of Scenography in the Twentieth Century

CHRISTOPHER BAUGH

palgrave
macmillan

First published 2005 by
PALGRAVE MACMILLAN
Houndmills, Basingstoke, Hampshire RG21 6XS and
175 Fifth Avenue, New York, N.Y. 10010
Companies and representatives throughout the world

PALGRAVE MACMILLAN is the global academic imprint of the Palgrave
Macmillan division of St. Martin's Press LLC and of Palgrave Macmillan Ltd.
Macmillan® is a registered trademark in the United States, United Kingdom
and other countries. Palgrave is a registered trademark in the European
Union and other countries.

ISBN–13: 978 1–4039–1696–9   hardback
ISBN–10: 1–4039–1696–9   hardback
ISBN–13: 978 1–4039–1697–6   paperback
ISBN–10: 1–4039–1697–7   paperback

This book is printed on paper suitable for recycling and made from fully
managed and sustained forest sources.

A catalogue record for this book is available from the British Library.

Library of Congress Cataloging-in-Publication Data

Baugh, Christopher
   Theatre, performance and technology : the development of scenography in
the twentieth century / Christopher Baugh.
      p. cm. – (Theatre and performance practices)
   Includes bibliographical references and index.
ISBN–13: 978 1–4039–1696–9 (hard.)
ISBN–10: 1–4039–1696–9 (hard.)
ISBN–13: 978 1–4039–1697–6 (pbk.)
ISBN–10: 1–4039–1697–7 (pbk.)
   1. Theaters—Stage-setting and scenery. 2. Theater—Technological
innovations. I. Title. II. Series

PN2091.S8B318 2005
792.02′5–dc22   2005047457

10   9   8   7   6   5   4   3   2   1
14   13   12   11   10   09   08   07   06   05

Printed in China

This book is dedicated to the memory of
Josef Svoboda, 1920–2002
Scenographer

Contents

List of Figures

General Editors' Preface

This series sets out to explore key performance practices encountered in modern and contemporary theatre. Talking to students and scholars in seminar rooms and studios, and to practitioners in rehearsal, it became clear that there were widely used modes of practice that had received very little critical and analytical attention. In response, we offer these critical, research-based studies that draw on international fieldwork to produce fresh insight into a range of performance processes. Authors, who are specialists in their fields, have set each mode of practice in its social, political and aesthetic context. The series charts both a history of the development of modes of performance process and an assessment of their significance in contemporary culture.

Each volume is accessibly written and gives a clear and pithy analysis of the historical and cultural development of a mode of practice. As well as offering readers a sense of the breadth of the field, the authors have also given key examples and performance illustrations. In different ways each book in the series asks readers to look again at processes and practices of theatre-making that seem obvious and self-evident, and to examine why and how they have developed as they have, and what their ideological content is. Ultimately the series aims to ask questions about what are the choices and responsibilities facing performance-makers today?

Graham Ley and Jane Milling

Preface

On Writing Theatre History and My Mother's Button Box

I am grateful to Professor Baz Kershaw, who some while ago urged me to read Jacques Derrida's *Archive Fever*, insisting that it should be essential reading for anyone who wanted to make a history of the theatre and performance. Reading *Archive Fever* with its dissection and reformulation of thinking about history, the archive and the making of archives, made me think about my mother's button box. Until I was about 7 years old, it was one of my favourite toys. It lived in the kitchen sideboard and I would take it to beneath the kitchen table to play. Emptied out onto a newspaper, the pile of buttons gave me hours of pleasure. The box in fact was a circular tin covered in patriotic and union flags and had been made to commemorate the coronation of King George VI. It had been a tin of 'Empire Biscuits' from the Barnsley British Co-operative Society and it had a photograph of Mr G. Willis (President) surrounded by the flags, on the lid. Inside were buttons of every description, shape and colour, a treasure house of disordered, random pleasure – Derrida reminds us of the linguistic correspondence of archive and (an)archy.[1] I used to make patterns with them, inventing games and arranging them according to colour, size, or shape. Sometimes I would look in vain for a three-holed button that I was sure that I had once seen. In the box there were also odd badges – some from chapel anniversary occasions, some from schools, or guide and scout groups – many with odd words and numbers on them like 'monitor', 'valour', 'Centenary 1911' and 'diligence', some bearing evidence of long forgotten associations, missionaries, mothers' unions and bible-reading groups.

At that age, playing with buttons was free, and uncluttered by rules or external requirements. But, of course, my play could not be *really* free, simply because the buttons were not any old buttons. They each had a history. Some were my mother's, some came from her parents, some from distant uncles and aunts and cousins – many had the shape and smell of the past. They had a history of function – buttons are, after all, essentially practical devices holding together night-clothes, blazers, sports clothes, greatcoats, plus-four trousers and Great-Grandma's boots. Some were bound up with distant memory and loss, military buttons of great-uncles, of fusiliers and sappers of the Great War. And of course my play depended very much upon how I felt as I poured over the buttons spread on the kitchen floor – today I'll find all the red buttons; today I'll pile up all the square buttons. My play was anything but free. The desire to make order out of the buttons was in constant confrontation with their histories and meanings.

As artists and scholars trying to make histories of theatre and performance, our desire is to find the 'truth', to somehow 'tell it how it really was'. We hope, as we rummage through the archive(s), to find a new set of buttons – a set of buttons that will make sense of a hitherto unclear past. Perhaps it may be a single fact – the illusive three-holed button – that will now throw everything into relief. Derrida says:

> The first, the *arch-example*, shows us the desire of an admirable historian who wants in sum to be the first archivist, the first to discover the archive, the archaeologist and perhaps the archon of the archive. The first archivist institutes the archive as it should be, that is to say, not only in exhibiting the document but in *establishing* it. He reads it, interprets it, classes it.[2]

Appia, Craig, Meyerhold, Neher, Svoboda (or indeed any artist or topic of our past theatre) present themselves as a huge collection of anarchically assorted 'buttons' – represented by copious writings, images and photographs, letters, documents, and memories. Others who knew or met them have left selected 'buttons' of their own memory for us to arrange. Some will have already been placed into archives, and we need to remember that the arrangements they make in those archives can only be temporary – 'selected letters', memoirs, correspondence, witness and anecdote. There can be no final archive, no definitive arrangement of buttons. We must beware the temptation to try to tell the final truth. John Donne reminds us that an archive, in his instance the Bible, may be so huge that the careful selection of phrases and statements (or buttons) may serve to 'prove' almost anything:

In this thy booke, such will their nothing see,
As in the Bible some can find out Alchimy.[3]

With theatre artists of longevity and stature such as Appia, Craig and Meyerhold, the button boxes are so large that, with careful selection, we can make any number of new archives and play any number of 'games' to match our own inclinations and passions: we can easily prove that Craig hated modern technology, or that he relished the opportunities offered by technology, or that he believed in an autocratic director, or that he believed in an ensemble collaboration of theatre artists. In this way our personal choice of buttons may 'mean' whatever we wish. But it isn't quite so straightforward, because, like those in my mother's box, the buttons are not neutral. We are rarely in the position of the archaeologist who finds an archive that has not already been archived. The archive of material relating to Craig at Eton College in Windsor is beautifully presented. Large leather-bound box files grace the shelves, each with gold-tooled inscriptions of its contents. The contrast between the handsome gilt and leather and the frequently scribbled scraps of letters and notes inside the boxes is marked. A slightly thicker, small file opens to reveal wooden pegs secured in a black velvet frame. On these pegs there are three small puppet heads carved and painted by Craig. Their presentation and their revelation as the box is opened in the archive bestow upon them great value, importance and historical significance. Whereas in truth (perhaps) they may have been carved very quickly; they may have been superseded by others; they may have been over-painted on several occasions; or alternatively, Craig may have considered these puppet heads to be the very finest that he ever made, and they may have enjoyed a place of honour and value in his studio, similar to that of their archive. How are we to form judgements about such buttons, and what games are we to play with them?

Like the very present-tense-ness of playing with buttons, as Derrida reminds us, an archive is not primarily a question of the past:

It is a question of the future, the question of the future itself, the question of a response, of a promise and of a responsibility for tomorrow. The archive: if we want to know what that will have meant, we will only know in times to come.[4]

I have become increasingly aware in writing this book that I have been playing with some old, favourite, well-thumbed buttons. I make no apology for the selection that I have made, and I am aware of the very significant contributions that have been made to twentieth-century scenography and its use of technology by artists who are not represented in this book. I offer these buttons as *an* arrangement, as a display of parallel energies and overlapping ideas that began their game in the last years of the nineteenth century, and are still in play today. These buttons seem to me to represent what *might* have happened. Contributing a new history of theatre and performance must always involve caution, power, and responsibility.

Christopher Baugh
University of Kent

Acknowledgements

My research has been supported by the Arts and Humanities Research Council (then but a mere Board) who awarded me funding under their Research Study Leave scheme in 2004. This extended the period of leave granted to me by the University of Kent and which, together, enabled me to complete the writing of this book.

I am grateful to the galleries, museums, institutes and theatre archives that have treated me with consistent courtesy in responding to my requests for images of productions. In this context Dr Jim Fowler of the V&A Theatre Museum, London, has been remarkably helpful. I want to thank Jean-Guy Lecat for his photograph of the Bouffes du Nord theatre, and Jerzy Gurawski for permission to publish his design for *The Constant Prince*. I am especially grateful to my friend Eric Alexander of the International Federation for Theatre Research who proposed, arranged and accompanied me to Prague in 1999 to meet and talk with Josef Svoboda in his studio. I particularly want to thank Svoboda's daughter, Šárka Hejnová, who has generously allowed me to include illustrations of her father's work.

This book has been a long time in preparation – in my mind, if not on the page. To that end, I am profoundly grateful to all my past students of scenography whose enthusiasm, opinions and questions have served as both inspiration and stimulus over many years.

Introduction

Stage technology, machinery and special effects have always been a part of the experience of theatre and performance. Often they have been used as a means to an end: to shift and illuminate scenery, or to simulate events and actions that could not easily be presented in performance – explosions, catastrophes and meteorology for example. But also technologies have frequently been used as ends in themselves, where the gasp of awe and amazement at their operation has been a significant aspect of the experience of performance. For example, the intense pleasure of the 'now you see it, now you don't' moment as a special effect takes place; the inexplicable transformation of one location to another in the baroque theatre; the flash of 'lightning' and accompanying sound effects when Mephistopheles appears as if by 'magic' on *Walpurgisnacht*, have all been reported as significant moments in the history of theatre and performance. Inevitably therefore during most periods of both occasional and institutional performance, technology has served as an externally presented representation and celebration of human skill and ingenuity.

But complex technologies in performance may also serve as symbols of power and authority, at the simplest where the stage knows or 'owns' something that the spectator does not. More subtly, in the knowledge and ownership of technology there may also dwell the colonial power of the nation, the patriarchal power of monarch, duke and state, the power of the owner of the theatre and its means of presentation. Dramaturgical power and efficacy may also reside in technology; the theatre of Greek antiquity used a *mechane* – a mechanized lifting arm or crane to suspend gods over the concluding action of its tragedy. Their suitably elevated status illustrated their ability to provide dramatic resolution to the drama – hence the *deus ex machina*, 'god out of a machine'. From the mystery and miracle plays of the Middle Ages to the late nineteenth century, technologies have striven to realize the metaphysical truths and beliefs of religions – from the expanding universe of angels suspended in Filipo Brunelleschi's construction in the *duomo* of the cathedral in Florence, to the mythic river maidens of the Rhine in Wagner's operas at the *Festspielhaus* in Bayreuth. The Renaissance very consciously used presentational technologies as framing metaphors for supreme political power. Monarchs, dukes and their favoured courtiers descended effortlessly as performers into the scenic world – often presented miraculously upon a cloud or a seemingly heaven-borne chariot. As servants of the dramaturgy of court spectacle, their appearance served to banish disorder and to bring order and calm to a troubled world through their technology-assisted miraculous appearance (Figure 1).

It is inevitable that there has always been an important link between scientific discoveries, technical developments and their presentation and use within the theatre. For example, the urban place of performance in Renaissance Italy with all its accompanying technologies and modes of presentation formed what Marvin Carlson terms 'the jewel in the casket',[1] the glittering showcase of authority and political

Figure 1   Inigo Jones and William Davenant, *Salmacida Spolia*: the concluding scene ('The Suburbs of a Great City') in which deities descend in clouds to bestow order and peace, 1640 (*The Devonshire Collection, Chatsworth*)

power, set within the palace or castle of Renaissance dukedoms. The seemingly miraculous scenographic and technical abilities of Bernardo Buontalenti or Inigo Jones to rid the Medici Court in Florence or the Court of Charles I of diabolic and politically subversive elements at the mere appearance of the crowned ruler illustrates the potent link between technology and spectacle, ownership and the rights of governing powers.

As power moved from the court and its places of privileged performance towards the market-places, town centres and metropolitan capitals during the late seventeenth and through the eighteenth century and on into the Industrial Revolution at its close, the technologies of theatre became commodified as 'the spectacle', a marketable and highly commercial 'show'. Witnessing spectacle and becoming absorbed, as audience, in the scenic products of technologies developed into a significant theatrical genre. During the 1770s at Drury Lane theatre in London, David Garrick called them simply 'entertainments'. They were a hybrid performance of very little narrative or literary content, but rich in recognizable topography, topical allusion and pictorial and spectacular presentation. Nevertheless, the technology and spectacle retained much of their earlier political power and upheld the dominant ideology of government, since most such entertainments concluded with some form of national apotheosis accompanied by patriotic songs that served to embrace the audience within the theatrical world. These entertainments represented an urban, mercantile spectacle that might be designed, constructed and delivered, away from the direct patronage of governing powers, to any who could pay the price, and the huge theatres of the metropolitan centres of the nineteenth century provided a range of prices that could accommodate all sections of society.

During the nineteenth century, theatre served as something of a showground for new industrial technologies – many encountered the products and inventions of the Industrial Revolution for the first time through the scenography of spectacular theatre. Thomas Drummond invented limelight (published in his *Philosophical Transactions*, 1826) to facilitate accurate trigonometric sightings for the military mapmaker. But the technology of focusing an enriched jet of burning gas upon a piece of lime quickly became public through theatre, and in the angled brilliant beam of light striking the stage from high to one side, offered the engraver and illustrator a potent and enduring image of theatre and performance. The distillation of coal products during the 1830s created aniline dyes that in turn enabled the production of

Noting movement
the introduction
+ of technology))

fabrics of a hitherto unseen brilliance. These excited great public interest through their use in theatre costumes in the 1840s and considerably influenced the new, spectacular *féerie* pantomimes of the Opéra Comique in Paris and of Madame Vestris in London.[2] By the latter half of the nineteenth century, the windows of shops were being transformed, through the rapid exploitation of plate-glass, into proscenium arches framing glittering displays of merchandise that offered tantalizing images of fashion and lifestyle. 'Cup and saucer' plays and society dramas of the period turned the proscenium stage into animated window-displays of furniture and accessories whilst women actors became mannequins for the latest fashions and fabrics. Hydraulic power was first displayed to the public through its use on stage in Paris in the 1860s; and many experienced incandescent electric lamps for the first time through their use in theatre in the 1880s. The spirit of display and of exhibition dominated scenographic language as much as the energy of theatre and showmanship permeated the exhibition hall and the museum.]

The inter-relationship, and indeed interdependence, between dramaturgy and technology is significant. Change in dramatic structure and genre has usually been mirrored by significant technical, architectural (and therefore scenographic) change. The technologies inherent in Italian Renaissance perspective scenery provided a view of the world controllable from the single viewpoint occupied by the ruler of the state. The synchronous translation and re-writing of Roman urban plays during the early sixteenth century was mirrored within the scenic opportunities that developed to present physically ordered and layered visions of urban society. The architectures of the *Teatro Olimpico* in Vicenza (1580), the *Teatro Olimpico* in Sabbioneta (1588) and the *Teatro Farnese* (1618) in Parma each in differing ways established a form of indoor theatre that reflected both the technologies of perspective scenographies and the viewing authority of their patrons.[3]

Similar scenic technologies combined within the architecture of the English Restoration theatre during the late seventeenth century to create a long-lived physical exemplar of the dramaturgy and ethos of plays and of attitudes towards performance. But alongside the excitement of perspective representation and the social needs of theatre patrons there was also the need to accommodate a tradition of acting that had established itself long before the theatrical exploitation of 'Italianate' scenic technology. The English theatre of the late seventeenth century was therefore a tri-partite building that offered, in skilfully designed compromise, a place for the patron, a place for the actor and a place for the scenery. The scenic technology of wooden grooves set upon the stage and suspended above, with sliding shutters supported between them, provided a flexible opportunity to store, and achieve rapid change from within, a stock of scenes.[1] Mirroring the scenic technology in performance, the actors' 'stock' of characters and their detailed 'points' of performance could be scenographically reflected in the theatre, where 'The Stage should be furnished with a competent number of painted scenes sufficient to answer the purpose of all the plays in the stock, in which there is no great variety.'[4]

The skills of the stage machinist and scenic artist during the early nineteenth century were such that their contributions became much more than the provision of apposite 'stock' backgrounds to the action of the late seventeenth century, or the intimate interior locations of the eighteenth-century theatre. The products of technology – the carefully constructed illusions of landscape and historical pageant – could as easily take on the role of protagonist as offer illustrations of the scenes of the drama. Whether at the service of Charles Kean and Shakespeare in his reconstructions of history at the Princess's Theatre of the 1850s, or in a theatrical reconstruction of the Crimean battle of Alma at Astley's Amphitheatre in 1856, scenography and its technologies became leading protagonists in the theatre. The plays of Dion Boucicault were frequently structured around a narrative presentation of event and topographical circumstance that relied upon scenographic presentation and which, inevitably, used the very latest theatrical technologies. The new technologies of gaslight mantles and the electricity of the last decades of the century offered the well-made play the opportunity to explore in detail the furnishings and property-filled world of the domestic interior. The naturalism of Zola, Antoine and Stanislavski chose not to reject out of hand the three-hundred-year-old technologies of perspective scenery. Although impelled towards change through the increase in illumination offered by electricity, they tended towards blending two-dimensional painted surface alongside three-dimensional 'carpentered' scenery to inject what was considered to be a greater degree of theatrical honesty. Strindberg's Preface to *Miss Julie* (1888) calls for real decoration and objects to replace the painted two-dimensional surfaces.[5]

But alongside this almost continuous presence of technologies within places of performance and their effects upon dramaturgy, have been the simultaneous laments of critics, actors and playwrights that the theatre and its audience were beginning to consider scenes and

Figure 2   Large-scale 19th-century popular technological spectacle –
a rocking ship from J.-P. Moynet, *L'envers du théâtre: machines et
décorations* (Paris: Librairie Hachette, 1874)

special effects as more important than the dramatic literature and the work of the actor. Spectacle, as *opsis*, after all, was quite low in Aristotle's list of 'ingredients' that he indicates in the *Poetics* as being proper within the performance of dramatic tragedy.[6] Especially in northern Europe, this authority of antiquity supported a dour Protestant dislike of images, where machinery, devices, simulacra and their associated technologies might be viewed as Catholic and 'Romish'. [The use of sophisticated technology has been most frequently associated with spectacle, and spectacle has been consistently associated with extravagance, waste and courtly indulgence, exemplified by the Stuart court Masque from 1605 to 1641. But in its commercialized and commodified form, in the sensation melodrama of the nineteenth century for example, spectacle is also associated with cheap thrills, visual indulgence and the commercial pandering to an audience who were supposedly too unlettered to follow or understand fine dramatic poetry and diction.] Perhaps also, because of the nature and strength of oral traditions in actor training, there has frequently arisen an atavistic tendency within the theatre that has focused on the primacy of the actor within the act of performance – you may rid the theatre of scene, costume, artificial light and even architecture, but you cannot remove the actor and audience. In this way, theatre histories have frequently presented the actor as being continually challenged and possibly threatened by technology and its associated spectacle. Ben Jonson reflects the fundamental importance of the idea made manifest through the word in the face of the image-making of Inigo Jones and the Stuart Masque, whilst Thomas Shadwell faced the challenges of writing poetic English within the scenographically extravagant Restoration heroic opera. Colley Cibber in his *Apology* (1740) regretted the new technology and architectural spectacle of Sir John Vanbrugh's theatre in the Haymarket of 1702, which made it more suited to spectacle, opera and music, preferring what he considered to have been the more 'actor-friendly', but architecturally more restrained and probably technologically inferior, Drury Lane theatre of 1674.[7] Richard Cumberland's memoirs of 1806 consider the enlarged stages of both the patent theatres of London to have become viewing places of spectacle rather than playhouses for hearing.[8]

But great periods of Western theatre, and indeed major non-Western theatre cultures, have all made performance that represents a complex collaboration and interaction between the living and the inanimate aspects of theatre. The Nō and Kabuki theatres of Japan, the Kathakali of Kerala and the sophisticated dance drama of Bali alongside what we understand of the theatre practices of antiquity and of the Renaissance, all indicate a seamless and complex interaction of image, sound and movement that may not be represented by a neat hierarchy of perceptual importance beginning with the actor at its pinnacle. This reductive account of the operation of performance may pertain in a theatre that is driven by dramatic literature, where the words spoken by the actor represent the first realization of dramatic text, but it is not an inevitable description of the way in which performance and theatre have operated or may operate in future. Technologies may have meanings in and of themselves, and are not simple servants to the mechanistic needs of scenic representation. They are an expression of a relationship with the world and reflect complex human values and beliefs.

Our thinking, our philosophies and modes of expression and understanding of humanity have been frequently governed by current technology and the capabilities of machinery. For example, the Renaissance understanding of the heart as a pumping device coincided with the mechanical development of water-pumping machines. The technologies of framing and placement developed in the late eighteenth century to represent landscape in the theatre conditioned our perception of the real world and, for example, generated the paradox of the landscape gardener, a Capability Brown or a Humphry Repton, using artificial (scenic) means to create a seemingly 'natural' environment. During the nineteenth century, the progressive and materialist science of Humphry Davy, Michael Faraday or James Clark Maxwell generated an understanding of the world that was increasingly expressed with considerable physical certainty.[9] Nineteenth-century science presented a world of toppling mysteries, of a more precise and more tangible understanding of the physical circumstances of existence. This science firmly believed that the application of work, money and experiment would convert the mysteries of the present into credible, tangible certainties of the future. Inevitably, therefore, technologies used in theatre and performance cannot exist in isolation from the larger issues of natural philosophy and science that, since Copernicus and Galileo, have attempted to explain the existence of the world, the behaviour of materials and objects, and of humanity.

The major consideration of this book will be to consider ways in which changes in technology over the last century have been reflected in the search for scenographic identity. Significantly, this search began almost precisely at the point where the material certainty and reality of science was rejected and exploded by revolutionary theories of uncertainty and relativity that shook consciousness and precipitated the culture of modernity. X-rays defied the seeming permanence and opacity of matter, and the view of the world when first seen from the air shattered the dominance of a centre of focus resting on earth, within human limits. Einstein's general theory of relativity of 1905 and its experimental proof during the solar eclipse of 1919 validated and further provoked a rejection of the material certainties of the past, and proposed a limited construction for the future based upon relative function. In this way, there are obvious synergies between the technologies of speed, electricity and construction and the futurism of Marinetti and the design manifesto of the Bauhaus, which gave aesthetic primacy to the relative function of that which was being designed. More recent science, and especially issues of chance and chaos, has continued to provide a store of metaphors and perceptions of relationships that are available to understand the ephemeral and impermanent nature of live performance. We are supported in our consideration and theorization of post-modern and post-dramatic performance by our awareness of and sensitivity to computing terms such as 'software', 'interface', 'multi-media', and 'inter-active'. For example, the inter-active nature of the computer aesthetic gives 'power' to the player of a computer game to freely control point of view and to wander at will around the site of computer performance. The computer 'audience' is not limited to a place and a space designed to accommodate it; it inhabits a place and a space that is specific to the nature of the performed event. Of course, the development of such a computer aesthetic does not in any way account for a pervasive contemporary rejection of formal architectural 'theatre', but it represents an interesting and significant synchronicity.

The over-arching theme of this book will therefore be to examine the inter-relationships between technologies, theatre and performance and the ways in which science has offered, and indeed required, powerful alternatives to traditional modes of narrative and representation. It will explore ways in which these technologies have urged forward and indeed in some cases dominated the development of scenography and, in more recent years, where a conscious rejection of technologies has similarly nurtured new scenographies and performance. I propose to examine the vein of atavism that, in the rejection of elaborated, extravagant and 'rich' forms of the more recent past, has sought inspiration in 'poorness', an artistic strength and purity in ancient and early modern theatre forms – Shakespeare's Globe for example. Many twentieth-century theatre artists have found parallels between a contemporary interest in the material qualities of scenography and an awareness of those qualities believed to have existed in the theatres of antiquity, of pre-Renaissance Europe, in the *commedia dell'arte* and in non-Western performance cultures.

An equally important and revealing theme within the period has been the attempt to integrate the place (the architecture) and the space (the scenographic location within the architecture) to the point in some instances where it is not sensible to separate a discussion of the architecture from a discussion of scenography. The inability of the twentieth century to design a successful theatre building is a significant indication of uncertainty over the function of theatre as much as it is an architectural and scenographic challenge. But running strongly throughout theatrical endeavour and experiment, from the initial rejection of the material realism of the nineteenth century to the present time, and serving as a *leitmotif* of scenographic energy, has been an urgent investigation of the *materials* used to make theatre and performance. A potent issue that unifies the ideas of artists as diverse as Edward Gordon Craig, Vsevelod Meyerhold, Caspar Neher, Jerzy Grotowski, Peter Brook, Josef Svoboda, Robert Wilson and Robert Lepage is a concern for an examination of the 'tools of the trade', the nature and qualities of the materials and technologies with which art may be made. Indeed, the manifestos of laboratories, workshops, schools of theatre, and experimental theatre studios throughout the period frequently isolate this exploration as one of their principal aims. The work of these theatre artists represents, in many ways, a celebration of the 'quiddity' of theatrical performance, the phenomenological actuality of the smells, colours, textures, sounds and movement of performance; in short a celebration of the lived experience of being in the presence of performance. Inevitably, therefore, the art of that compound experience itself becomes the theoretical and experimental focus of the twentieth century. Their conclusions propose an art that is independent of dramatic literature and that will generate artistic self-sufficiency within itself. Moreover, their achievement and their manifestos propose a vision of theatre where there is a seamless and creative interface between theatre, performance and technology.

1 Performing Great Exhibitions

A Nineteenth-century Speciality

'Material realism' would be an appropriate term to describe the basic scenographic language used in the theatre of the nineteenth century. Although it had clear antecedents in the perspective principles and scenic technologies of the Italian Renaissance, material realism as a theatre language may be considered to begin in the late eighteenth century, and can be attributed to new scenographic values instituted by the painter Philippe de Loutherbourg during his short, but extremely influential, period of work at Drury Lane theatre from 1772 to 1780.[1] After he left Drury Lane, he created what was to become a highly successful and influential miniature theatre experience, the *Eidophusikon*, at his home in Lisle Street off Leicester Square. He returned to the theatre once more, to Covent Garden in 1785, to design and to collaborate with John O'Keefe in the production of the spectacular travelogue pantomime *Omai: or, A trip around the world*. Although he wrote little, and certainly nothing that could be thought of as offering a theory of scenography, his practice and its implications for theatre and performance established attitudes and approaches that were to remain in force, effectively, until they were radically questioned and overthrown by artists such as Aurélien-Marie Lugné-Poë at the Théâtre de l'Oeuvre in Paris in 1893, Edward Gordon Craig when he left the London Lyceum Theatre in 1896, Adolphe Appia in his book *La Musique et la Mise en Scène* of 1898, or Vsevelod Meyerhold in the New Studio of the Moscow Art Theatre in 1905–6.[2]

11

The innovation represented by Loutherbourg's work in the late eighteenth century should be seen as initiating not merely a new scenic style with significant technological implications, but also a period of seismic transition in the *functioning* of the theatre. To illustrate something of the extent and significance of this change, the chart in Table 1 contains two columns: on the left there is a listing of attitudes and qualities that may be associated with European theatrical presentation from roughly the middle of the seventeenth century until the closing years of the eighteenth century – that is, until the practice of Loutherbourg. On the right are corresponding qualities that may be associated with European theatrical presentation from the close of the eighteenth century until they were rejected and/or challenged during the early twentieth century. It is obviously important that these implied transitions should be seen as *tendencies* and marks of a developing and changing aesthetic, many of which developed haphazardly and over varying and in some instances considerable, periods of time. For example, it would be true to say that Loutherbourg's scenic practice proposes, or at least indicates, a significant darkening of the auditorium, whereas lighting technology (and ultimately the social and artistic impetus that inspired that technology) did not achieve this until quite late in the nineteenth century. Similarly, many theatres maintained stocks of generic scenes that were in use throughout the nineteenth century, although the preference in the principal theatres may have been for custom-designed and custom-painted scenes. In contrast to this, the architecture of theatre rather rapidly implemented change quite early in the nineteenth century as it enshrined the viewpoint and framing of the proscenium arch as a fundamental quality and determinant of theatrical aesthetic.

The concerns and achievements of individual artists may be examined in the light of this contrasting of attitudes. It would, for example, be possible to think of David Garrick's most significant achievement as an actor as his ability to become so absorbed into character for brief moments, and with such an intensity of presentation, that he was able to temporarily transport his audience. He expanded the socially constructed understanding of acceptable performance for brief moments by *becoming* in some way the character of Hamlet rather than *showing* the character of Hamlet to the audience. His acting therefore may be described as proposing a crossing of the sharply contrasting attitudes indicated in the chart: on Garrick's first appearance in London at Goodman's Fields theatre in 1741, the

Table 1   Changes in European theatrical presentation

c.1650–1800	c.1800–1900
• The actor was raised on a platform in the same architectonic space as the audience – a large forestage, a 'liminal space' set within the auditorium.	• The actor was raised on a platform in a different architectonic space from that of the audience – beyond a framing proscenium arch.
• Costume served as a codified 'trade uniform' of acting with a charade-like indication or emblem of character and historical period.	• Costume was consciously researched and designed, and tried to fully realize the dramatic character and the historical period.
• Actors and audience shared much of the same light that illuminated the entire theatre.	• Actors occupied a brightly illuminated acting space with a corresponding reduction in light on the audience – the darkened auditorium became a reality by the last decades of the nineteenth century.
• The audience shared an intense awareness of its individuality and of itself as a group.	• The audience was invited to 'lose' its individuality in the act of public spectatorship.
• The actors had an intense awareness of the presence of the audience.	• Actors had less awareness of the audience – Stanislavski urged his actors to perform as though the audience were not present.
• Scenery was drawn from stock – used over and over again – painted by artists as generic scenes.	• Scenery was custom designed and made for the production.
• Scenery was considered as a capital investment. Italian artists (the Bibienas, Cipriani, Servandoni) toured Europe supplying theatres.[3]	• Scenery was increasingly considered to be disposable when the production was removed from the repertory.
• Technology was on display and enjoyed as part of the spectacle – scene changes were visible.	• Technology was still enjoyed as part of the spectacle, but was hidden behind architecture and scenic illusion – scene changes were hidden.
• Scenery served as an apposite, decorative background to the performance – it did not provide an embracing, physical environment for the dramatic action.	• Scenery aimed to provide an embracing environment for the dramatic action.
• The mode of theatre tended towards the presentational and rhetorical; the audience shared in the experience of performance; they admired, they wept, they laughed, and they applauded the display of consummate skill.	• The mode of theatre tended towards the representational; the audience witnessed a harmoniously conceived 'other' world; they were invited to be transported; to become absorbed, anonymous spectators.

leading actor of the previous generation, James Quin, stated: 'If this young fellow be right, then I and all the other actors are wrong.'

This change in attitudes is manifest in scenography and its pendant technologies. Scenery and costume that traditionally *showed* the audience an emblem of a location, character or historical period, now began the attempt to persuade an audience that they were observing an actuality, a simulacrum, indeed in some cases to try to convince the audience that they were looking at the thing itself. When Louther-bourg negotiated his job description by writing to Garrick in 1772, he had little doubt about his own abilities and the radical extent of his proposed changes:

> I must invent scenery, which will have the effect of creating a new sensation upon the public. To this end, I must change the manner of lighting the stage so as to serve the effects of the painting. I must also change the method of pulling off simultaneously an entire scene – and generally, alter such machinery as might be necessary to the aspiration of my talents. ... Furthermore, I must make a small model of the settings and everything that is needed, to scale, painted and detailed so as to put the working painters and machinists and others on the right track by being able to faithfully copy my models. ... I shall draw in colour the costumes for the actors and the dancers. I must discuss my work with the composer and the ballet-master.

Figure 3   The 18th-century theatre of rhetoric: a riot at *Artaxerxes*, Covent Garden Theatre, 1763 (*London, V&A Theatre Museum*).

... If you were to give me full authority over all of your workers, I would use this trust as an honest man and treat your interests as my own.[4]

Loutherbourg's demand for complete aesthetic control over all visual aspects of production, and his belief in the centrality of the designer's place within the production company, closely echoed the work of Jean-Georges Noverre who wrote *Lettres sur la danse et les ballets* (Lyons, 1769) and whose theory reached beyond matters of choreography: 'Let the poets come down from their sacred mount: let each artist in his department at the opera, act in concert, and give each their mutual assistance.'[5]

Demands and exhortations such as these give a clear indication of the future values and attitudes of nineteenth-century theatre. Its implementation enabled the aesthetic unity and pictorial harmony that would eventually integrate the costumed actor within the scenic environment that was to be established on the stage. In the meantime, during the late eighteenth century, the actor, way down on the forestage wearing an increasingly accurate and detailed costume, was beginning to be something of a pictorial anomaly within the architectural and social context of the contemporary theatre. The desire, therefore, to remove the actors from their forestage set within the audience space and to locate them further up stage, placing them within the scenic frame, was a significant factor that influenced change in the architecture of theatre in the early years of the nineteenth century. Changing acting styles, new scenic techniques and technologies, new approaches to stage costume and authenticity, and correspondingly new architectural solutions, all centred upon attempts to find ways of absorbing the audience into the fictional world offered by the theatre. Theories of absorption of the spectator into the mental 'other' worlds generated by art are not, of course, uniquely theatrical in their application, and indeed, they are reflected in all art forms and provide a foundation of romantic activity throughout Europe.

In Britain, Loutherbourg's reputation and especially the *Eidophusikon* model theatre, which long outlived his full-scale theatre work, served as a manual of aspirations and techniques for the generation of scene painters of the 1820s and 1830s such as Clarkson-Stanfield, David Roberts and the Grieve family of artists.[6] It is likely that his inability to implement fully his scenic aspirations at Drury Lane was a significant factor in his creation of the miniature theatre, over which he had complete artistic control. For example, Loutherbourg had ambitions for lighting the stage and representing meteorology that went far beyond illumination. Newspaper reviews and audience response indicate that he wanted lighting to establish mood and to represent changes in atmosphere, but this almost certainly exceeded the capability of the lighting equipment available, whereas the desired effects could be created on the miniature stage at his home – possibly experimenting with the Argand lamp, which used a tubular wick in place of a flat ribbon.[7]

Outside Britain, where many theatres enjoyed royal and courtly patronage, considerable energy and money were spent in developing stage machinery that enabled the individual elements of a scene to be combined so that the manipulation of a single winch could bring about a unified transformation of the entire scene. The essence of such technology involved the mounting of individual wing flats onto below-stage wheeled trucks, rather than having them running in surface-mounted grooves, which required corresponding upper grooves to support the flats. All the trucks might then be linked with ropes to 'drum and shaft' winches below stage and to similar machinery for the cloud and ceiling shutters in the flies above the stage. Although some significant changes were undertaken at Drury Lane when Loutherbourg arrived, there is no indication that such major infra-structural change was carried out. The model stage, however, could more easily present the benefits of such new technology. Writing his reminiscences some thirty years later, William Henry Pyne reports that the painter Gainsborough was so entranced by the effects of the *Eidophusikon* that for some time he talked of little else and 'himself a great experimentalist, could not fail to admire scenes wrought to such perfection by the aid of so many collateral inventions'.[8] Pyne was especially impressed with the extensive use of sound effects, the subtlety of which would have been lost in the full-size theatre, and credits Loutherbourg with the introduction of a new art, the 'picturesque of sound'. The *Eidophusikon*, therefore, seems to have enabled the aesthetic harmony, the controlled integration of visual and aural elements, that was implied in Loutherbourg's letters to Garrick but which may well have been unachievable at Drury Lane theatre.

The implications for theatre management and for the processes of production that were embedded in Loutherbourg's proposals were to underpin the developing concept of production and the emergence of the director during the nineteenth century: from the Kemble family's archaeologically accurate reconstructions at Covent Garden Theatre in the early years of the century to the careful precision of Henry Irving's pictorialism at the Lyceum Theatre and, throughout Europe, to the highly influential work of the touring Saxe-Meiningen company and its director Ludwig Chronegk during the 1880s.[9] For example, the ambitions of Alexandre Dumas, père, at the Théâtre Historique in Paris in the 1840s, or Charles Kean at the Princess's Theatre in London in the 1850s, may be understood as being focused attempts to integrate all personnel and all aspects of production in order to create a credible spectacle of another world, a transport into a coherent, harmoniously designed past where the very considerable technologies that the theatres utilized would be hidden from the immediate consciousness of the audience.[10]

For most of the nineteenth century, there seems to have existed very little doubt as to the overall direction and aesthetic aim of the theatrical process (although there was frequent debate and doubt as to what might practically be achieved). The period increasingly believed in the ability of the new technologies of the scientific and industrial revolution to offer ways whereby human experience might be converted into physical reality – to 'realize' the essence of human experience in theatrical form.[11] More widely, the century's pursuit of 'realism' and 'verisimilitude' found its progress and focus through its commitment to scientific experiment. Michael Bell suggests:

> Throughout much of the nineteenth century natural science had been the paradigmatic form of truth statement; as was evident in the way the fiction of the period constantly modelled itself, whether literally or metaphorically, on science. Zola's naturalism, theorized in The *Experimental Novel* (1880), was the culminating example.[12]

The scenographic implication of this, and its impact upon the overall functioning of the theatre, was identified long before Zola, when the mid-century Examiner of Plays, William Bodham Donne, summarized the totality and effects of this concern with the visual and its material realization: 'To touch our emotions,' he explained, 'we need not the imaginatively true, but the physically real. Everything must be embodied for us in palpable form [and] all must be made palpable to sight, no less than to feeling.' He concludes with some regret that the spectators' lack of imagination 'affects equally both those who enact and those who construct the scene.'[13]

The dominant nineteenth-century ethos of the 'progress' of civilization suggested and supported the inevitability of scientific discoveries and their consequent technologies. Great exhibitions (and huge metropolitan department stores by the end of the century) served as benchmark displays of achievement and nationalistic celebration, and the public awareness of the progress of invention (such as the railway and other forms of mechanized transport and engineering) seemed to assert that if you met with failure today, new scientific discovery and new technologies would lead inexorably to success tomorrow. Throughout the nineteenth century, scientific practice and repeatable experiment de-mystified the physics of heat and light, and refined Newton's laws of movement. The qualities and behaviours of electricity, magnetism and optics were understood and established within mathematically verifiable equations. Trust in the biblical account and religious faiths were challenged as the longevity of the earth was given scientific credibility, geology as a science was invented and, most significantly, a scientific and rational (if not altogether palatable to its first audience) account of the origin and development of *Homo sapiens* was articulated.

It is within this optimistic, progressive, and frequently aggressive context of the rational progress of civilization that the attitudes expressed in the memoirs and handbooks of theatre artists such as Jean-Pierre Moynet (*L'Envers du théâtre: machines et décorations*, Paris, 1873), Frederick Lloyds (*Scene Painting*, London, 1875) and Georges Moynet (*Trucs et décors*, Paris, 1895) were articulated. Whilst generally displaying considerable pride in what had been achieved and how it had been realized on stage, the over-riding assumption for the future was one of an almost breathless excitement at what the theatre might achieve. These authors perceived the stage as a significant beneficiary and as an exhibitor of the very latest technology. The business of making theatre was understood to have become an increasingly industrialized, institutionalized and mechanized operation. Hence, within the architecture of theatre during the latter quarter of the century, there was a movement towards large, more sophisticated stage houses facilitated by steel technology that allowed the flies and the below-stage spaces to become highly mechanized, and there was inevitably a concomitant growth in the numbers and significance of the stage machinists and technicians. Mass-produced components of iron and steel – beams, plates, hinges and brackets, for example – enabled designers and stage technicians to bridge gaps that timber structures could not achieve; to swing, flip and pivot large scenic units that could, if need be, support significant numbers of actors. The tradition of receding wing flats of timber and

Figure 4   Water nymphs rising from the depths, from J.-P. Moynet, *L'envers du théâtre: machines et décorations* (Paris: Librairie Hachette, 1874).

canvas that were linked with suspended 'cloudings' and backed by shutters or a backcloth had been an effective and elegant system that had defined scenic technology (and therefore theatre architecture) since late in the Renaissance. But these two-dimensional painted, flat scenic components (and the timber stage that stored and manipulated them) were now augmented by three-dimensional, fully built-up scenic 'practicables' that employed new, sophisticated technologies. Within the three-dimensionality of these scenes were scenic opportunities and challenges that could no longer fit comfortably within the architectural 'two-dimensional' technology of the traditional stage. The *asphaleia* system incorporated into the Budapest Opera House in 1881, and vigorously advocated elsewhere in Europe, proposed a fully mechanized stage supported, in sections, on hydraulic platforms that could enable entire scenes, consisting of three-dimensional 'practicables', to be raised or lowered from beneath the stage. The additional *asphaleia* proposals consisted of embracing the stage with a curved cyclorama, and the ability to suspend scenery as and where desired, while the hydraulic lifts and the subsequent electric stage bridges

Figure 5 Interior of the Bayreuth *Festspielhaus*, 1876 (*Festpielhaus Bayreuth Bildarchiv*)

collectively pronounced the demise of the systematic codification of the scenic world into grooves, and their flat, sliding shutters.

But inevitably the poetic and the metaphoric then, as now, resisted transliteration into physical form, and inevitably also technology all too frequently failed to offer an artistically acceptable solution. Although few could offer radical alternatives, there was considerable dissatisfaction expressed with what appeared to be an inevitable commitment of the theatre to ever more scenic expansion. Richard Wagner spared no expense in delivering the most technologically advanced auditorium and stage to present his music dramas. The *Festspielhaus* at Bayreuth (1876) was a revolutionary architectural solution that removed galleries and provided a unified auditorium offering an unencumbered 'spectatory' to experience and to become absorbed in the 'other' world created by the very latest technology on the stage. Wagner carefully considered the question of absorption and realized that the framing of the image was of crucial importance – on the one hand to compose and to delineate, whilst on the other to engage and embrace. The *Practical Magazine* reports in 1874:

> In front of the orchestral space the architect devised a second proscenium, the effect of which will be, in its relation to the proscenium proper, to produce the illusion of an apparent further removal from the scene. The effect will be that the audience, though fancying the scene to be far removed, will nevertheless perceive it with the clearness of immediate vicinity; and then a further illusion will be produced that the persons on the scene will appear in increased size, in superhuman form.[14]

However, nineteenth-century theatrical sensibilities were committed to painting and its corresponding pictorial aesthetic and composition, and Wagner employed the finest painters he could attract, encouraging meticulous and detailed scenic research. Nevertheless, his exasperation was acute, for example, at the inability of designer Max Brückner and the finest scene painters and machinists to adequately 'realize' the chapel of the Holy Grail on stage for his production of *Parsifal* in 1882. All he achieved was a splendid painted peepshow – a kind of *Baedeker* guidebook to accompany a Thomas Cook's tour of the Baptistry in Sienna, which served as Brückner's model. Referring to the below-stage orchestra that he had incorporated into the theatre at Bayreuth, he said: 'having invented the invisible orchestra, I now wish I could invent the invisible stage!'[15]

Percy Fitzgerald wrote *The World Behind the Scenes* (1881) as a passionate theatregoer rather than as a practising theatre artist, and

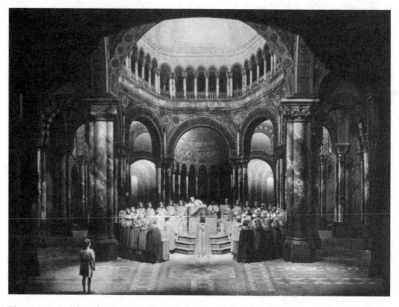

Figure 6   Richard Wagner, *Parsifal*, Bayreuth *Festpielhaus*, 1882
(*Festpielhaus Bayreuth Bildarchiv*)

he welcomed the structural development that culminated in the
concept of theatre as a 'window on the world' becoming a physical
reality. He applauded its architectural achievement in C. J. Phipps's
reconstruction of the Haymarket Theatre in 1880, where '[a] rich and
elaborate gold border, about two feet broad, after the pattern of a
picture frame, is continued all round the proscenium, and carried even
below the actors' feet'. The result, he claimed, is increased illusion,
since 'the actors seem cut off from the domain of prose; there is no
borderland or platform in front; and, stranger still, the whole has the
air of a picture projected on a surface'.[16] This was a significant and
timely choice of final image since the Lumière brothers would shortly
achieve such a 'projection' in their *cinématographe* in 1896. None the
less, Fitzgerald expressed considerable doubts about the extent to
which his contemporary theatre was embracing new technology and,
more significantly, he identified what proved to become a dangerous
quality of self-destruction within the overall ambition of theatre:

The mistake in modern scenery is the attempt to combine the hostile
elements of pictorial and artificial distance, shadows, &c., with *real* effects

of distance. Each must necessarily destroy the effect of the other. A real chair will make a painted chair look flat and poor, while the painted chair will make the real one look dull and prosy. To imitate real objects by the agency of colours and painting requires a flat surface; therefore, constructed set pieces, retiring at right or acute angles to the footlights, are false in principle.[17]

The incidence of this 'mistake' in scenic expression that Fitzgerald identified could easily become a tyrant – especially to the manager of a small theatre. Squire Bancroft's Prince of Wales's theatre was small, and the programme note for *The Merchant of Venice* in 1875 suggested that grand-scale scenic illustration had to be rejected in favour of William Godwin and George Gordon's more precisely observed architectural detail. Bancroft and Gordon undertook a research trip to Venice, where: 'in the Palace of the Doges we saw at once that the Sala della Bussola ... was the only one capable of realization within our limited space; and this room we resolved should be accurately reproduced for the trial'. Ominously for the future of this scenic approach, however, Bancroft reports in *The Times* (19 April 1875):

> Mr. Gordon ... devoted months of labour to the scenery, which was very realistic; elaborate capitals of enormous weight, absolute reproductions of those which crown the pillars of the colonnade of the Doge's palace, were cast in plaster, causing part of the wall to be cut away to find room for them to be moved, by means of trucks, on and off the tiny stage.

Such a scenic approach was further threatened by rapidly developing technologies of illumination. Brilliant light generated by an arc of electricity sparking between carbon rods had been used in the theatre since the 1860s. The considerable direct current needed to do this effectively was initially provided by a large number of batteries connected in series and stored in large basement rooms below the stage. However, although the light was brilliant, its duration was short and this method tended therefore to be used for special effects such as moonlight, a flash of lightning, a sunrise effect, or for mysterious special effects in pantomimes and *féeries*. When dynamo-generated electricity and lighting by incandescent lamps was intro-duced into the Savoy theatre in London in 1881, it was hailed as a triumph by the inevitably partisan *Engineering* of 3 March 1882:

> In an artistic and scenic point of view nothing could be more completely successful than the present lighting of the Savoy Theatre. The illumination

is brilliant without being dazzling, and while being slightly whiter than gas, the accusation of "ghastliness", so often urged against the light of the electric arc, can in no way be applied. In addition to this the light is absolutely steady, and thanks to the enterprise of Mr. D'Oyly Carte, it is now possible for the first time in the history of the modern theatre to sit for a whole evening and enjoy a dramatic performance in a cool and pure atmosphere.

The gas industry retaliated quickly and by 1885 had developed the gas mantle. This was a beehive-shaped mesh of knitted thread impregnated with lime that, in miniature, converted the naked gas flame into, in effect, a lime-light. Nevertheless, as the *Engineering* report indicates, the pressure to achieve audience comfort, convenience and, above all, the safety that electricity provided ensured that electric technology was rapidly introduced (supported by licensing regulation in some cities in Europe), so that by the end of the century gas lighting served in most theatres merely as supplementary or stand-by lighting in corridors and passages.

In spite of the praise lavished by such reports as that in *Engineering*, early incandescent lamps offered a blunt and, because they were used in very large quantities, a rather garish illumination of the stage. As with the introduction of any new technology, it was scarcely within the thoughts of its inventors and first users to offer the invention at anything less than its full potential – why develop a new technology that can achieve a significant improvement only to operate it at well below its full capabilities? 'Never was a stage more brightly lit', 'the entire stage illuminated by the light of over 500 incandescent lights' reflects the tone of contemporary stage advertising. Even were this enthusiasm for the technology to be resisted, effective dimming was not achievable until early in the next century. Although destined to be quickly outmoded, gas lighting did have the significant advantage of over half a century of experiment with dimming, blending and the colouring of light. The lighting of the nineteenth-century painted scene required an intimate artistic collaboration between the gas technician and the painter to blend the real shadow with the painted ones on canvas, and to complete the overall pictorial composition. Moynet refers to the scene painter as having the principal responsibility for lighting and says that the painter should be responsible for marking on the back of painted canvases the kind of lighting and the number of lights that were to be used.[18] So although he was an advanced and sophisticated stage director in so many ways, it is probably not surprising that Henry Irving chose to reject the complete installation of electric stage lighting at the Lyceum Theatre during his management. At the heart of his pictorialism was a consideration of the entire stage as a scenographic canvas. Its lighting represented a major way of visually unifying and harmonizing the disparate elements of painted scene, three-dimensional scene, meticulously selected properties and furnishings and, of course, the carefully costumed actor. Indeed, a common comment on Irving's stage pictures was that they resembled the composition of easel paintings being brought to life in the theatre.

Although sophisticated and careful lighting with gas may have extended the life of the essentially painted perspective scene, the introduction of electric lighting from the 1880s ultimately served to expose the inherent artificiality of both the carpentered and painted stage forms – to make the two-dimensional look even more two-dimensional in contrast to its three-dimensional scenic partners, and to cause the illusion of the painted canvas surface to appear as rather tawdry artifice. No scene painter could ever paint the illusion of a shadow that was as dark as the shadow created by the absence of light. Upon a stage that was lit by the gentle light of oil and the relatively soft light of gas, Fitzgerald argued, the reality of the three-dimensional actor could blend comfortably within a scenic environment of skilfully painted, two-dimensional surfaces. But maintaining the balance between the light which fell upon the actors and that upon the scenes was critical, and the fundamental brightness of electric lighting served to seriously disturb and expose this fragile relationship (Figures 7 and 8).

The theatre responded to this challenge by throwing even more technology into the gap of representational credibility introduced by electricity, and invested in three-dimensional structures that could withstand illumination by bright lights without seeming false. But the architecture of the theatre and the stage house was planned and constructed for the management of two-dimensional scenery. In spite of recent technical innovation, the stage itself still consisted of a systematic arrangement of grooves, traps, sloats (long, thin traps traversing the width of the stage, which allowed ground-rows to rise from beneath the stage) and grid-lines that all ran parallel to the front of the stage. All were designed to hold, store and shift two-dimensional pieces of painted timber-framed canvas. The three-dimensional 'practical' units employed by Bancroft and regretted by Fitzgerald clogged this system: they ignored the traps and sloats and traversed the grid-lines; they were heavy and needed extensive

Figure 7 *Midsummer Night's Dream*, 1900, Beerbohm Tree, Her Majesty's Theatre, London – 'You can't see the Shakespeare woods for the Beerbohm Trees', George Bernard Shaw, *The Sketch*, 7 February 1900 (*London, V&A Theatre Museum*)

Figure 8 Conflict between painted and built scenic detail: *Much Ado About Nothing*, 1895, St James Theatre, London (*London, V&A Theatre Museum*)

handling, they could not be easily stored in the flies or below stage, and scene-changes became cumbersome and long. The brighter the stage lighting, the more the painted scene looked false, and the more the theatre responded by ever more intricately carpentered architectural detail and the introduction of real properties and furnishings. Plays (especially those of Shakespeare) became heavily cut and re-ordered, sometimes serving as little more than supporting narrative for ever more spectacular tableaux. Beerbohm Tree, managing Her Majesty's Theatre with less taste and true pictorial sense than Irving, resorted to extravagant and extensive detail – 'You can't see the Shakespeare woods for the Beerbohm Trees' quipped George Bernard Shaw on Tree's production of *A Midsummer Nights Dream*, in January 1901.

Of course, painted scenes in their use of perspective had always contained within them the seeds of their ultimate artistic failure and destruction. The earliest Italian scenic artists warned that close proximity between the reality of the human actor and the painted surface ought not to be allowed. The painted palaces, temples, mountains and forests placed up stage would instantly lose their power should the actor stray too close. While scenery spoke an emblematic language of suggestion and decoration, and the dramatic action was placed down stage, the painted scene gave an atmosphere that provided an aesthetic distance for the rhetoric of the actor and celebrated the fundamental artifice of theatre. The actor might *show* the audience the rage of King Lear or the love of Juliet, whilst the corresponding scene typified and indicated the *kind* of location. But neither actor nor scene would pretend to so identify with the emotion, or the place, that they might transport the audience into belief in a non-existent reality. Fitzgerald understood the extent of the loss in 1881 when he said that the 'old' system offered 'typical scenes of a general character, such as: "a street", "a forest", serving nearly every piece', whereas, he said, '[t]he modern fashion ... loses itself in an extravagance of details which must be arbitrarily selected, as all the details in real life *could never be brought on a stage at once*'. He urged his contemporary theatre to believe that the '"understanding of a leg of mutton in its quidity [*sic*]," should be the rule as applied to scenery: a logical generalisation of the leading features is all that should be attempted'.[19] Precipitated, therefore, by a blaze of electric light, the aesthetic grammar, syntax and functional 'quiddity' of this three-hundred-year-old theatrical and scenographic language collapsed.

Fitzgerald's concerns were for the maintenance of a scenographic propriety, which he believed should be achieved by a more
rigid adherence to traditional forms: a rejection of new mechanical
technologies and a (nostalgic) return to simplicity. Others shared
some of Fitzgerald's concern with 'new' techniques of stage realism
and cautioned us about the care needed with such slippery terms as
'realism' and 'naturalism'. W. J. Lawrence, one of the earliest scenic
historians, argued in his 'Realism on the Stage: How Far Permissible?'
in 1891:

> Realism is a grateful auxiliary so long as it leaves the imagination
> unshackled, and remains subservient to the play of action. We must draw
> the line sharply where it ceases to assimilate with its surroundings, where it
> inclines to become of itself quite uncontrollable. Illusion is the aim of Art,
> and Realism is permissible so far as it aids that aim. When Illusion is thrust
> on one side, Realism, even when reigning in its stead, has not the slightest
> right of existence.[20]

But alongside the promoters of scenographic change made possible by
new technologies there were other, far-reaching forms of artistic
rejection that exposed the problems created by such technologies; and
this rejection spread throughout Europe. A majority of those who
rejected the language of the stage did so in the name of a greater truth
and 'reality'; for many this was the desire for a physical and emotional
truth that the current theatre of the late nineteenth century did not
provide. It may, of course, be argued that every phase of change in
theatrical presentation has been urged forward by a claim for greater
'realism' – a greater truth to life. Every new actor who has burst
upon the stage to great acclaim, has done so on the grounds of
being more 'true to life', more 'real' than their predecessors. At this
point in the history of performance, when there was a millennial
frenzy of artistic rejections and manifestos for change, we should
treat with care a 'Darwinian' view of theatre history that implies
a progressive movement towards enlightenment, a true-to-life, more
realistic future proceeding from a primitive, untrue-to-life, and artificial past. Stage 'reality' is so self-evidently and clearly relative, and
theatre is such a complex social construct, reflected in the codified
actions of both actors and scenes, that such making of a history of
theatre is less than useful. Painted perspective scenery, artificial and
conventional as it was, could, for example, very effectively represent
and serve as performed metaphors for important qualities within a

hierarchical, structured society. Scenes could show that some characters were more important than others; they could reflect and provide a frame for important social and philosophical difference through painted size of representation, and in this way be very accurately true to the life at, for example, the court of the Medicis or of the Stuart monarchy.

During the last decade of the century, a circuit of small, independent and experimental theatres sprang up to satisfy those who sought a different material 'reality' in the theatre. In some cases these theatres and companies represented acts of rejection of the aesthetic values and scenography of mainstream theatre, but most were established because the mainstream theatre, and the society that it reflected, rejected the language, morality and structure of the new dramatic literature that these theatres wanted to present. André Antoine opened his Théâtre Libre in Paris in 1887; Otto Brahm created Die Freie Bühne in Berlin in 1889; J. T. Grein opened The Independent Theatre in London in 1891; W. B. Yeats co-founded the Irish National Theatre Society, which served as the basis for the creation of the Abbey Theatre in Dublin in 1898; and Konstantin Stanislavski co-founded the Moscow Art Theatre in 1897. Within this network of alternative venues, however, stagecraft and technology were rarely able to match the ambitions of the artists and provide the kind of physical reality on stage that their playwrights believed to be necessary. Without major financial investment, the theatre buildings were usually inappropriate for theatrical experiment and generally had inadequate scenic or electrical resources. Furthermore, although the ambition was high, technical skills were generally low and, in many instances, both the technicians and the actors were amateur. John Stokes notes that the ambition to create a theatre that permitted socially relevant new writing was easier to accommodate than one that aimed to overturn existing scenographic values: 'the staging of Independent Theatre productions attracted almost no attention at all: the play and, to a much lesser extent, the acting was the thing ... [a transition] from the theatre as "movement" or as "picture" towards the theatre as "literature"'.[21]

Nevertheless, the attempts by these companies to turn the theatre into a forensically accurate window upon the real world, whilst being generally considered as representing the beginning of modern drama, may also be thought of as an additional example of nineteenth-century progressive science. In his founding statements on naturalism, Emile Zola used the language of science to articulate his attitude towards artistic function, regretting the tardiness of the drama in rising to the challenge of rational analysis:

> It seems impossible that the movement of inquiry and analysis, which is precisely the movement of the nineteenth century, can have revolutionised all the sciences and arts and left dramatic art to one side, as if isolated. The natural sciences date from the end of the last century; chemistry and physics are less than a hundred years old; history and criticism have been renovated ... an entire world has arisen; it has sent us back to the study of documents, to experience, made us realise that to start afresh we must take things back to the beginning, become familiar with man and nature, verify what is. Thenceforward, the great naturalist school, which has spread secretly, irrevocably, often making its way in darkness but always advancing, can finally come out triumphantly into the light of day. ... An irresistible current carries our society towards the study of reality.[22]

Zola saw the artist of the future as a forensic pathologist who experimentally dissects society in order to anatomize it. He articulated the powerful idea that showing (exposing) a reality must precipitate social and political change – much as investigative journalism is considered in our own day. But to do this scenographically needed as much skilful artifice, and ultimately a falseness that was equal to that being rejected on the commercial, mainstream stage. Even using the actuality of real materials (Stanislavski's barrow loads of autumn leaves strewn on the stage for his production of *Uncle Vanya* in 1899) could never communicate a reality when presented within the structural artificiality of a stage scene that was witnessed in public by an audience. This early naturalist approach may therefore be understood as one of greater integrity and truth to nature *within* the prevailing scenographic language, rather than its outright rejection. None the less, the political ambition of Zola as the 'investigative journalist' of art may rightly be used to identify the beginning of a new theatre and its dramatic literature, and serve also to identify a particular and long-lasting quality of rejection of the values and methods of nineteenth-century theatre. Indeed, it still finds a place within the ambitions of some theatre and performance of the twenty-first century: the belief that in attempting to show a greater reality – putting the 'real thing' on stage – the theatre might somehow shock an audience into the understanding of a greater truth.

Although it is interesting to examine the milestones within this movement – real door-knobs instead of painted ones, real cooking utensils on real shelves, real enclosed rooms as settings (although still with an absent fourth wall), real furniture, costumes and properties – probably the major contribution to making a history of the development of scenography should be seen in its formal rejection of a systematic and unified perception of stage technology: a technology that converted the visual experience of the world into a codified collection of scenic apparatus – the backcloth, the wings, the borders and the ground-rows. This abandoning of system by the early avant-garde was further precipitated by the rejection on the part of the mainstream theatre of much of the new dramatic literature, and the need, therefore, for the naturalist movement to create stages and performances in non-theatre spaces, or at least in small, technologically unsophisticated theatre clubs. From the point of view of a designer therefore, rather than asking 'What shall we paint on the wings and the back-drops, and what shall we hang in the flies?' the issue became one of questioning the very existence of, or need for, a system of wings, back-drops and flies. Within this environment of production, scenography rapidly found ways to become more of an artistic *partner* within theatre-making, as opposed to simply playing a formulaic role of interpretation. The need for the circuit of small, experimental, little theatres on the part of naturalist artists therefore created an infrastructure of experiment that was to rapidly enable the emergence of a wide range of alternative and divergent scenographies. Following very quickly in the wake of the initial naturalistic experiments of Antoine, Brahm and Stanislavski, a significant few chose a degree of rejection that goes far beyond the plea for the real rather than the painted, and seems to represent a wholesale rejection of the entire scenic language and its accompanying technology. The possibility of making theatre outside the mainstream institutions, of creating experimental theatre spaces that were not controlled by state censor or audience expectation, generated an explosion of alternative approaches to theatre and, inevitably, to its scenography.

Early in 1896, Auguste and Louis Lumière presented their exhibition of moving pictures throughout Europe – the *cinématographe*. There is an historical 'niceness' in seeing projected moving photography as offering the ultimate solution to the late nineteenth-century aesthetic problem of theatre and its scenographic technology: that, with the alleged gasp of shock as the flickering image, upon the screen, of a railway train moved across the projected tracks towards the audience, the ambition of Loutherbourg for involvement and absorption had finally been achieved. The new technology of the camera, for taking moving photographs, and of the projector may be thought of as a more economic and – given the many attempts to portray train crashes and disasters on stage – timely replacement for the increasingly cumbersome and 'well-upholstered' stage. In its earliest manifestations, however, it is probably truer to say that the moving pictures did not present any threat whatsoever to the established theatre. The new technology of the *cinématographe* was simply the latest (and possibly the last) manifestation of the material realist technology of the nineteenth century with its commitment to the imitation and impersonation of the real world. In this context, it rightly took its place within the theatre building and served as yet another 'special effect' and attraction within the entertainment of the music hall and variety theatre. Nevertheless, its rapid development into a major form of entertainment and putative art form shortly before 1914 served as an additional encouragement to those who sought a more complete and more thoroughgoing rejection of theatre and its scenographic values, and looked for their replacement with new forms of performance and theatre art.

Notwithstanding, the values and attitudes initiated by Louther-bourg and his fellow artists were remarkably invasive and powerful – indeed they still occupy a significant place within much contemporary scenographic theory and practice. A powerful and distinctly unifying feature amongst the disparate European avant-garde of the twentieth century has been an assertive, and occasionally violent, rejection of the values of the theatre and scenography of the nineteenth century. For example, our interest in Brecht's re-functioning of theatre focuses in considerable part on distinctions that are very similar to those that were described to explain changes in attitude between the rhetorical and emblematic stage of the eighteenth century, and the presenta-tional and descriptive stage of the nineteenth century. Although it is understandable that Brecht selected Aristotle in his articulation of the functioning of theatre as the 'villain' within his theory, a significant argument could be established for suggesting that Loutherbourg and his fellow workers throughout the beginnings of Romanticism in Europe could equally represent the focus of his antipathy. The revolution in acting brought about at that time may be thought of as Garrick's rejection of earlier attitudes to acting – probably close in many ways to Brecht's concept of the *gestus*; whereas the decision by Brecht's scenographer Caspar Neher to deny the appropriateness of the title *Bühnenbildner* (literally 'stage-picture maker') expressed the rejection of the pictorialism of the painter as scenographer in favour of the emblematic – the *gestic* stage construction reflected in earlier eighteenth-century practice, and indicated by Neher's preferred title of *Bühnenbauer*.

This chapter has aimed to represent more than an introduction or preface; it has tried to present an ontology of the attitudes and scenographic values that have so uniformly presented themselves as a focus for rejection by the twentieth century. That they are still clearly understood, and, in only barely modified forms, still experienced in theatre and performance, indicates both their potency and the need for such a prologue in a discussion of scenography and technology within performance over the last hundred years.

2 Rejection of the Past
A Modern Mode of Thought

[T]he avant-garde as a whole seems united primarily in terms of what they are against: the rejection of social institutions and established artistic conventions, or antagonism towards the public (as representative of the existing order).[1]

From the very early years of the twentieth century, progressive artists considered the act of 'disengagement' with the past and with existing artistic preoccupations as a necessary part of the artistic condition; of the fundamental alienation experienced, and in many cases actively sought, by the artist. Perhaps there have always been artists who viewed their artistic practice in this way, although until the beginning of the twentieth century the apprenticeship and 'studio'-based nature of training discouraged this. However, since rejection of the past became a consistent and potent unifying force within modernism in all its artistic manifestations, it has been, and continues to be, an ever-present artistic condition of modernity. Given its ubiquity, it is of value, therefore, to consider the nature and idea of rejection since with very few exceptions, rejection of past styles, values and forms of art has been a universal starting point for all artists working in all disciplines – the establishment of a personal *tabula rasa* upon which to create new values and forms.

If the primary act of rejection has united the artistic impulse throughout the twentieth century, then the creation of manifestos, the articulation of aesthetics, and the development of programmes and academic curricula have been an inevitable result. As much as the process of rejection has served to unify artistic effort, so too does the need to study and learn and to create programmes for this

34

purpose. The school, the *atelier*, the experimental theatre, the work-shop have all acquired positions of unparalleled artistic importance since the beginning of the twentieth century. These new schools of the modernist twentieth century would no longer operate by examining the best practices of the existing professions and creating programmes of study designed to provide new entrants for those professions.

Rejection of the past – the clean sweep – invited the artist to propose the kind of radical re-evaluation that only an equally radical school could provide. Equally also, complete rejection of the past invited kinds and depths of study hitherto not contemplated in the training of the artist. For example, Stanislavski rejected the training provided by the traditional apprenticeship within Russian theatre, and developed a radical and systematic programme of study in the early years of the century in the hope of producing a new kind of performer. Meyerhold totally rejected existing practice after he left the Moscow Art Theatre in 1906, and instigated studios and workshops where an entire redefinition of the nature of performance was attempted. Craig rejected both these positions and established a school at the Arena Goldoni in Florence in 1912 whereby the very need for the living actor was thrown into question. Simultaneously, Appia was working with Emile Jacques Dalcroze at the Hellerau Institute in Dresden, where he began to reject the architectural basis and emotional relationship that existed between performer and spectator, and proposed the act of performance as a shared celebration of living art. In the early 1960s, Grotowski rejected the suffocating richness and complexity of contemporary Polish theatre and proposed the dour rigour of a 'poor' laboratory theatre in Wroclaw. Early in the 1970s, Peter Brook rejected a similar richness and the artistic assumptions generated by theatres of national and institutional responsibility and proposed an international institute of research dedicated to simplicity, to reduc-tion, and through these, to aim for a concentration and distillation of performance. Each of these well-known, and sometimes iconic, theatrical 'rejections' has resulted in the formation of the *atelier*, the learning studio, as the logical and indeed the only place of work and experiment for the contemporary artist.

Within the formal academy of art the act and process of rejection have, since at least the late 1950s, become a structured part of the teaching syllabus. Programmes of study unfailingly commence with periods of structured 'unlearning': an active disengagement and an abandoning of what has already been learnt. It is generally presented as an opportunity for students to learn to 'think for themselves', to discover what art might mean for the individual rather than accepting or even building upon existing values and assumptions. The academy of art that I attended as a graduate student to study painting had the exhortation 'Abandon all you already know about art all ye who enter here!' written above the studio doorway. In many ways paradoxically, therefore, training as an artist is very much about expunging and extirpating what has gone before, what is already known, and what is therefore assumed to be stylistically stale, conventional and lacking relevance. It is an attitude of rejection predicated upon the degree of difference between the experiences of contemporary existence, between the distinctiveness of living in the present and a relationship with the future, and the world of memory and the past. Reconsiderations of the universality of art, the existence, status and validity of a canon of exemplary work, all form part of this process of rejection. Speed of social, political, scientific, technological and cultural change has made and makes the artist actively consider even the most immediate past to be in some ways irrelevant to the functioning of a truly modern art.

Rejection has therefore, in a variety of ways, been a primal, organizing feature of twentieth-century art, and its earliest manifestations might well be considered as the most significant and explosive. The effects of the artistic 'big-bangs', the creative violence of the Dada cabaret, and the howls of rage of the modernism of the first three decades of the century have dominated activity in all art forms for another half century, to the extent whereby, as Michael Levenson wrote in the very late 1990s, '[w]e are still learning how not to be Modernist'.[2]

The preceding chapter suggested that the scenographic ambitions of the theatre, and the technologies employed to realize them, contained internal fatal flaws that the most recent technologies, especially the introduction of electric lighting, of the 1880s and 1890s mercilessly exposed. But rejection of the past has more fundamental foundations than a rejection of aesthetic style and their forms as they may be revealed by new technologies. The technologies of the industrial revolution, of iron, steel and mechanized movement, that were harnessed to achieve the aims of material realism in the theatre, were inevitably technologies generated by new scientific knowledge. Scientific understanding of the world, and of the perception of humanity within that world, during the early years of the twentieth century undermined, and indeed precipitated a far greater and more thoroughgoing need to re-evaluate the purpose of, art and its social functioning.

As the establishment of experimental science had propelled the nineteenth-century belief in a quantifiable material reality (and therefore a reality capable of rational observation, imitation and artistic representation), so it was science that played a crucial role in dislodging traditional values, in urging the forces of rejection, and in precipitating the possibilities of radical redefinitions of art in the years before the First World War. For the late nineteenth century the reduction of matter to its smallest conceivable particle, the atom, confirmed the finite nature of material existence. Material reality expressed through the surface appearance and texture of millions of accumulated and arranged (although still invisible) atoms, shared a quality of trust alongside other similarly absolute certainties. Certainties such as Isaac Newton's perception of infinite space, a quality that was self-existent and without any dependence on anything else – like time.

The period 1895–1905, which saw the launching of crucial alternative strategies of theatre practice, also saw widespread attacks upon existing scientific theories of material reality, and important new discoveries were made. In particular, the physics of matter and of electromagnetic radiation examined by Marie Curie and Ernest Rutherford began to reach conclusions that focused upon radioactivity, and the activity and the behaviour of the individual atom. Understanding of the radioactive nature of matter eventually enabled a more precise dating of the Earth and of significant geological events, which, however tentative, put paid finally to belief in the traditional biblical account of the origins of life on Earth. Wilhelm Röntgen discovered the X-ray in 1895, and the famous photographic image of the skeleton of his wife's hand with its bulbous wedding ring was published in the European popular press in the following year. From the artist's point of view, the ability of the X-ray to display an existence *beneath* surface reality rendered the surface appearance of reality to be insignificant in contrast with more significant truths that may lie buried beneath. In this way, as Michael Bell suggested, 'the X-ray remains a suggestive image of modernism'.[3] Crucially, therefore, for the forward-thinking artist, surface appearances lost their state of artistic reverence – the definitive quality of truth that had been the principal object of study for the pre-Raphaelite painter of the nineteenth century, and the lodestone of endeavour for the scenic artist and painter in the theatre.

Of course, surface appearance could not be denied and in some ways it gained a new importance, though less as the finite representation of a greater internal truth or reality; but rather acquiring the possibility of an artistic independence from its role within representation. For example, the young Wassily Kandinsky's reaction to Claude Monet's painting *Haystacks in Snow*, which he saw in Moscow in 1891, was that: 'the [recognizable] object was discredited as an indispensable element of the picture'.[4] The haystacks could exist in a pictorial form purely as expressions of shape, position and colour. The artist's ability to exploit these qualities became of far greater significance than the ability to tell, for example, the story of a field where hay is mown and formed into stacks for preservation and storage. Such an attitude and outcome of rejection has enormous implications for the scenographic ambitions of Craig, Appia and Meyerhold, whose first considerations, following their own initial acts of rejection, were to instigate rigorous analysis of the materiality of their spaces and means of performance.

In 1897 the Manchester scientist J. J. Thomson announced in a public lecture: '[T]he assumption of a state of matter more finely divided than the atom is a somewhat startling one.'[5] By this urbane understatement he shattered the dominant material perception of the world by his experimental proof that there was considerable activity *within* the atom itself, experiments that resulted in his isolation of the electron (or 'corpuscle' as he first called it). From this point onwards, the future of the physical sciences for the next hundred years was to lie at a subatomic level, much as the future of art was to lie beneath the surface material realities of everyday appearances.

Further scientific events during the first decade of the century confirmed that rejection of the past must be the proper, indeed the only, artistic attitude to adopt. Newton's mechanical laws, which assumed the regularity of motion and acceleration, the inevitability of physical cause and effect and the fixity of matter, had prepared the technologists and merchants for the vast exploitation of the world's resources and huge technological developments during the late eighteenth and the nineteenth centuries. The post-Newtonian perception of time was that it flowed always at the same steady reliable speed, and that space was immovable. However, during the early years of the twentieth century, Albert Einstein theorized ways whereby the universe might not obey these seemingly finite and immutable laws. His theories, published in three papers in 1905, said that time adopted variable and relative tempi, and that space itself could be both mobile and flexible. For almost half a millennium the western world had been artistically ordering the universe by converting its supposed fixed reality and material rotundity into planes of two dimensions, and by placing these planes carefully one behind the other had created an illusion of reality within the mind of the spectator. The relativity of space and time proposed by Einstein now threw the seeming inevitability of this artistic process, and the science that underpinned it, into confusion and conjecture. The fundamental skills of observation, analysis and draftsmanship that were required to re-present the world in this traditional way had established the benchmarks of the artist's training, and furthermore formed the basis of the critical response to art. In the academy and conservatoire, the life-class and the re-presentation of the nude human figure had been the principal pedagogical method for acquiring and developing these skills.[6]

New scientific understandings inevitably created new technologies, and these further challenged perceptions of the world and of the artist's relationship with it. In December 1901, Guglielmo Marconi proved in his transmission of a carrier signal that was modulated by the voice from Cornwall to Newfoundland that radio waves could defy linearity and transcend the curvature of the Earth. The unseen and mysterious power of electricity further confounded the natural ordering of time; it lit the night sky and moved humanity with unheard-of speed in carriages and trains.[7] Its illumination enabled moving pictures of the Boer War to mediatize warfare for an audience by recording, for the first time in history, images of the common soldier in action. In so doing, it effectively terminated the heroic military subject as being one of the oldest of artistic genres. The work of Einstein and Gustav Hertz to understand photo-electricity and the spectrum of electromagnetic waves established the primary scientific framework upon which the permanence, uniqueness and authenticity of the artwork would be thrown into question by mechanical reproduction and dissemination.

The location of humanity at the centre of power and authority were crucially important in the artistic formulation of a method of representation during the Renaissance. The rules of linear perspective imposed a material order and conferred an acceptable reality upon the perception of the world; they organized objects so that they seemed to recede towards a vanishing point, and theatres were built to reflect this framed artistic analysis. But the vanishing point of perspective may be considered a fiction because, of course, there does not exist a point at which objects truly vanish. Moreover, it was a fiction based upon the humanism and political hierarchy of the Italian courts, which prioritized the artistic vision of the single, highly privileged, static viewer. Heavier-than-air, powered flight by Orville and Wilbur

Wright at Kitty Hawk, North Carolina, in December 1903 offered a radical alternative to this illusory perspective representation of the world. The appearance of the world dwindles and simultaneously reforms when seen from an aircraft as it rises from the earth. The moving aircraft becomes the centre of the temporary point of view on which all lines converge. The radical movement available to the pilot enables an equally radical selection and change of viewpoint, a multiplicity of framing, much as cubist and expressionist paintings offer varied and multiple points of view.

The period 1910–14 was especially, and in the light of the evolving science, inevitably, remarkable in the development of modernist ideas. Conceived from the premise of rejection of the past, radical and frequently violent artistic strategies were proposed that created powerful modes and models, many of which still energize contemporary artistic thought. According to the Futurist Manifesto with its decisive concern for modernist precision, space and time perished precisely in 1909. Whether futurist or not, the convergence of spatial planes in cubist paintings by Georges Braque and Pablo Picasso, and the jumbled time schemes of the literary narratives of Ezra Pound or James Joyce, proved to be key indicators of modernism; 1910 was the year of Kandinsky's first abstract painting and of Georges Braque's *Violin and Pitcher*, of Stravinsky's *The Firebird* ballet, Diaghilev's *Ballets Russes*, and of E. M. Forster's *Howards End* and Bertrand Russell's *Principia Mathematica*; it was the year when Craig took out a patent on his 'screens' representing a revolutionary new approach to stage setting, and it was the year when the craze for the tango dance swept the western world. As a later response to the significant art events of the year 1910, which in London centred on the post-impressionist exhibition at the Grafton Gallery, Virginia Woolf claimed that: 'On or about 1910 human character changed.'[8]

The universal sense of rejection, the enormity of the sense of difference, and the heady, but frequently isolated and alienated state of the artist, who was well aware of the epochal nature of his or her position, was well summarized in 1912 by the painter Franz Marc, who wrote in *Der Blaue Reiter*, which he co-edited with Kandinsky:

> nothing occurs accidentally and without organic reason – not even the loss of artistic style in the nineteenth century. This fact leads us to the idea that we are standing today at the turning point of two long epochs, similar to the state of the world fifteen hundred years ago, when there was also a transitional period without art and religion – a period in which great and

traditional ideas died and new and unexpected ones took their place. Nature would not wantonly destroy the religion and art of the people without a great purpose. We are also convinced that we can already proclaim the first signs of the time. The first works of a new era are tremendously difficult to define. Who can see clearly what their aim is and what is to come. But just the fact that they *do exist* and appear in many places today, sometimes independently of each other, and that they possess inner truth, makes us certain that they are the first signs of the coming new epoch – they are the signal fires for the pathfinders. The hour is unique.[9]

As Marc indicates, the new and future guide to artistic activity will be measured by its 'inner truth' rather than a relationship with external appearance. The thoroughness of the scientific revolution and the (seemingly) comprehensive vision of fundamental physics supported the totality of the act of artistic rejection. But such a revolution also led to the belief in the potential for a similarly far-reaching meta-narrative of human existence based upon an equally fundamental analysis of the relationship between humanity and modern science and technology. Truth within the mind of the artist and truth to the materials being used became the foundational criteria for all redefinitions of art and would prove to be far more significant than placing both at the service of representational verisimilitude and external, preexistent, reality. Hence the early focus by modernist theatre artists upon the expression of self and upon the materials – the 'quiddity' as Fitzgerald would have termed it – of the means of expression. As a foundation of new art, these offered a far greater assurance of meaningful truth than a scientifically devalued verisimilitude. By 1911 Kandinsky wrote in his *Concerning the Spiritual in Art*,[10] in the first of what were effectively to become manifestos of abstract painting, that the phenomenological qualities of pigment and paint surface should cease to be merely the means of art, but should become the future subject matter of the painter.

Although sharing very many similar concerns and a similar violent rejection of the past, in many ways of course, theatre was very distinct from other art forms. For a start, at the beginning of the twentieth century theatre was not generally considered to be an art form at all; after all, the theatre could hardly share the creativity of the fine arts when its principal function was considered to be the realization of dramatic literature. Its mode was therefore understood to be one of interpretation, and given the complex nature of the collaboration involved, it could not aspire to the sense of uniqueness and 'authorship' that properly only existed in the world of the 'fine' arts. The struggles of Craig, Appia and Meyerhold both to reject the past and to identify and redefine theatre and scenographic theory should be viewed not only within the larger context of radical changes within science, technology and art, but also within the by no means insignificant context of their claim that theatre should be thought of as an art in its own right. To do this inevitably meant that clear distinctions between the art of dramatic literature and the art of theatrical expression had to be articulated and examined. Was it possible, for example, to make a work of theatre without a prior work of dramatic literature? Was it possible to create a work of theatre art out of the materials of the theatre itself? Might an audience respond to the core materials of theatre *in their own right* – much as one might respond to abstract colour, texture and form? Given that the theatre could not be thought of as existing without the presence of the audience, what was, or might be, the role of the spectator in a possible new 'art' of the theatre?

But of course the initial acts of rejection in the theatre were fundamentally hindered by the entrenchment and seeming permanence of prevailing attitudes and styles. Denis Bablet begins his seminal analysis of scenographic change within the twentieth century by saying: '1880. The Italianate theatre reigns and its structures seem immortal: two worlds face each other through the magic curtain of "the fourth wall".'[11] Much as one might reject such theatre, one might also suspect that to many, the mainstream 'Italianate' theatre of the last decades of the nineteenth century presented itself as an immovable, overblown experience, a rather baroque *Gesamtkunstwerk* of extravagance and excess where the increasingly self-evident theatricality of its techniques might actually be enjoyed – Bernard Shaw reviews the theatre of the period with (for Shaw) an almost benign presentation of its utter irrelevance. Even Gordon Craig, who spent his life rejecting 'this false-witnessing Realism – this traitor to the Imagination – this idolatry of ugliness to which the Realistic Theatre would compel us',[12] never lost his sense of pleasure in the quality of splendid and overt theatricality that Henry Irving created, for example, in his production of *The Bells* at the Lyceum Theatre.

To the audience and to a majority of professional theatre workers, including the adherents of Zola's vision of naturalism in the theatre, reformation along the lines of that proposed by the Meiningen Theatre Company seemed desirable and eminently achievable. Early attempts at such reformation, however, made things considerably worse. The productions of the Meiningen, which became exemplary in mainstream theatre following their European tours during the 1880s, presented a theatre of earnestness and craftsmanship, which displayed a studious attention to detail. The rigours of their production methods appealed to scholarly theatre managers of the period, and seemed to be restoring a welcome conscientiousness, rationality, industry, and above all a proper sense of managerial hierarchy to a debased and star-dominated stage. But it was the degree to which the permanence and entrenchment of this fundamentally pictorial theatre was extended to meet the claims of naturalism that finally revealed its artistic baselessness. Its essential absurdity became especially clear to a significant few when this scenographic style of heightened material realism was applied and developed within the staging of new and important dramatic literature by writers such as Strindberg, Ibsen and Chekhov. In 1908, Meyerhold summed up the extent of Stanislavski's assiduous pursuit of a fully representational *mise en scène*:

> The naturalism of the Art Theatre is the naturalism adopted from the Meiningen[13] players; its fundamental principle is the exact representation of life. ... Everything on the stage must be as nearly as possible real: ceilings, stucco cornices, fireplaces, wallpaper, stove doors, air vents, etc. ... A real waterfall flows on the stage and the rain falling is real water. I recall a small chapel built out of real wood, a house faced with thin plywood, double windows with cotton wool padding and panes coated with frost. Every corner of the set is complete in every detail. Fireplaces, tables and dressers are furnished with a mass of oddments visible only through binoculars, and more than the most assiduous and inquisitive spectator could hope to take in during the course of an entire act. ... Through the window a real ship is seen crossing a fjord. On the stage not only is there a whole set of rooms but it is several storeys high, too, with real staircases and oak doors. Sets are both struck and revolved. The foot-lights glare. There are archways everywhere. The canvas representing the sky is hung in a semicircle. When the play calls for a farmyard the floor is strewn with imitation mud made out of *papier maché*.[14]

But even at the Moscow Art Theatre, where the longevity of this approach to *mise en scène* seemed most theoretically supported, and in many ways extended, its ultimate reliance upon such physical materiality was questioned. In *My Life in Art*, written in 1924, Stanislavski considers his frustration in 1904 at the demands of such a stage:

> 'My God!' I cried to myself. 'Is it possible that we, the artists of the stage, are fated, due to the materiality of our bodies, to the eternal service and

expression of coarse realism? Are we not called to go any farther than the realists in painting went in their time? Can it be that we are only forerunners in scenic art?'[15]

The rejection of scenographic material realism set alongside the theatre's struggle with the material reality of the living actor has served as a benchmark of theatrical experiment throughout the period. Although, therefore, the act of rejection is an important statement about circumstances early in the twentieth century, rejection remains a constant and consistent attitude and mode of thinking to the present day. This consistency of rejection may prove to be an indicative feature of twentieth-century theatre – especially in its search for meaningful scenographic identity within post-dramatic theatre. For the generations of artists before the close of the nineteenth century, young assertive artists would reject the styles and techniques of the mainstream and their teachers, but then slowly a dominant new approach would emerge and would, over time, create a new mainstream that, in its turn, would be challenged and re-formed. However, the acts of rejection at the close of the nineteenth century, precipitated in no small part by the enormity of scientific discovery, were so radical and thoroughgoing that no new dominant aesthetic was to emerge – no accepted modernist mainstream was created to replace, in the western world, the universality of nineteenth-century realism. Rather, a multiplicity of manifestos, attitudes, styles and techniques were thrown into the vacant spaces created by rejection, and hotly debated.

In addition, and most significantly, the events of two world wars and their accompanying genocides, the totalitarian ideologies, the terrorisms and the rebirth of nationalisms have all served as major challenges to the cultural possibilities proposed by modernist meta-narratives. The appeal to a universality of understanding and shared sets of reference and perceptions, which the modernist artist thought could only serve to unite peoples and nations, have been rejected by social complexity and diversity, which together have hindered the establishment of universally acceptable cultural forms comparable to those of the late nineteenth century.

It would probably be true to say, therefore, that in the early twenty-first century the artist, although working within a significantly different condition of theatre and performance, still operates in a condition of constant rejection of past and existing forms, whilst at the same time being faced with an ever expanding range of artistic and technological opportunities and solutions. In the early years of the twentieth century, 'know your enemy' had a coherent meaning that might be shared by the modernist painter, architect, poet or theatre artist and that would have served to focus and unite their acts of rejection. But for the last years of the century, as Baz Kershaw says 'post-modernity signals an acute destabilisation of the cultural climate throughout the world: an end to all the human certainties of the modernist past'.[16] The act of rejection is therefore more than a mere 'preface' to beginning to make new theatre and performance; it is not an attitude that the artist outgrows and leaves behind upon gradua-tion; it seems to have become an ever-present condition of making new work.

Perhaps this is made even more so by the continuing validity of the approaches, solutions and 'energies' generated through earlier seminal acts of rejection. The solutions and propositions that were created by Craig, Appia, Meyerhold and Stanislavski have not been superseded in either practical or artistic usefulness – unlike, for example, ideas and solutions of early twentieth-century physics and technology. Their work co-exists alongside later approaches and newer solutions. The following chapters, therefore, look at a range of these solutions and 'energies' and treat them as ongoing conditions of contemporary scenography – rather than as historical precursors. For example, the approach that thinks of the stage and its scene as a machine and a place for performance (rather than a setting upon a stage) might be said to begin with Craig and Meyerhold, but it continues to chal-lenge work in performance today. The desire to eradicate any useful distinction between architecture and scenography, which has its origins equally in the ideas of Appia and Craig, still serves to focus the desire to create proper sites of performance. The rejection of the increasing technological presence in theatre throughout the century has urged many to atavistically examine early historical forms, such as the theatre of antiquity, the *commedia dell'arte*, and Renaissance theatre, along-side non-western aboriginal ways of making performance. In all of these, the fundamental qualities and abilities of light, first theorized by Appia, have also served to focus and generate new work. And just as the new technologies reformed theatrical experiment in the early years of the twentieth century, so we may be prepared to reject all existing material forms in pursuit of a virtual performance space enabled through the newest of information technologies.

3 The Scene as Machine, 1

Scenography as a Machine for Performance

In this chapter I want to consider some of the initial alternatives proposed by early twentieth-century artists and thinkers following their thoroughgoing rejection of nineteenth-century approaches to scenic language. For example, if the stage scene should no longer exist in order to imitate or impersonate a pre-existing material reality, then what should it look like? How should the stage scene, if it were to become 'non-real', relate with the real actor? How should it function as a location for performance? If the scene increasingly begins to acknowledge, and indeed to celebrate, that it looks like nothing other than itself, then what does this mean for the relationship between dramatic literature and scenography? What, therefore, is the purpose of scenery? Is there a meaningful significance in considering a distinction between the 'scene' of performance and the 'place' of performance? All theatre artists have had to (and still do) contend with the complicated inter-relationship between the real-time existence of the living performers and the physical actuality of their surroundings – their place of performance. Just as the actor must acknowledge the performative tension between him/herself and the dramatic fiction, so must the scenographer engage with the actuality of the wood and fabric and metal, alongside any representational purpose that they may have. In this discussion, I want to suggest that the metaphor of the scene as a *machine* – as a physical construct that theatrically locates and enables the public act of performance – represents one of the earliest, and has proved to be one of the most long-lived, *leitmotifs* of scenographic research and experiment during the twentieth century. There is a significant parallel between the radical scientific enquiry into the innermost operation of all matter by clearing away surface texture and detail, and the discarding of all attempts at a scenic illusion in order to examine the inner mechanics of the place of performance. Around such examinations and alternatives, the identity and distinctiveness of modern scenography has been built.

The core of this new scenographic endeavour was articulated within the first decade or so of the twentieth century, and indeed some of its most significant and long-lived ideas were generated during the five-year period before the outbreak of the First World War, and in this and the two subsequent chapters I want to try to locate this within the larger context of artistic endeavour of the period. I want to establish this metaphor of the scene as machine from its probable earliest manifestations in the work of Gordon Craig, who, carefully articulating the distinction as he worked on his proposal for stage 'screens' in 1910, tried to define the stage setting as a *place* for performance rather than a *scene*. I will then consider the concern of Adolphe Appia to create what he called the 'study site' as the location for the living performance space that he sought. The self-reflexive scenography that was begun in St Petersburg studio theatres by Vsevelod Meyerhold, and his concerns to conceive of the stage as a performance construction, initiated the exposure of the technology of its expression; it produced a conscious revelation of the physical reality of the resources of the stage house, the lighting equipment, flying winches, and associated machinery.

In similar ways, Brecht's collaborator and scenographer Caspar Neher consistently revealed the mechanics of the stage construction. Crucial to his concern to 're-function' the working of theatre, in terms of both the rehearsal process and the performance, was his focus upon the title of his profession; he insisted on a fundamental distinction between the existing *Bühnenbildner* – the stage picture-maker, and his more acceptable title of *Bühnenbauer* – the stage builder. Neher distinguishes between the designer of a stage picture, which cannot in any sense be real, because it imitates an earlier reality, and the construction (hence the verb *bauer*) of a place on the stage that has its only significant reality at the moment (at the building) of performance, and therefore has a true theatrical reality. The metaphor, and the implications, of the scene as machine still have considerable contemporary relevance, and it will be useful to look at the work of Josef Svoboda and his concern for the 'material reality of the stage' as in some way representing a culmination of modernist scenographic ambitions during the twentieth century.

Considerable critical attention has been given to the long period of rejection and, according to some, of failure that occupied almost half of the long life of Edward Gordon Craig (1872–1966). It is inevitably easy to allow this debate to influence and condition our understanding of the intensely rich and creative period of artistic activity that he underwent following his departure from Henry Irving's Lyceum Theatre in 1896 until, say, the publication of his book *Scene* in 1923. In 1910, Craig was 38 years old and at the height of his artistic power, and seemed to be close to achieving the recognition, and opportunities for the implementation and consolidation, of his ideas for performance and scenography. The volume of essays published by Heinemann in 1911 under the title *On the Art of the Theatre* consolidated his writings, bringing together the important essays that he had written in the period 1905–8, and including the 'Art of the Theatre' dialogues. The book also contained the complex and critically highly damaging 'The Actor and the Über-Marionette', which many critics and most of the theatrical profession understood as a desire by Craig to banish the actor from the theatre and create a theatre of purely scenographic action animated by marionettes. During the period 1910–13, his radical vision of theatre (although with a predominant focus upon his scenographic proposals) was being recognized internationally, and in the preface to *On the Art of the Theatre* he identified a powerful international grouping of like-minded artists with which he confidently associated himself: a grouping that included Stanislavski, Meyerhold, Fuchs, Antoine, Wyspiansky, Yeats and Appia. He concluded the preface:

> It is a great honour for me to feel that among my friends are the names of the first artists in Europe. And I think we can all feel happy on the progress which our movement has made, a movement which is destined ultimately to restore the Art of the Theatre into its ancient position among the Fine arts.[1]

To substantiate this, two of the most important 'art' theatres of Europe, the Moscow Art Theatre, and the Abbey Theatre in Dublin, were actively seeking his collaboration; and, through exhibitions, his name was beginning to be linked alongside that of Adolphe Appia as theatrical co-founder of scenographic modernism. Two years later in 1912, plans that he had begun to develop in London in 1904 for establishing a school for the art of the theatre would be achieved in practice at the Arena Goldoni in Florence. It is therefore important to set aside the knowledge and interpretation that we may have of Craig's later life and consider the period 1910–14 as an extremely positive and optimistic one for his career. He would probably have considered all his productions, his scenographic designs, and his writing since his very personal and strikingly formal act of rejecting the Lyceum Theatre in 1896, as a period in which traditional ideas were abandoned and a new clarity and artistic conviction took their place. Craig expressed something of this when, at the age of 85, he summarized his artistic situation in 1907: 'From now to the middle of 1913 is a very productive period of my life. All came along this year – 1907: Screens, and SCENE, the "Übermarionette", Black Figures, *The Mask*.'[2]

Early in 1910, on 24 January, Craig submitted to the King's Patent Agency Ltd office[3] in London a provisional specification for what he quite modestly called 'Improvements in Stage Scenery'. Almost three months later on 15 April, he submitted the complete specification describing his scenic proposals in detail and accompanying them with four sheets of technical drawings. Under the terms of the Patents and Designs Act (1907), a search would then have been made through the last 50 years of patent submissions to ensure originality. This having been completed, his patent submission was published on 1 September 1910. The patent that Craig now owned was for the design for a stage scene, created by what he called 'screens'. He described the screens in his book *Scene* (1923):

> They stand on the stage just as they are; they do not imitate nature, nor are they painted with realistic or decorative designs. They are monotone. ... 'A nice place', said a dear old friend to me on looking at the model of the scene [probably W. B. Yeats] ... and I have always thought this was the best word to use – far better than scene – it is a place if it seem real – it is a scene if it seem false.[4]

Craig was concerned to emphasize the mechanical reality of the stage construction that he proposed, but then he very clearly described its relationship with the living performer:

> For the foremost characteristic of this scene is that it is an architectonic construction with a life of its own. It is a solid, three-dimensional unit which adapts itself to the actor's movements, a group of screens which stand up by themselves.

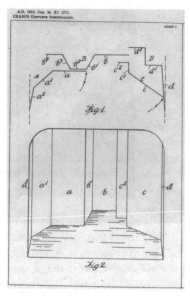

Figure 9   Ground-plan of Gordon Craig's 'screens' from his Patent Specification, 1910 (*London, V&A Theatre Museum*)

Figure 10   Computer reconstruction by Christopher Baugh, Gavin Carver and Cat Fergusson for the Kent Interactive Digital Design Studio (KiDDS), 1999 (University of Kent)

Although free-standing they were not inert for not only could they relate with the physical movement of the actor, they might also, like a musical instrument, be brought to life through performance:

> The relation of light to this scene is akin to that of the bow to the violin, or of the pen to the paper.[5]

In crucial ways, the scenography proposed by Craig's screens was not only central to his thinking, but through its functioning within performance, firmly established the idea of the scene as machine. Neither the formally structured geometrical screens, nor their surface treatment of untreated, unbleached canvas, represented anything; they neither imitated nor (arguably) represented any relationship with the real world. This, of course, was an essentially modernist concern, operating in theatrical terms that rejected the imitation of the past (or in fact anything that already existed) as the prime motivator and function of scenographic effort. In this way, Craig's patent proposal exemplified the famous 'prophecy', or at least what might be thought of as the agenda for the future of theatrical art that he proposed in 1907: 'Today they *impersonate* and interpret; tomorrow they must *represent* and interpret; and the third day they must create. By this means style may return.'[6]

For the easel artist, whose relationship with the appearances of the natural world was historically engrained, the situation was equally acute. Stemming from a similar impetus of representation during the Renaissance, the easel and the stage had inevitably followed parallel tracks ever since. Although a little in advance of the theatre, easel painting had indulged in a welter of minutely detailed verisimilitude during the latter half of the nineteenth century, both in anticipation of photography in the early years and later as a response to photography. 'I wished to copy nature,' said Cézanne, 'I could not. But I was satisfied when I had discovered that the sun, for instance, could not be *reproduced*, but that it must be *represented* by something else ... by colour.'[7] In a similar way, Craig's screens did not try to reproduce the constituent parts of a pre-existent place – a room, a street, or a palace. They *might* serve as a device or construction to *represent* such places should the act of performance so indicate. In this way, the screens created a place for performance that might represent imaginatively whilst simultaneously responding to the movements of the actor. None the less, their fundamental realism was that of their material presence before an audience – hence Craig's description of them as a 'place' rather than as a 'scene'. 'Place' also de-localized scenographic effort and allowed it a freedom that Craig considered to be central to his ambition to restore (rather than reform) theatre: 'Yet the aim of the Theatre is to restore its art, and it should commence by banishing from the Theatre this idea of impersonation, this idea of reproducing Nature; for, while impersonation is in the Theatre, the Theatre can never become free.'[8]

Looked at in a different way, but within a contemporary context to that of Craig when he was writing about the screens in *Scene* in 1923, this may be thought of as similar to the energy and values that an artist such as Mies van der Rohe committed to the design of furniture at the Bauhaus during the early 1920s. For van der Rohe, a chair has a formal purpose that may be defined by use and function, by ergonomics – it does not 'imitate' the past – its design aesthetic is determined not by style, but by purpose, by its need to 'perform' the functions of being a chair. In this way determining and designing the form of a chair from function and ergonomics will undoubtedly create the 'style' of a chair – and as Craig said, 'by this means style may return'. In a similar way, the purpose and aesthetic of a scene by Craig may be defined by performative function rather than by imitative, representational, or even aesthetic purpose. Furthermore, and in a very practical way, the screen scenes tried to achieve the relationship between theatre architecture and scenic design that underpinned so much of Craig's thinking whether expressed in models, words, or designs. As a clear statement of scenographic intent he wrote in his daybook in 1909: 'I wish to remove the *Pictorial Scene* but to leave in its place the *Architectonic Scene*.'[9]

Craig's belief in the aesthetic and functioning of the screens underpinned his scenography for the production of *Hamlet* that he undertook at the Moscow Art Theatre in 1912. In spite of the personal tensions and technical complexities of realizing the scenography, Stanislavski appreciated this ambition:

> It seemed that nothing simpler than the screens could be imagined. There could be no better background for the actors. It was natural, it did not hurt the eyes, it had three dimensions, just like the body of the actor, it was picturesque, due to the endless possibilities of lighting its architectural convexities which gave freedom of play to light, half-tone and shadow. ... The public was to come to the theatre and see no stage whatsoever. The screens were to serve as the architectural continuation of the auditorium and were to harmonise with it.[10]

Stanislavski's understanding of the scenography is evident and he deeply regretted the inability of contemporary theatre technology to achieve the functionality which they both wanted:

> What a tremendous distance there is between the scenic dream of an artist or a stage director and its realisation upon the stage. How coarse are all the existing scenic means of incarnation. How primitive, naive and impotent is scenic technique. ... Why is it that the same mechanics are so coarse and primitive where man strives to satisfy not his personal bodily needs but his best spiritual longings which arise from the clearest aesthetic depths of the artistic soul? In this region there seems to be no inventiveness. The radio, electricity, light rays, create wonders everywhere but not in the theatre, where they could find a completely exceptional use in the sense of beauty and forever banish from the stage disgusting glue-paint, papier-mâché and properties. May a time come when newly discovered rays will paint in the air the shadows of colour tones and the combinations of lines.[11]

Nevertheless, in spite of the challenges and all the technical problems, Stanislavski concluded:

> The production of *Hamlet* met with great success. Some people were enthusiastic, others criticised, but everybody was excited, and debated, read reports, wrote articles, while the other theatres in the country quietly appropriated the ideas of Craig, publishing them as their own. ... Apparently we could not expect a greater success.[12]

Hamlet remained in the Moscow Art Theatre repertory for three seasons, with a total of forty-seven performances in all.[13] Sadly for serious critical attention, Craig's achievement has been overshadowed by Stanislavski's frequently referenced irritation and loss of patience. But his anger was very clearly concerned with the technical problems that arose, and not with Craig's overall scenographic vision of what amounted in practice to the complete 're-functioning' of the Moscow Art Theatre stage. The screens were in process of being hastily re-set following a late rehearsal, ready for the first performance, when they collapsed, and the angry irritation of the director of the theatre is understandable. However, the problems were resolved very shortly before the audience entered the auditorium for the first performance, and there is no evidence that similar technical problems were to hinder any of the performances in Moscow or when the production toured to St Petersburg.

Craig's concern for the architectonic qualities of 'place', rather than the imitative qualities of 'scene', stems especially from his response to theatre architectures of the past. In 1913 he wrote:

> Once upon a time, stage scenery was architecture. A little later it became imitation architecture; still later it became imitation artificial architecture. Then it lost its head, went quite mad, and has been in a lunatic asylum ever since.[14]

Figure 11   Edward Gordon Craig, plate 15 from *Scene* (London: Humphrey Milford; Oxford University Press, 1923)

The theatre structures of antiquity, the 'artificial' architectural theatres of Palladio and Scamozzi at Vicenza and Sabbionetta in northern Italy, the bare *commedia* trestle stage, the large forestage of the eighteenth-century English playhouse, all of these seemed to structure within their architectonic frame a liminal place, a place that might 'become' anywhere that the act of performance might wish. Most importantly for Craig, it was not an act of building and painting scenes that should achieve this, but the act of living performance as it encountered the imagination of the audience. He suggests that the act of theatre takes place upon this liminal place of meeting, and that therefore the arts of scenography and architecture must combine to create these places that generate the potential for performance. As liminal places, they are not, of course, impositions by architect or actor. Their potential and their acceptance as places of performance, as exciting places of possibility and imagination, whether under the hot Greek sun, or within the dim and smoke-filled playhouse of the eighteenth century, were an expression of the complex social contract that performance involves. Craig's struggle to articulate this distinction between 'scene' and 'place' initiated this most critical of debates for contemporary scenography. More recent, anthropologically-led studies of theatre and ritual[15] have articulated more clearly the role of the liminal in performance, upon which, along with Craig's example, many contemporary scenographers and architects have grounded their work.

Adolphe Appia's rejection of past forms and values was no less wholesale than Craig's. Appia (1862–1928) splendidly demolished the scenic processes of the past by saying that once the paint has dried upon a surface it is static, whereas dramatic action and human emotion changes and grows. Therefore placing dramatic action, which lives, against a painted scene, which is static, is nonsense – therefore abolish painted scenery. However, unlike Craig who was born and bred in the theatre and worked for eight years as a well-regarded professional actor in a major metropolitan theatre, Appia's background and his responses to theatre and scenography were developed as a spectator, and more especially as a spectator for the music dramas of Richard Wagner. It was the firmly entrenched nineteenth-century material realism of Wagner's scenography at the *Festspielhaus* in Bayreuth that Appia chose as the initial battleground for his demands for both rejection and reform. In this way, perhaps, the initial contribution of Appia may seem somewhat less radical than that of Craig. For example, for much of his creative life, Appia maintained an adherence to his understanding of scenography as being fundamentally placed at the service of dramatic energy, which would be provided by musical and dramatic literature. In some ways Appia's view of the scene as machine may therefore be understood as consisting of a machine whose function would be defined by, and remain fully at the service of, a controlling dramatic action. Possibly for this reason, his reception by subsequent theatre artists and theorists has been less problematic than the uncompromising and almost mystical ideas expressed by Craig.

Furthermore, there is an issue of presentation. Both Appia and Craig were always most anxious to point out the difference between a two-dimensional design on paper and its realization in living time in performance. Nevertheless, contemporary theatre photography (albeit quite primitive), the account of the eye-witness, the evidence provided by designs and sketches, all carry a heavy burden in enabling the scenic historian to assess the concerns and ideas that lie beneath the ink and chalk. Craig spent his entire life creating beautiful, haunting graphic images of possible stages. They resonate with qualities of space, contour and mood; they also suggest possibilities of stage lighting that only became technically achievable towards the end of the twentieth century. But they are not images *of* the stage; they are representations of the *qualities* that the stage might create. Craig was very clear about this:

> When I make the same scene on the stage it is sure to be quite different in form and colour, but it will create the same impression on you as this design ... a design for a scene on paper is one thing; a scene on the stage is another. The two have no connection with each other. Each depends on a hundred different ways and means of creating the same impression. Try to adapt the one to the other, and you get at best only a good translation.[16]

In comparison, Appia's drawings reveal little, other than in contrast with the designs and photographs of stage scenes by his contemporaries. They are workmanlike in their presentation of three-dimensional space and they have an interestingly hazy and atmospheric quality that gives an indication of some of the qualities of light that he sought. He has a sufficient command of technical matters such as perspective to enable the viewer to thoroughly understand his spatial propositions, but in the light of their soaring ambition, his limitations as a draftsman are very evident. Care must be taken, therefore, when trying to compare the frustratingly evanescent, sometimes mischievous, propositions of Craig alongside the more sombre and occasionally dour designs by Appia. The puritan practitioner, the 'man of the theatre' such as the American stage designer Lee Simonson writing in the 1930s,[17] for example, welcomed the workmanlike simplicity and depth of Appia's drawings and the serious challenge of his theory, but was irritated by the catholic excess and deliberate mystery of the images of Craig and the sometimes irritatingly fanciful language of his writings.

Appia's scenographies for Wagner's music dramas are 'machines for performance', and like any good machine they work in intimate partnership with those who control their perception in time. Appia rightly insisted that his scenography might only serve to energize a truly living space when lit with skill and artistry and when fully brought to life in performance. Considerable imagination is therefore needed to envisage the full implications of Appia's proposals. I shall consider his ideas concerning light and the scene in more detail in a later chapter when I come to examine his revolutionary premise that lighting should serve not only to expose, but also to function as the living partner of, dramatic action.

Figure 12   Adolphe Appia: rhythmic space ('The Staircase') 1909, entitled 'Escalier en face' (*Deutsches Theatermuseum, Munich*)

Although Wagner was ever present in thematic influence upon him, during the period 1909–14, Appia temporarily stepped aside from his life's mission to create scenographies for Wagner's music dramas and worked in collaboration with Emile Jacques Dalcroze at the Dalcroze Institute in Hellerau, a carefully planned 'garden city' suburb of Dresden. In any understanding of the role, Dalcroze was not a theatre director, nor indeed someone especially concerned with theatre. He had, however, an important belief in the educative and social powers of performance. He was a musician and a teacher, who believed that training the human body to respond in movement to the rhythms and tones of music would serve as a liberation of the conscious mind and of the inner self, and as such might prove to be a profound force in the development of society and community. He called this practice, and the techniques of learning that he devised, 'Eurhythmics'.

Understandably, Dalcroze's work with his students was not primarily created for presentation to an audience – indeed he was concerned that his work with students should not in any way be conceived of as a process of rehearsal for performance. The work and its values were to be achieved in the personal and artistic fulfilment acquired by the participants through the learning sessions. Appia wrote in 1912:

> Eurhythmics is recognised as the art that arouses in us a sense of bodily musical rhythms and thus permits us, through the gradual realisation of that rhythm within space, to become fully aware of its beauty and to enjoy its beneficial power.

He is, however, aware of the complex relationship between the participants and those who watch, and he tries to account for the act of spectatorship in performance.

> If an earnest pupil stepped before a mirror to perform a rhythmic exercise, he would perceive immediately that he had made a most serious error, having taken the wrong direction in attempting to modify from the outside what he ought to approach from within. The mirror takes his image and in reflecting, falsifies it. No relation is possible between the student's experience during free exercises in space, as he follows his inner rhythm alone, and that image dutifully reflected in the mirror. Here your eyes, sir, play the part of the mirror. As incorrigible spectators, they seize upon the external form of Jacques-Dalcroze's students and reflect a falsified image. Undoubtedly some of the students must be uncomfortably aware of this, for more things occur here between the auditorium and the stage than are

dreamt of in your spectator's philosophy. The student comes to the Hellerau Institute not to study the aesthetic life of the body, but to awaken the same life in his own body.[18]

Nevertheless, the 'demonstrations' and the sharing of work in progress that took place at the Institute acquired the status of performances, and observers the status of an audience, and it would be true to say that Appia, although the most reclusive and retiring of theatrical collaborators, perceived the performance potential of Dalcroze's work more than its originator. But because of this, he was especially aware that his contribution differed significantly from that which would be applied to creating the scenography for a perform- ance that had been entirely planned for public viewing. His work at Hellerau proposed the scene as a machine for performance in a way that extends the potential of that metaphor, because of his need to deconstruct the relationship between performer and spectator, and therefore between stage and auditorium. He realized that he was creating a scenography for a performance that shared its emphasis and focus between an aesthetic event undertaken with a view to being

Figure 13   Adolphe Appia: Hellerau Studio – *Orpheus* setting, 1912 (*Richard C. Beacham, University of Warwick*)

witnessed by an audience, and an event that primarily existed as an extension of the personal and emotional learning concerns of the participants. Scenographic solutions must therefore propose spatial ways of uniting the performer's act of self-discovery alongside the aesthetic experience of an audience watching the performer.

Although there are profound architectural implications in almost all that Gordon Craig proposed and achieved, and he wrote passionately about the interaction between architecture and scenography in his articles and books on theatre history, nevertheless, with some exceptions, his ideas stir the *imagination* of the architect and theatre planner, rather than offering achievable architectural solutions. Appia, on the other hand, whilst undertaking the great majority of his theatre practice in very traditional opera houses, did propose through his work at Hellerau with Dalcroze, the first coherent practical vision of the experimental theatre space, the *atelier*, or the studio or workshop theatre. Furthermore, Appia's conception is more than just an efficient architectural shell, a scenic *tabula rasa* upon and within which scenographers may articulate a space of performance suitable for a specific project. His description seems to indicate the desire for an empty, aesthetically neutral space to serve as a venue for performances of all kinds aided by a skilfully planned and a very complete lighting installation – a machine of sorts that does indeed become the scene of performance, but of a uniquely holistic and involving nature. There are no drawings of Appia's 'study site', but a good sense of his thinking may be gained from the designs and photographs of the 'living spaces'; the constructions of platforms, levels and steps that participated in the movement of the performers. The radical decision to abolish any form of architectural division between audience space and performance space was matched by the even more remarkable decision to include the audience within the atmosphere of performance by sharing the lighting. The audience would not be placed in a darkened room and asked to observe a brightly lit spectacle placed beyond a segregating archway. Although light provided emphasis for important moments of performance, Appia's design for Hellerau was one that could make the entire interior structure of the hall a machine that could reflect the atmospheric qualities of the performance and physically embrace all participants. The further significance of Appia's achievements in proposing the 'study site' and in lighting at Hellerau will be considered in later chapters.

Although the focus in this chapter has been upon some of the distinctions between Appia and Craig, there are crucial ideologies

which link their work. There was a universal rejection of a scenographic past based upon the scenic impersonation of the natural
world. In the work of both artists there was an acknowledgement and
indeed a celebration of the 'quiddity' of the materials of the stage.
Both saw the stage, or performance space, as being fundamentally
incomplete: scenographies did not exist as pictures, nor were they
sculptures; they should have no existence other than as collaborators
in performance. Therefore the artist must explore seemingly non-
representational, abstracted neutral surfaces. Both artists understood
that the physical scenography would be given form, colour, texture
and possibly even dimension by the use of light. Light would
accompany the actor to bring the whole to life. Most importantly,
Appia and Craig, arriving from quite distinctive starting points,
appreciated the quality of performative 'tension' in the liminality of
the empty stage space or 'study site'; both saw it as a place that could
achieve its ultimate artistic life through the act of live performance.

4 The Scene as Machine, 2

Constructing and Building the Scene as Machine

The work of Vsevelod Meyerhold (1874–1940) shortly after the October Revolution in 1917, which created the Russian Soviet Republic, is that which is probably most associated with the concept of scenography serving as a machine, a constructed, functional place for the making of theatre – a physical framework for performance. Modernist Utopian ideas that a society might operate as a machine, with all its parts co-operating and interlocking, were clearly reflected in the theatre. Lyubov Popova was responsible for the scenography of *The Magnanimous Cuckold* in 1922 for Meyerhold's company. Fernand Crommelynck's play is about a pathologically jealous husband who tests his wife's fidelity by offering her to his friends, thereby goading her in order that she might confirm his suspicions. In a society that had dispensed with privacy and, technically, the bourgeois monopololistic tendencies of marriage, Crommelynck's hero seemed genuinely to operate in the best interests of a new society, magnanimously donating his wife for the common good. Popova illustrated this new and unexpected social moral in a kinetic stage construction, which, with some imagination, might be taken to represent a schematic, sectional view of a windmill. She made a stage construction that consisted of grinding wheels and revolving sails, steep ladders, pulleys and delivery chutes: she physically realized a mechanism of desire that allowed the community economy to be illustrated in furious, hyper-efficient and hyperactive stage action. Actors scrambled over the bare structures, ran along catwalks and slid down ramps, physically presenting the socialist transformation of work into fun. It proved to be an ideal stage for the display of biomechanical

Figure 14   The stage as performance construction – Liubov Popova's setting for *The Magnanimous Cuckold*, 1922 (*University of Bristol Theatre Collection*)

performance, 'a spring-board for the actor which quite rightly was compared to the apparatus of the circus acrobat'.[1] In a lecture given in the same year, Meyerhold outlined the principles behind his theory of biomechanics:

> Since the art of the actor is the art of plastic forms in space, he must study the mechanics of his body. This is essential because any manifestation of a force (including the living organism) is subject to constant laws of mechanics (and obviously the creation by the actor of plastic forms in the space of the stage is a manifestation of the force of the human organism).

He then united this theory of the operation of the human body in performance with his scenographic interest in the construction of stage space:

> In art our constant concern is the organisation of raw material. Constructivism has forced the artist to become both artist and engineer.

Arts should be based on scientific principles; the entire creative act should be a conscious process. The art of the actor consists in organising his material; that is, in his capacity to utilise correctly his body's means of expression.[2]

The social and political circumstances of Soviet Russia in the early 1920s and the language of revolution and the building of a new social order coincided to enable Meyerhold's concerns to flourish. In fact, he had been experimenting for almost twenty years with the component elements of the stage 'machine', and this period may be considered as a conclusive period of quite consistent development towards this view of constructed scenography and performance.

In 1905, Stanislavski gave Meyerhold artistic control of the experimental studio attached to the Moscow Art Theatre. Stanislavski hoped the studio would result in finding solutions to the *mise en scène* of symbolist plays, and in so doing he hoped also to expand the ideas for his developing system for training the actor. However, Meyerhold saw the studio as symbolic confirmation of his own personal act of rejection of an existing theatre. In the late eighteenth century Loutherbourg had used the importance of the painted cardboard scenic model to typify the aesthetic harmony and scenographic control that he sought – it was central to his job description. A little over 125 years later, Meyerhold exemplified in the dominance of the scenic model an attitude towards making theatre that he most wanted to reject:

> So after we had completed a whole series of models representing true to life interiors and exteriors, the atmosphere in the workshop became uneasy, with everyone waiting patiently for someone else to give the order to burn or break up every model. But there was no regret, for this labour had served a specific purpose: everyone realised that once the glue on the models had set, the entire machinery of the theatre was set with it. As we turned those models over we seemed to be holding the entire contemporary theatre in our hands. In our desire to burn and destroy them we were already close to the desire to destroy the obsolete methods of the naturalistic theatre.[3]

Beginning in such symbolic acts of rejection there developed Meyerhold's method of working with a technique of impressionistic 'plans'. He would prepare diagrams and plans of stage space, in collaboration with his company, that would serve as a starting point for building a performance in rehearsal. He consistently resisted the premature finality that a detailed painted model or mock-up could illustrate, before work with the actors was even under way. Marjorie Hoover says:

In his later account of the Theatre Studio Meyerhold saw [the] partnership thus: 'the director contributes a drawing (the plan); the artist in accord with this drawing contributes the harmony and colours, the disposition of colour patches ... the director's conception in charcoal or pencil of the movements of lines or ... the artist's sketch of the setting in colours – this is quite enough to move to the stage, bypassing the mock-up.[4]

Furthermore, the circumstances at the new Moscow Art Theatre Studio created a working environment where there was really very little alternative but to find new methods since there were few resources, no budget and only a tiny acting space in which to work. Accordingly, what emerged from Meyerhold's work with the young actors was a heightened consciousness of the materiality, and therefore of the essential artifice, of theatre: the actors were so close to the spectator that the presence of the actor *as actor* became increasingly as important as the actors representing their dramatic character. The realist, illusionist art practised by Stanislavski in the main house of the Moscow Art Theatre effectively dissembled the medium of theatre by using art to conceal art. Modernism and Meyerhold would increasingly use art to call attention to art. In any circumstances, the scenic environment of the Studio, without either the size and distance or the technical resources of an equipped stage house, could at best offer a mere suggestion of location and atmosphere. These imposed conditions of theatrical 'poverty' (a pedagogy of theatrical learning that was to be frequently self-imposed throughout the century) indicated a route that Meyerhold's future understanding of a theatre-making process and its scenography would take.

The Studio lasted only until the following year and it gave no public performances. However, Meyerhold had learned that his act of rejection needed to be more fundamental than could be readily accommodated within the structure of the Moscow Art Theatre as it was instituted under the charismatic control of Stanislavski. The work already undertaken by Meyerhold and the Studio company during that one year indicated the need for a more thoroughgoing reappraisal of theatre and its processes than could be carried out in an environment that had been planned as little more than a training space for young actors, who would 'graduate' into the main theatre. Therefore in May 1906, Meyerhold concluded:

it struck me that an acting school attached to a theatre is death for the actors studying there. An acting school must exist independently and must not teach the current style of acting. It must be organised so that a new theatre arises out of it, so that there is only one possible path leading from it: if the pupils do not go into the new theatre which they have created for themselves, they go nowhere. ... The Theatre-Studio was a theatre in search of new scenic forms.[5]

Meyerhold accepted an invitation to work at the theatre run by Vera Komissarzhevskaya in St Petersburg. The theatre was renovated and elegantly redecorated in white, and Leon Bakst painted a house curtain that showed white nymphs dancing against foliage and the Doric columns of an Elysium temple. *Hedda Gabler* opened there on 10 November 1906. It is clear from Meyerhold's detailed description of the production, and the scenography that he planned with his designer Nikolai Sapunov, that the quality of counter-illusion and stylization that he sought in the production might be found in a focus upon the studiedly artificial theatricality of the staging. He described the approach:

> *Hedda Gabler* on the stage of the Dramatic Theatre is *stylised*. Its aim is to reveal Ibsen's play to the spectator by employing new unfamiliar means of scenic presentation, to create an impression (but only an impression) of a vast, cold blue, receding expanse. Hedda is visualised in cold blue tones against a golden autumnal background. Instead of autumn being depicted outside the window where the blue sky is seen, it is suggested by the pale golden tints in the tapestry, the upholstery and curtains. The theatre is attempting to give primitive, purified expression to what it senses behind Ibsen's play: a cold, regal, autumnal Hedda. ... The huge armchair covered with white fur is meant as a kind of throne for Hedda; she plays the majority of her scenes either on it or near it. The spectator is intended to associate Hedda with her throne and carry away this combined impression in his memory.[6]

It is clear that Meyerhold's and Sapunov's ambition was to construct the *play* of Ibsen and not necessarily the *location* of the play of Ibsen. They were using quite new criteria for their roles as theatre makers: they were transferring their energies from visualizing and creating a fictional reality for the play, to an attempt to physically build a structure to illustrate the dramatic action of the play. Their scenography gave a meaning and significance to the story, rather than simply a display of the story within a detailed reconstruction of the socio-economic realities of the Tesman household. Hoover cites the conclusions of contemporary critics that the setting had not so much ignored Ibsen as gone beyond the text to show 'the dwelling of Hedda's spirit'.[7] Significantly, this was the first major re-working, or reconstruction of a classic play, for which Meyerhold was to be famously noted in his later work on plays by Ostrovsky and Gogol.

Productions by Meyerhold in the Komissarzhevskaya theatre in St Petersburg and the studio theatres where he worked over the next decade were typified by an exploration of the theatricality of theatre along with its scenographic implications, and the more significant realization within this broad generality, that the process of theatre must be thought of as a three-way event. The Stanislavski and Meiningen ambition (as had been Loutherbourg's) was to create a complete world of scenic detail that could be presented fully designed and completed to an audience (the realized version of the scenic model) and this was fundamentally a two-way process – the spectator confronted by the finished art work. Of course, everyone acknowledged that a living audience was essential to any act of theatre; but Meyerhold grew to consider the precise implications for the scenography and the entire *mise en scène*, of the 'liveness' of his audience. He realized that theatre could not be completed by actors and scenographers on the stage and then offered 'ready-made' to its audience: a view that parallels his earlier rejection of the scenic model. An audience should be thought of not as a body of passive, inert *voyeurs* peering into the Tesman household, but as individuals who bring their lives and their concerns into the auditorium. The real, significant act of theatre therefore takes place in a third place, in the liminality of the space that serves as the meeting place between artist and spectator. The architecture of the theatre and its internal scenography should be conceived as the 'imaginative possibility' that is generated where there is a meeting between spectators and the work of theatre artists. As Jane Milling and Graham Ley suggest: 'Meyerhold's focus on the spectator was a powerful and fresh element to his rhetoric and work. Moreover, as he conceives it the spectator is more than simply interpreting, she is completing the creative task of the stage.'[8] In order to achieve this necessary imaginative space, he needed to find ways to establish a creative tension between an audience's enthralment in the action upon the stage, and an awareness of their simultaneous presence at a theatrical event. However, to do this would need more physical freedom than the St Petersburg theatre could, or would, provide.

On 30 December 1906, Meyerhold's production of Alexander Blok's play *Fairground Booth* (*Balaganchik*) tried to create a greater sense of plasticity in the movement of the actors and their greater integration within the scenic structures, and also to counter the tendency of symbolist scenography to create quite static 'significant' poses on a narrow stage set in front of an overtly 'artistic' painted back-scene. In this work he found tremendous support, and indeed life-long inspiration, in his study of the *balagan* – the Russian folk tradition of wandering players performing at carnivals and fairs – and in his simultaneous study of the practice of *commedia dell'arte*. He planned to open the second season at the theatre, in 1907, with a production of Fyodor Sologub's *Gift of the Wise Bees* 'in the round'. This was strongly resisted by Fyodor Komissarzhevsky, the technical and administrative director of the theatre, and Vera's brother, on the grounds that such a rearrangement of the theatre would contravene licensing regulations. A production of *Pelléas and Mélisande* roused further discontent in the theatre management. It was probably an ill-advised decision by Meyerhold since Vera, at the age of forty-three, was challenged in playing the youthful *Mélisande*. Nevertheless, the scenic experiment continued and the production was staged on a small platform set upon the stage proper, and surrounded by the orchestra. Towards the end of the season, Meyerhold was effectively dismissed, but was appointed to the position of Stage Director at the Imperial Alexandrinsky Theatre and at the Imperial Marinsky Opera. He remained at these theatres until the October Revolution in 1917, but continued his experimental work at several smaller studio theatres. It is, of course, significant that he chose to work in these studios under his *commedia*, *doppelgänger* name of Doctor Dappertutto (Dr Everywhere), which he had adopted in 1911 (initially so that he could avoid contractual problems while still employed at the Imperial theatres).

Meyerhold's regular designer of the period was Alexander Golovin, and they collaborated on Molière's *Dom Juan* (9 November 1910) at the Alexandrinsky Theatre and extended the exploration of the *commedia dell'arte*. He continued to explore ways in which the scenic reality of the event might be heightened and in itself become fundamental to the theatre performance. In a letter to his scenographer, Meyerhold describes his 'plan':

The stage to be divided into two parts:

1. The proscenium, constructed according to architectural principles, intended exclusively for 'reliefs' and the figures of the actors (who perform only in this area). The proscenium to have a forestage projecting deep into the auditorium. No footlights. No prompt box.

2. The upstage area, intended exclusively for painted backdrops, is not used by the actors at all, except in the finale ... and even then they will appear only on the dividing line between the two areas.[9]

Sganarelle remained on stage throughout, sitting on a stool close to the audience on the forestage. Stage assistants based upon the *kurogo* of Japanese theatre practice were used as prompters and as scene and property shifters, and to rearrange actors' clothing. In addition, small 'blackamoor' servants ran about the stage sprinkling perfume and 'assisting' actors by, for example, picking up a lace handkerchief dropped by Don Juan. They offered a stool to a theatrically 'tired' actor, or fastened Don Juan's shoe-laces as he argued with Sganarelle, and they removed cloaks and rapiers from the stage after Don Juan's fight with the brigands. They appeared with lanterns when the stage was plunged into semi-darkness, and they summoned the audience with small tinkling bells and, in the absence of a curtain, announced the intervals. The entire action was lit by hundreds of wax candles in chandeliers and candelabra.

The large forestage that was built for *Dom Juan* was very significant for Meyerhold and Golovin. As a 'mechanism' of performance it not only had historic authenticity to Molière's theatre, but also had clear links to absolutely primal scenographies of making theatre – the *orchestra* of Greek antiquity, the Italian *proscenium*, the eighteenth-century forestage, the fairground booth stage, and the Russian *balaganchik*. Employing the original term for the space in front of the scene, Meyerhold says:

But what of the proscenium? Like a circus arena hemmed in on all sides by a ring of spectators, the proscenium projects right out to the audience so that not a single gesture, not a single movement, not a single grimace of the actor is lost in the dust of the wings. And note the conscious adroitness of every gesture, movement, pose and grimace of the proscenium actor. ... How his [Molière's] grotesques sprang to life once they were free to perform without hindrance on a deep, projecting stage area. The atmosphere which fills this space is not stifled by the wings, and the light projected into the dust-free atmosphere falls directly onto the lithe figures of the actors so that the entire surroundings seem to be designed for the intensification of the play of bright light – both from the stage lighting and from the lights in the auditorium which were left on throughout the performance.[10]

The accepted liminality of a forestage seemed to provide the quality of social and creative tension that Meyerhold felt was needed between the actors and the audience. The efficacy of this tension sprang from the binary qualities that the forestage possessed: it seemed to show another world, the world of Don Juan, and yet it was a world that was self-evidently not 'other', since it was not separated from the audience. The dramatic world was therefore both real and false. The excitement of the forestage for Meyerhold was that it could become a more freely accessible, socially licensed halfway place, a place of becoming and of endless possibilities.

The October Revolution in 1917 served to re-energize, concentrate and focus Meyerhold's long period of studio experimentation. He was a committed and energetic participant in the Revolution and held passionate and clearly articulated views about the ability of theatre to play a vital role in the construction of a new socialist culture. He saw his theatre serving as an arena in which 'the new man' – the concept of the revolutionized and modernized proletarian that the events of 1917 created – could both understand and demonstrate personal and social freedom. In 1920 he drew up plans for constructing a trapeze in the open air for acrobats, whose bodies would express the very essence of revolutionary theatre, and also serve to illustrate the enjoyment of the physical struggle in which the new society was engaged. The Revolution understandably gave a clear impetus both to confirm and intensify Meyerhold's rejection of the past, and to progress his interests in popular theatre forms towards an active engagement with a new proletarian audience. The decorative and architectural elements of the *balagan* and of Molière's use of popular *commedia* dramatic forms that Meyerhold had used, were now channelled into the harsher environment and performance aesthetics of the 'cabotin' – the manifest theatricality of the scruffily dressed mountebank performer 'working' the crowd from an equally obvious cheap fit-up platform stage. The trauma of the First World War, alongside political revolution, created a cultural caesura that violently accelerated the processes of rejection and change towards a movement that in many ways closely followed Gordon Craig's three-phase 'agenda': from impersonation to representation to creation. Meyerhold wrote in 1913:

> The actor may get bored with perfecting his craft in order to perform in outdated plays; soon he will want not only to act but to compose for himself as well. Then at last we shall see the rebirth of *the theatre of improvisation*.[11]

From a scenographer's point of view, it is hard not to be excited and enormously invigorated by the totality and the lengths to which

Meyerhold and his team of collaborators went in their scenic and technical revolution during the first decade of the Soviet Republic. The 'cabotinage' of banding together and barnstorming a performance with an audience who might have no formal previous experience of theatre united the immediate political circumstance alongside theatre history in a remarkable manner. The sheer relish of completely taking over a theatre and, in today's terms, treating it as a 'found space', and then building an entire place of performance from hitherto non-traditional materials, is irresistible. Their overall scenographic manifesto was clear:

> Now a word on the sets. For us 'decorative' settings have no meaning; 'decoration' is for the Secessionists and restaurants in Vienna and Munich; spare us 'The World of Art', 'Rococo' and the painstaking detail of museum exhibits. ... We have only to talk to the latest followers of Picasso and Tatlin to know at once that we are dealing with kindred spirits ... we are building just as they are building. ... For us the art of manufacturing is more important than any tediously pretty patterns and colours. What do we want with pleasing pictorial effects?
>
> What the *modern* spectator wants is the placard, the juxtaposition of the surfaces and shapes of *tangible materials*!
>
> To sum up, both we and they want to escape from the box of the theatre on to the wide-open stage – and our artists will be delighted to throw away their brushes and take up axes, picks and hammers to hack stage sets out of the materials of raw nature.[12]

Erast Garin, a student on Meyerhold's two-year drama course, which he established shortly after the Revolution, describes the beginning of the fit-up of Popova's constructivist setting for *The Magnanimous Cuckold* (1922) in the former Zon theatre: 'all his pupils appeared promptly that morning ready for the dirtiest cleaning job ... we had to clear the whole stage area in the huge theatre of "junk", as the master put it'. Garin says 'a pillar of dust' rose up when the accumulated sets and stage furniture from decades of performance were thrown out into the courtyard, adding, 'we simply tossed out the bourgeois theatre with all its crockery'.[13] In all the theatres that he worked in, beginning with the Free Theatre Company, which he called the RSFSR Theatre No. 1 (Rossiskaia Sovietskaia Federativnaia Sotsialisticheskaia Respublika), in 1920, the stages were stripped to their structural architecture, exposing bare brick surfaces and, at the sides in the wings, the counterweight tracks and machinery of the flying system. The proscenium arches were purged of their bourgeois plasterwork and gilded cherubs, and steps, ramps and platforms were built across from the stage into the auditorium. With the removal of the borders, tormentors, and 'teasers' that traditionally concealed the workings of the proscenium stage, spotlights and huge, industrial, 'acting area' lights hung in full view of the audience. The walls of the foyers and the auditorium itself were hung with placards and banners and the aisles through the audience served as entrances for cast and machinery – Meyerhold once roared into the theatre and through the audience on a motorcycle. Meyerhold and his team established a distinctive scenographic identity during the first decade of the Soviet Revolution. In many ways it was an identity whose attitudes and values were to dominate theatre practice for the remainder of the twentieth century.

Probably the most influential *mise en scène* was his production of Nikolai Gogol's *The Government Inspector* (9 December 1926). The acting space was delineated by a semicircular, highly polished mahogany screen containing eleven double doors (plus two more in each of the wings). High above the stage was a dull green border and below this, in full view, were three large suspended industrial area

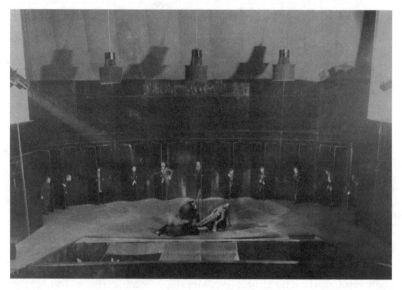

Figure 15   Vsevelod Meyerhold, *The Government Inspector*, 1926, episode 9 ('Bribes') (*University of Bristol Theatre Collection*)

lights. The centre section of the rear, curved screen could be opened to allow a small stage-truck to be pushed silently forward on runners towards the audience with furniture, actors and setting already in place. At the end of the scene, the rear screen re-opened and the truck was pulled off the stage, to be replaced by another similarly set up. All but four of the play's scenes were played on the trucks. The setting for the Inn scene at the beginning was lowered from the flies. The remaining scenes occupied the forestage, which spread out over and around the orchestra pit, and the final tableaux overflowed into the auditorium. The basic architecture and structure of this stage – neutral backing, large forestage that allowed access into the audience, and exposed lighting and stage technology – remained with Meyerhold and were formalized in the plans for the Meyerhold Theatre, which was structurally built, but never fitted out, during the late 1930s.

In 1926, Meyerhold worked with El Lissitsky and Sergei Tretyakov to make a theatre for a proposed production of *I Want a Child*. Lissitsky created a scenography of multiple stages that took over the complete interior of the theatre, entirely obliterating the division between stage and audience. So complex was the project that Meyerhold postponed it until the building of the new theatre. He did not live to see this happen and, as Edward Braun said, 'a production was lost which, to judge from the model and photographs which survive, would have exemplified the spatial and functional concepts of constructivism'.[14]

As has been suggested, Meyerhold characterized his rejection of the immediate theatrical past by casting away the detailed scenic model of card, paper and paint. He committed himself to an idea of building performance throughout the collaboration of the rehearsal process. In doing this he posed a significant theoretical problem that still challenges production practice in contemporary theatre. He rejected the idea that a detailed, finished conception of the scenography should be prepared right at the outset of the production process – usually before rehearsals have begun. Most would agree with the theoretical premise of this. Consider, for example, the parallel status of the completed costume design. If finished costume designs are presented to members of the cast at the *beginning* of their work then, in effect, the designer of those costumes is saying that although the process of discovery has not yet begun in rehearsal, nevertheless these are the clothes that will be worn by the, as yet, undiscovered characters. The theoretical basis both of this and of what Meyerhold typified in the scenic model, makes a nonsense of the reasonable notion that the rehearsal is a process through which a group of theatre artists discover the possible meaning and significance of (typically) a piece of dramatic literature, and that during this process, practical strategies are created for communicating their findings to a future audience. If theatre artists have believed (as they progressively have throughout the twentieth century) that the art of theatre is indeed a *Gesamtkunstwerk*, one that represents a compound and composite of stimuli – aural, visual and temporal – then to determine the visual (or indeed any other) qualities in advance totally contradicts the theoretical meaning and purpose of the rehearsal. Inevitably, of course, the economics and management of the processes of production have tended to retain the illogical theory of the scenic model. Within traditionally organized theatre companies, which must allocate prescribed periods of time to the process of production, it is argued that decisions must be made well in advance in order to enable scenic artists to complete the physical realization of the work.

A further implication of Meyerhold's act of rejection and his adoption of the 'plan' suggests that the director should also undertake the work of the scenographer – the division between directorial and scenographic *mise en scène* is so questionable as to render a meaningful 'job description' unhelpful. The collision that can occur between the ideals of working as collaborative artists alongside the vision of a unified art of the theatre is self-evident and has been illustrated throughout the twentieth century. Aspirations to political and social democracy and more generally collaborative working methods, which have progressively affected most aspects of life, cannot easily accept the idea of theatre art being artistically dominated by a single individual. Few have achieved this combination of skills and talents, although some exceptions, such as Josef Szajna in Poland, David Ultz in Britain or Robert Lepage in Canada, are significant.[15] How therefore to integrate a theory, with which most would unquestioningly agree, within an equally acceptable and creative artistic practice of theatre making?

Caspar Neher (1897–1962) consciously grappled with the challenge to the process of theatre making posed by the rejection of the scenic model. As I have summarized elsewhere, '[Neher] deconstructs the human complexity of the "director–designer relationship" and offers a mode of creating theatre which in an organic way links not only the end-products of dramaturgy and scenography, but also centralizes within this process, the working practices of dramatist, director and scenographer.'[16] The basis of his solution (or rather the solution generated by the creative team with which he worked) was to extend the metaphor of the scene as machine and to suggest that we should conceive of the making of theatre (the rehearsal process) as the constructing of a machine for performance: a machine that naturally includes the physical elements of scenography – setting, costumes, wigs, make-up, properties, furniture – but also a machine that includes the less tangible elements of performance such as idea, tension, repose, movement, light, sound and time. Since all these elements and more operate variously and concurrently during a performance, the *processes* of their creation must surely reflect this. The final, live act of performance becomes the setting in motion of a multi-dimensional structure consisting of many components, which engage and intermesh in complex semiotic formations across both space and time and achieve the ultimate purpose of the 'machine', which is to engage with the imagination of an audience. This immediacy can, according to Neher, provide the only acceptable usage of the word 'reality' in connection with theatre and performance: '[a] picture is never realistic, the stage is always realistic. That's why I maintain that the "realistic stage picture" is a nonsense.'[17]

Neher's relationship with Bertolt Brecht (1898–1956) was initiated by play and theatre fantasy together as schoolboys in Augsburg before the First World War. Probably on account of such an intensely personal collaboration they were able to propose working solutions to the practical problems brought about by the rejection of the predetermined artistic solution to a production that was represented by the scenic model. The problem for Neher and Brecht is typified by their concern to find a proper job title, since they both rejected the names traditionally used in German theatre: *Bühnenbildner*, or *Bühnenmaler* – stage picture-maker or stage painter. Brecht describes the problem:

> Normally the sets are determined before the actors' rehearsals have begun, 'so that they can start', and the main thing is that they evoke an atmosphere, give some kind of expression, [and] illustrate a location; and the process by which this is brought about is observed with as little attention as the choosing of a postcard on holiday. If at all, it is considered with regard to creating a space with some good possibilities for performance. ...
> It seems very strange that set designers (*bühnenbildner*) who feel and claim that they are artists with a 'vision' which they must realise, seldom reckon with the actors, maintaining that set designers can work just as well, or even better, without actors.[18]

Whilst on the other hand, Brecht argues:

> The good scene designer (*bühnenbauer*) proceeds slowly and experimentally. A working hypothesis is based on a precise reading of the text, and substantial conversations with other members of the theatre, especially on the social aims of the play and the concerns of the performance, are useful to him. However, his basic performance ideas must still be general and flexible. He will test them constantly and revise them on the basis of results in rehearsals with the actors. The wishes and opinions of the actors are wells of discovery for him. He studies to what extent their strengths are adequate and intervenes. ... This is how a good stage designer (*bühnenbauer*) works. Now ahead of the actor, now behind him, always together with him. Step by step he builds up the performance area, just as experimentally as the actor.[19]

Neher went further and thought of the term *Bühnenbildner* as a 'Nazi' term since it pretended to offer as being 'real', a coherent and completed view of the world, a *Weltanschauung*, and therefore theatrically suggested someone who could create an aesthetically coherent, harmonious and unified stage picture. As such, the *Bühnenbildner* works so as to deliver to the audience a completed interpretation of the play's meaning. The scenographer as *Bühnenbauer*, on the other hand, believes that the job is to build a scene as an integral component within what Brecht termed the 'practical dramaturgy' of the play in performance. Working in this way, therefore, the scenography must be conceived as an act of performance: as a combination of thinking and its associated active intervention. The scenographer will be responsible, along with others, for the construction of theatrical 'components' within the overall machine. In this context, Brecht's use of the term *gestus* as an action of showing the character to an audience needs to be expanded to include the scenographic *gest*. This is a very different attitude from that which assumes that the designer's prime function is to create the stage setting as a completed interpretation of the drama expressed in the scenic model, and the costumes expressed in painted designs.

At the very beginning of his career in the early 1920s, Neher rejected not only past realist and naturalistic theatre, but also what he similarly thought of as the overly pictorial 'effects' of expressionist art and stage design. He rejected the harsh, distorted angular lines and tightly focused, steeply angled light sources and the use in the theatre of fashionable filmic dramatic shadows. Throughout all his work, and in keeping with this resistance to pictures and pictorial effects, he tried to find the theatrical equivalent of the sketch. He tried to find ways of giving timber canvas and stage paint a softness of definition similar to the tentative and suggestive effects achieved by drawing and writing with ink upon damp watercolour paper; a medium that Neher particularly favoured. In this way, for example, his drawings of characters in the play (importantly *not* conceived as costume 'designs') were intended as points of departure and as a focus for debate and development during rehearsal.

To achieve this integration of artistic means, there naturally had to be the closest possible creative collaboration between theatre artists. This was not only vital for the development of an appropriate stage aesthetic and new working practices, but vital for the development of an artistic philosophy that was attempting such a total 'refunctioning' (*Umfunctionierung*) of theatre and the processes of production. The ability for director, writer and scenographer to consider *all* aspects of theatre without following an established theatre etiquette of professional 'areas of responsibility' lies at the heart of the collaboration between Neher and Brecht. A significant and provocative description of rehearsing with Brecht and Neher is given by Egon Monk, who was present during rehearsals of *The Tutor* at the Berliner Ensemble in 1950:

> Brecht and Neher sitting next each other at rehearsal. Both of them leaning back, their knees pressed against the seats in front. Brecht appreciatively studying his cigar; Neher, his eyebrows exaggeratedly raised or exaggeratedly frowning over his glasses, more severe. ... They are rehearsing 'by interjections'. Each interjection is prefaced by Neher or Brecht naming its originator. 'Neher thinks ...', 'Besson thinks ...', 'Brecht thinks ...', 'Monk thinks ...' The interjection is listened to then tested. If a detail works, then Brecht giggles with pleasure and Neher gives him a look of amusement. ... This lasts a long time.

A significant practical method employed by Neher and the Company was the use of his *Arrangementskizzen*, which were made both before and, importantly, during rehearsal. These sketches resemble a story-board presentation of the play. However, as used by Neher and his successor at the Berliner Ensemble, Karl von Appen, they were much more. Their focus was upon the actor and upon the ability of theatrical performance to create an integrated *gestus* of significance. Therefore, they were not simply a moment-by-moment transcription of dramatic text into visual text *en route* to becoming a completed performance text, and they were not a preliminary stage in the process of design, which would be superseded by more detailed drawings and a scenic model. Monk continues:

> They [Neher's sketches] always lay ready to hand on the director's table, with the scene currently being rehearsed on top. Nearly all the blocking of the Berliner Ensemble derived directly from Neher's sketches. If there was a particular scene, or a particular moment within a scene – a 'nodal point' as Brecht and Neher would call it – that had no sketch, or if Neher for once was not there (a rare occurrence in the first years of the Berliner Ensemble), then that rehearsal might well be broken off. As for instance when the last scene but one of *The Tutor* was being rehearsed: 'Engagement in a Snowstorm'. This had to appear as an idyll, amiable at first but gradually undermined by malice. ... On stage, a large number of actors, glasses in their hands, drinking a toast (yes, but how?). Projected behind them, falling snow. Brecht rehearsed somewhat indecisively, asked first one then another of his aides to try blocking the scene, looking helplessly at the actors on stage, who looked equally helplessly down on him, then finally said: 'It's no use, we'll have to wait till Cas gets here.'

At the Berliner Ensemble the sketches became a constant part of rehearsal methodology. Far from serving merely to animate the discussions between director, scenographer and technical crew (as is the traditional function of the story-board), they drew strength from the actors, were fed back to them and served as models for stage blocking and textual development. Monk concludes:

> Friedrich Maurer as Wenzeslaus the Schoolmaster. ... One hand holding Neher's sketch, the other holding the long quill pen with which the sketch shows him driving Count Vermuth and the Major's armed domestics from the room. A most impressive moment, clarifying the scene as no subsequent performance could do.[20]

Neher and Brecht's developed practice of creative collaboration in making theatre exemplifies a practical scenography standing side by side with a practical dramaturgy. As the text of performance slowly emerged, component parts within the overall machine were built up by confrontations between actors and scenographic material. More than adding the element of three dimensions to dramatic literature this raises a further, and very important issue in connection with the identity of scenography.

Craig, Appia and Meyerhold had all endowed scenography with the independent and the collaborative power of bearing significance

Figure 16   Caspar Neher: a place on stage that has its reality in performance: *Threepenny Opera*, at the Theater am Schiffbauerdamm, photograph, 1928 (*Bertolt-Brecht-Archiv: Stiftung Archiv der Akademie der Künste, Berlin*)

and communicating meaning. Neher and von Appen, through their practice with Brecht, pursued this to a logical conclusion. But how should the results of such collaborative creation be viewed beyond the time of the original performance? Dramatic literature naturally lives on through print and thereby has an important, although incomplete, after-life; but what of the scenography, the original stage mechanism for its performance? Brecht called the overall construction a 'model'. From the collaboration between Elizabeth Hauptmann, Bertolt Brecht, Caspar Neher and Kurt Weill that created *The Threepenny Opera* at the Theater am Schiffbauerdamm, during the summer of 1928, emerged the first production in which the idea of an entire *mise en scène* achieved the status of a 'model'. The argument runs that if the scenography offers a layer of performance and significance that is integral to the entire meaning of the performance, then it *should* theoretically be as inappropriate to separate it from future productions as to omit sections of the written dialogue or the musical score. Brecht acknowledges the problem in a typically slippery manner as he introduces the *Courage-Modell 1949* and proposes a theoretical resolution to the problem of the 'model', one that illustrates resistance to permanence in *any* aspect of theatre:

> Provisional structures must be erected, and there is the danger that they may become permanent. Art reflects all this; ways of thinking are part and parcel of ways of life. As far as the theatre is concerned, we throw our Models into the gap. ... And the Models will be misused by those who accept them and have not learnt how to handle them. Intended to make things easier, they are not easy to handle. Moreover, they are not made to exclude thought, but to inspire thought; they are not made to replace artistic creativity, but to compel it.[21]

To the practitioner this may be easier to say than to do since, in so many instances, the scenographic identity created by the original team of collaborators is as persuasive and beautiful as the written text. Should the question of what we *do* with the image of Mother Courage's cart on the revolving stage and her famous 'silent' cry of anguish be as relevant as what we *do* with Brecht's written text? Kenneth Tynan's review of the visit of the Berliner Ensemble to the Palace Theatre in London in 1956 illustrates the problem:

> Let me instance the peasant wedding in *The Caucasian Chalk Circle*, a scene more brilliantly directed than any other in London. A tiny cell of a room, ten by ten, is cumulatively jammed with about two-dozen neighbours and a sottish monk. The chances for broad farce are obvious, but they are all rejected. Reality is preferred, reality of a memorable and sculptured ruggedness. I defy anyone to forget Brecht's stage pictures. No steps or rostra encumber the platform; the dominant colours are browns and greys; and against a high, encircling, off-white backcloth we see nothing but solid, selected objects – the twin gates in *The Caucasian Chalk Circle* or Mother Courage's covered wagon. The beauty of Brechtian settings is not of the dazzling kind that begs for applause. It is the more durable beauty of <u>use</u>.[22]

But perhaps a key to an understanding of the problem posed by the production 'model' may well lie in Brecht's notion of throwing them 'into the gap'. Is this the gap in which 'provisional structures' *must* be erected? Are the assertive 'must' and the present tense of 'ways of thinking' an indication of both the necessity and also the immediacy of the staged production? How might the future status of such an inevitably temporary staged solution differ from the status of the written dialogue of a play-text? Perhaps the act of 'taking on' words and dialogue that may be many years old is qualitatively different for an actor, from that of a scenographer who might 'take on' the scenographic gestures of Neher? After all, we happily adopt the words of Chekhov (or *The School for Scandal*) but not the scenographies of Stanislavski (or Loutherbourg). Notwithstanding the degree and extent of scenographic collaboration and integration, perhaps the 'gap' of understanding can only be related to the immediate conditions of performance, and as these change, so, inevitably, will the gap and so too must the solutions that are proposed. So, although proposing a working methodology for achieving some of the possibilities for scenography that had been suggested by Craig, Appia and Meyerhold, Neher's practice has also raised significant theoretical issues that continue to be of considerable interest for both the identity and the practice of scenography.

5 The Scene as Machine, 3

The Kinetic Stage Machines of Josef Svoboda

In several ways, the work of Josef Svoboda (1920–2002) represents something of a culmination of the scenographic ideas that have been considered in the context of Craig, Appia, Meyerhold and Neher. The sheer output and wide range of his theatre, coupled with the comprehensiveness of vision make it appropriate that his work should be considered across the distinctions that have been chosen as chapters in this book. In this chapter, and by way of introduction, I want to introduce Svoboda's central concern for the kinetic potential of scenography and for his creation of what he called a 'psychoplastic' space. I hope to suggest that the movement of the scene (whether realized by physical movement or by movement of light) represents the final breaking down of the unhelpful dichotomy that had been noted by earlier artists – characters and dramatic action move, but are usually set against an immobile background and within a fundamentally static environment – the scene may be a machine, but it does not move. In a later chapter that focuses upon lighting and its technologies, I shall return to a further consideration of Svoboda's contribution and a consideration of the way in which light served both as a material of construction within the scenographic machine and as the technology that gave kinetic force to the stage.

In 1910 the painter René Piot visited Craig in London and was shown his model of scenic screens. He reported back to the director of the Théâtre de l'Art, Jacques Rouché:

> Craig wants his scenery to move like sound, to refine certain moments in the play just as music follows and heightens all its movements; *he wants it to*

advance with the play. ... I don't know how far this idea can be put into practice; but the idea itself is first-class, and if it were carried out it would revolutionise the art of scene-designing; for there has always been an antagonism between the movement of the plot and the immobility of the scenery; if the scene could change in harmony with the development of the plot, this would provide an entirely new source of expression.[1]

Svoboda's practice and his writing about the organization of 'theatrical space' continuously and consistently addressed this issue. His professional practice began in Prague in 1943 with a production of Hölderlin's play *Empedocles* at the Smetana Museum theatre, and he was still active as an international scenographer, and also as the Artistic Director of the Laterna Magika theatre in Prague, until very shortly before his death in 2002. The longevity and the artistic consistency of the principles that underpin his practice are important, and they serve as an interesting extension of the scenographic work of Meyerhold and his collaborators, and of Neher and Brecht. Furthermore, Svoboda was remarkably focused and articulate in interview, discussion and in his several publications. He was also a committed teacher and spent many of his final years touring the world attending seminars and dialogues and giving master-classes. In these, he was always very open in acknowledging the debt of influence and inspiration that he received from earlier theatre artists, and in locating his work and ideas within a continuum of developing practice and theory. He saw the ideas and practice of the earlier artists as establishing the framework of principle and concept of scenography for which he had the theatrical infrastructure, and the opportunity to develop the technology to implement and develop it. He responded especially to their commitment to the importance of the imagination; their absolute faith in the importance of theatre within a civilized community; and their belief that the theatre artist should work from a powerful sense of artistic and social 'necessity'. He concluded a seminar 'Towards a Visual Dialogue', in London in May 1998, by saying:

Of course I was influenced by Craig – he was an artist who understood the necessity, the necessity of the imagination, and the necessity that theatre is an art. Europe needs many, many, many more Craigs today!

In addition, during the late 1960s and through the 1970s when Svoboda was arguably at his most prolific and influential, his work, as it increasingly became familiar to the West, became synonymous with the establishment of the word 'scenography', where hitherto 'stage designer' or 'theatre designer' or even 'stage decorator' had been the most commonly used terms. The word 'scenographer' is now universally accepted and is used to describe the artists who have responsibility for all the visual and aural contributions of theatre and performance: the stage setting and properties, costume design, lighting and sound design. To those who 'discovered' the work of Svoboda during the late 1960s, it appeared to represent a degree of synergy and integration that went far beyond a seemingly straightforward bringing together of visual and aural ingredients. The musical metaphor of accompaniment has frequently been used to indicate what might be the proper partnership between scenographic support and the actors, and as we shall consider later, the flexibility of stage lighting has been consistently involved in enabling such a relationship. However, as Craig discovered (at great cost to his ultimate reputation) with the screens setting for *Hamlet* in Moscow, the achievement of a seamless movement of scenes was a considerable challenge to the available stage technologies. None the less, Svoboda always considered movement of all kinds – both physical and atmospheric – to be essential, and committed his work to finding some resolutions to the 'antagonism between the movement of the plot and the immobility of the scenery' to which Piot referred.

Svoboda's ambition for scenography was that it should embrace the complete realization and staging *in time* of performance (the language is inadequate to encompass this all-embracing totality, but although still retaining the static quality of placement, *mise en scène* comes closer). To achieve this he focused attention upon the conceptualization of a production idea that, in itself, would become the major activity of realization involved in determining the *mise en scène* – in this sense a logical extension of Meyerhold's concern to stage the dramatic action of *Hedda Gabler* at St Petersburg in 1906. The fullest possible collaboration of artistic materials and means implied in this ambition must, of course, be similarly paralleled with human collaboration amongst the team of scenographers, actors, and with the entire production team. The implementation of 'scenography' in the fullest sense of Svoboda's meaning and the employment of 'scenographers' have profound effects upon all aspects of the production process and the technical management of the theatre. It has been the totality of Svoboda's vision of the kinetic possibilities of scenography and his active engagement with complex new technologies to achieve this, and his ability (most importantly in collaboration with others) to make a 'palette' out of the total means of theatre, that have influenced the practice and especially education for theatre worldwide from the 1960s until the present day.

In many ways Svoboda's work and approach might also be thought of as a culmination of the ideologies of essentially modernist theatre artists of the first half of the twentieth century. His approach was coherent and he was committed to rationality and scientific precision. In searching for new solutions he was as radical in the rejection of past ones as any architectural or product designer at the Bauhaus of the 1920s. As his principal chronicler and biographer, Jarka Burian, says: 'Svoboda himself, educated as an architect and later a Professor of Architecture, has an inherent sense of discipline and is impatient with any sign of dilettantism; he respects the past and has tirelessly striven to understand and perfect his medium on a scientific basis.'[2] And yet, as Burian also shows, it is probably too simplistic to summarize Svoboda's achievement in this way. Rational, scientific, ordered, structured, coherent – most certainly, but he also displayed a post-modern tendency and will to mix media and to juxtapose; to frequently incorporate a self-reflexive theatricality; and as Ruggero Bianchi identified, an ability to create 'a neo-Baroque style that expresses an artist's enchantment with the contemporary world of perfected technology and media and his desire to share his enchantment with the spectator'.[3]

In 1999 whilst working on a model proposal for an assertively 'modernist' staging of Verdi's *La forza del destino* for the opera stage in the Verona arena, he was also creating a complex media installation in the Laterna Magica theatre. This was a production that he had 'written' in collaboration with the choreographer Igor Holováč, called *Past (The Trap)*, which explored the interface between the spaces of a real and a virtual world. The technology behind the scenography was a modern re-working of the nineteenth-century 'ghost' illusion known as 'Pepper's Ghost'. It consisted of a bare stage space, dominated by a vast screen of 50 per cent reflectivity made of tightly tensioned plastic material that spanned the entire stage width and was angled at 45 degrees to the floor of the stage. Through sophisticated moving and still projection from both in front and behind, this screen enabled the appearance, disappearance and half-appearance of actors and objects. It was frivolous, eclectic and at times seemingly flippant, and referential to all of the Svoboda 'trademarks' of mysterious projected imagery, and yet it was fundamentally serious and disturbing in its presentation of the real/non-real world of modern computer living. Whilst Svoboda is therefore capable in many ways of being called the ultimate modernist scenographer, his work frequently under-cut the idealistic modernist sense of trying to create the 'perfect' or the definitive design for a production. Perhaps a keen sense of the temporary, and circumstantial, nature of the 'gap' into which he threw his scenographic propositions encouraged the self-reflexivity that marks his work.

Within the context of this immediate discussion, Svoboda's vision of the resources of theatre serves to amplify, extend and also to transcend the metaphor of scenography as a 'machine for performance' as presented so far through the work of Craig, Appia, Meyerhold and Neher. This is, of course, not to say that Svoboda is 'better', or more sophisticated, simply that his longevity and his position as senior scenographer in a very substantially funded state theatre system, and his major role in the education of future scenographers, allowed him the opportunity to experiment with newly available technologies and structural solutions in a manner that had previously not been attempted. For example, his desire to find new surfaces to receive and to transmit projected images, or the need to move large sections of staging smoothly and silently, necessitated both the establishment of a highly skilled research team at the workshops of the Narodni Divadlo in Prague, and also the need to build relationships with industrial research and manufacture that were quite new to the making of theatre.

Beyond the opportunity to put into practice and develop some of the solutions proposed by the early artists, Svoboda's over-riding and crucial contribution has been to realize the consequences for scenography and technology of the time-based nature of performance. Actors move, narrative moves, emotions, feelings and actions move, and, of course, meaning and significance move and change within performance. If the scene aspired to be a true machine for and of performance, then it too should be capable of movement. Of course, since the Renaissance work of Bernardo Buontalenti at the court of the Medici, and Inigo Jones at the Stuart court, the endeavour of the stage had been to enable movement, and to provide the *frisson* of excitement as the scenic world dissolved and reformed before your eyes. The eventual lowering of the curtain to conceal movement and change on the stage was a late nineteenth-century practice to mask the inability of contemporary technology to render movement and change aesthetically pleasing, and to provide a 'shutter-like' revelation of the world on stage. But the movement of the scene proposed by Svoboda is of a different and quite a particular kind. The stage must, according to Svoboda, be a kinetic place of performance, not in the historical sense of changing scenes to change locations, but a kinesis that will create and change the qualities of liminality within the environment of the stage.

As has been discussed, a liminal stage space, such as the formal space of the Nō theatre, the platform of Shakespeare's theatre, or the forestage of the eighteenth-century playhouse, is one that is both scenic and formal; it is simultaneously representational and presentational, rhetorical and illusionary. But for Svoboda this was a space that, through performance, would be transformed in time as the performance progressed. Within the large, urban Italianate theatre buildings within which Svoboda spent his career, his kinetic scenography converted the box of the proscenium arch stage into an architectonic structure that was fitting and apt for the presentation of the play, and that kinetically reflected the emotional movement of the drama – what he termed a 'psycho-plastic space'. Svoboda said that he always began his work of making a scenography by staring into the void of the empty stage. He would attempt to project himself and his thoughts about the drama into the 'possibilities of the void' – not in order to attempt a conversion of the space into, say, the Verona of *Romeo and Juliet* or the Elsinore of *Hamlet*, but to make a space that would become the dramatic space of their performance. And furthermore as a partner in that performance, it could not remain a static space; it had to be one that would reflect the movement of the drama.

The kinaesthetic energy was to be generated by the interplay of performance alongside all the resources of scenography. For example, he described a scenography for a proposed production of *Faust* in 1970 with director Alfréd Radok, in which a crucial conceptual understanding was that Mephistopheles and Wagner, Faust's student and domestic servant, were one and the same person, and, of course, one and the same actor. The stage box was an empty and seemingly void space, shaped only by huge, very dark brown, barely distinguishable wall surfaces to the back and sides. The stage floor was steeply raked and apparently flagged with stone. A crucial feature of this floor was that beneath the stage were to be fitted felt-covered 'dampers' that could, by the action of silently operating pistons, be made to press against the under-surface of the stage and render it silent. As Faust prepared his occult pentagram down stage to 'conjure' diabolic forces, the stage would echo with the sound of his and Wagner's footsteps. Wagner, however, would not engage or assist in

Faust's conjuring practices; he would turn and make to leave, walking up stage, and his echoing footsteps would be heard. As he reached the farthest limit of the stage he would turn and walk back down the stage in total silence to stand before Faust – everyone in the theatre would know that in that transition of sound from echoing noise to silence he had become Mephistopheles. Who and what had created this scenography and its meaning? Is this set design, lighting design, sound design or costume design? Is it the work of the actor in the bare space? It is, of course, all of these, and, argued Svoboda, illustrates his understanding of the word 'scenography'.[4]

This illustration furthermore exemplifies Svoboda's belief that the stage should use technologies to retain a sense of distance from representation. In other words he consciously used the strangeness, the mystery of effects and their frequently complex technologies to keep the scenography on the level of the inner feelings and meaning of the play. Svoboda's stage existed as a place of transformation and magic, a place that would employ high technology to generate mystery and metaphors of complex human experience, although he did not use the stage to valorize technology or simply to display its powers. His fundamental concern was to use technology to reveal the human condition of the drama: to explore the ability of theatre to make an authentic new reality on the stage that 'testified to more important discoveries about the human spirit than any [individual] technical characteristic could provide'.[5]

Importantly also, Svoboda's stages would remain profoundly modern in appearance, and although he may frequently make reference to past forms and styles, for example using sections of skilfully painted representational imagery, the audience were never in doubt as to the absolutely contemporary nature of the art that they were experiencing. The scenes would most certainly never pretend to transport the audience to any far off place or time. It was Svoboda's view that it was through an assertive modernity that the stage achieved its relationship with its audience and accordingly acquired its 'licence' to become a liminal space: '[o]nly that which is contemporary on stage can thoroughly interest the spectator and affect him strongly. ... Contemporary art should present a ground plan of life, the life-style of its time.'[6] The inter-relationships of scenic details and their capacity for association with contemporary life outside the theatre created, from the abstract and undefined space of the stage, a transformable, kinetic and dramatic space. Svoboda's continued use of the phrase 'psycho-plastic space' identifies the links between three-dimensional space and its ability to relate with the psychological realities both of the dramatic action and of the audience. But the qualities of such dramatic space must be controllable: space may be cheerful space if it needs to be so, but it may also be a tragic space should the drama change. Good scenography can therefore transform itself synchronously with the progress of the action, with the course of its moods, and with the development of its conceptual and dramatic line. As identified by Craig and Appia, space, time, rhythm and light are the core elements that possess this dynamic ability, moreover they are intangible elements and they indicate the essential characteristics of scenography. Svoboda would qualify these qualities by calling them 'dramatic space', 'dramatic time', 'dramatic rhythm' and 'dramatic light', and it must be the scenographer's function to know how to generate and to manipulate the synthesis of these elements that make 'time-space' – what Svoboda calls the fourth dimension of the stage – since dramatic movement implicates both space and time.

How is Svoboda's understanding of the stage a 'machine'? Lyubov Popova took the brutally stripped, and 'liberated', stage of Meyerhold's theatre and made a construction of timber, metal components and minimal paint for *The Magnanimous Cuckold* in 1922. Actors ran, walked and manipulated the 'machine' in their performance: the stage framework and its apparatus remained assertively that, and together, actors and construction became an orchestrated device to *illustrate* and *represent* the themes and ideas of Crommelynck's play. Svoboda's scenographies include the potential for all of this, but he considerably expands and re-figures the constructional elements available to the machine maker. Naturally, with his extensive reliance upon the use of light and projected imagery, these represent significant materials, but it is also his distinctive view of the stage both as a 'building board' and as a crucial component of the machine itself that distinguishes his work. The key to understanding this distinction may lie in the fact that Svoboda made almost every one of his scenographies in large, extremely well equipped proscenium arch theatres. Almost every other innovative theatre artist of the twentieth century has begun his or her work with a rejection of this form, alongside the rejection of the approach to *mise en scène* that has been associated with it.

It may well be that Svoboda wanted to maintain the capability of the theatre experience that the proscenium arch form can offer, to absorb and emotionally involve the spectator – but not as Loutherbourg or Stanislavski would have wished. In a scenography by

Svoboda the spectator is absorbed into the mental world of the action of the drama as opposed to merely its location. As in a Stanislavski *mise en scène*, the spectators are invited to 'lose' themselves, but not to take on the role of voyeurs into a supposedly real scene being played out on stage. Svoboda wanted a more active engagement, an engagement with, for example, the inner worlds of Oedipus or Hamlet and their turbulent action, but one that is interactive to the extent that the involvement is ultimately contemporary, modern and returned to the audience. In other words, Svoboda's insistence upon a direct relationship with the modern and circumstantial world of his audience prevents a 'Disney-like' exploitation of technology that may merely produce a gasp of wonder. The machines that Svoboda constructed to achieve this may well have employed identical technologies of image generation and manipulation, but the motives and functioning of the machines in their relationship with the audience were quite distinct.

For the production of *Tosca* that he made with Karel Jernek (Theatre of the 5th May, Prague, 1947) he constructed a stage that showed the massive rotundity of baroque architecture. But as its angles and perspective swayed and teetered, it invited its audience to consider (and respond to?) an indulgent and otiose society that was being toppled through the action of extreme emotion and personal indulgence. The superb scene-painting skills used to make the painted *trompe l'oeil* perspectives of colonnades and cathedral dome would have been the admiration of a Loutherbourg, or any nineteenth-century scenic artist, and yet the machine served its contemporary critical function by its geometric distortion and the fact that the audience could see behind the scenes to observe the artifice of the social culture that it portrayed. *Oedipus Rex* (Smetana Theatre, Prague, 1963; director, Miroslav Machánek) assertively showed a seemingly endless flight of steps that descended from the distant recesses of the stage and burst through the proscenium arch, over the orchestra pit and into the auditorium. No iconography of the classical world was used: the steps were a brutal presentation of inevitability, not in themselves, but only in interaction with the measured tread of the actor. From the sides of the stage, parallel with the treads, small platforms slid silently across the stage with the determination of a choral response.

Between 1974 and 1976, Svoboda undertook perhaps the greatest of contemporary scenographic challenges when he worked with Götz Friedrich to make a *mise en scène* for *Der Ring des Nibelungen* at the

Figure 17   Josef Svoboda and the material reality of the stage: Sophocles, *Oedipus*, National Theatre at the Smetana, Prague, 1963; directed by Miroslav Macháček (*Šárka Hejnová*)

Royal Opera House, Covent Garden in London. His stage used the silent, unseen and awesome power of electronic technology to manipulate a platform that, effectively, replaced the floor of the stage. Beneath this, a huge single centrally placed 'fist' supported the platform, effortlessly turning, twisting and tilting the stage. As the

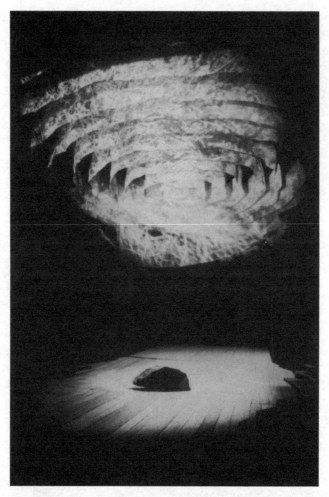

Figure 18   Josef Svoboda: the projection becomes a material reality –
Goethe, *Faust*, Teatro Piccolo, Milan, 1989 and 1991; directed by Giorgio
Strehler (*Šárka Hejnová*)

platform tilted high, the mirrored underside of the platform revealed
another world deep beneath the stage that was the source of both the
electronic and the mythic power. The scenography was aggressively
modern in that it seemed to be a naked display of technology and
hidden powers of control, and as such it was as mysterious and awesome as the operation of some ballistic missile silo that seems to be

in thrall to an unseen and unstoppable authority. In this way, the myths and gods of Wagner's music drama, and more importantly their significance and power, were shared with an audience through Svoboda's kinetic machine.

More recently Svoboda twice worked with Giorgio Strehler at the Piccolo Teatro, Milan, in 1989 and 1991, to stage Parts 1 and 2 of Goethe's *Faust*, and these were rare occasions when Svoboda worked outside a proscenium stage. As with many of his most successful scenographies, his work consisted of a fundamentally simple and single component within the overall machine. In this case he conceived a vast hanging of fabric held in a deep spiral above the large thrust stage of the Piccolo. The fabric seemed to be the self-colour of an unbleached and an undyed material, and it had a uniform, somewhat 'un-ironed' appearance. At once, by its size and height, it was oppressive, but by its spiral form it looked planned, controlled and controlling. Its shape tantalized and beckoned, and lured you tighter and tighter into its spiral track. As a metaphor it was a powerful simulacrum of divinities that simultaneously attract, tempt and ultimately control. In practice, as a 'machine' suspended above the stage it served to receive a bewildering array of projected images and undermined the organization of its spiral structure to become whatever Faust, and Goethe, wished. This was achieved primarily by the fullest possible integration of light within the mechanics of the scenic machine – light both created and changed space, and therefore the structure of the machine.

By taking the empty void of stage space and not simply building a machine to stand on the stage, Svoboda persistently converted the entire space into larger, endlessly transformable machines. His scenography brought together the moving scenes of Craig and the constructed, self-referential theatricality of Meyerhold, and he extended the 'Neher/Brecht-like' quality of creating a 'text' of performance using the materials and technologies of theatre as a palette of opportunities. That palette of materials became dominated by the theatre's ability to employ the atmospheric, unifying and transforming accompaniment of light as proposed by Appia. It was the acceleration of technological development during the last half of the century that enabled him to conceive of that light in ways that went beyond illumination, colour or effect, and which allowed him to treat the light as a material reality and therefore as a structural component within the stage machine.

6 The Century of Light, 1

Diffused and Living Light

> Where the other arts say, 'that means', music says, 'that is'. When forms and colours seek to express something, light says, 'I am; forms and colours will come into being only through me.'
>
> Adolphe Appia, *La Vie Musicale*, 1 April 1908

Electric power and lighting have been the major new technologies in the theatre of the twentieth century. The manipulation and movement of scenery have become easier and more sophisticated first through hydraulic power and then through electric motors and latterly moving 'cushion' air pallets and through computer control. To a greater or lesser extent, however, these are improvements in operation to the existing scenic manoeuvres of lifting, lowering and sliding; whereas electric light created a distinction of such significance in comparison with oil or gas lighting, that its introduction may be thought of as a radically new ingredient within theatre and performance. In this chapter I want to examine the development of electric lighting within the theatre and to consider the theories that have emerged to account for its use in performance. However, whilst stage lighting may well be considered to be the new, and possibly dominant, scenographic element in use, of equal interest and significance are the implications which a more detailed consideration of stage lighting has produced, and the impact which lighting has had upon dramaturgy and our understanding of the nature of the arts of performance.

For example, the manipulation of electric lighting revealed quite graphically that the theatre was essentially a form that happened in time, and that furthermore its revelation through time involved movement, and that movement was created by, and in turn would create, rhythm. This process of revelation achieved by the existence

94

(or otherwise) of light has presented theatre as a distinctive phenomenon of perception, a thing apart and, most importantly, quite distinct from the realization of dramatic literature, and so has presented a radical alternative to the role of literary interpretation as being the presiding rationale for theatre. Therefore, the theatre – the very act of living performance that was revealed and expressed by light – might have meaning and significance in and of itself. In turn also, the immediacy of the illuminated stage and its rightful deference to lighting has focused attention upon the act and quality of reception by an audience and its imaginative relativity. The stage and its artists make work that has no completion, no finished state until received and imagined by a living audience.

Realization of the essential 'quiddity' of the theatre, and the living plasticity of the theatrical experience and the relativity of its reception by an audience, have consequently provided the bedrock of theory and practice ever since Craig's insistence upon the independence of the art of the theatre in his early essay 'On the Art of the Theatre' (1905). It has affected dramaturgy in the way in which the act of writing for performance has increasingly become integrated within the creative studio of the rehearsal room, and it has affected the subject of performance since performance itself (as a phenomenon of perception) may well be the true subject matter of performance.

The introduction of electric light during the last twenty years of the nineteenth century, as has been described earlier, played a major part in precipitating the decline of nineteenth-century scenic language. Higher levels of illumination than had been achieved by gas lighting served to expose the hitherto acceptable painted two-dimensional scenery as being inadequate and tawdry, and, especially in contrast with the urgent political and social concerns of naturalist writers, the stage only seemed capable of offering a world of tricks, effects and falsity. It should be remembered, however, that until the period 1912–14, electric filament bulbs were only comparable in light output with the latest gas burner and mantle technology. Thomas Edison's invention and initial commercial exploitation generally fix the birth of the filament lamp as taking place in 1879, and by the 1880s, large-scale industrial manufacturing was under way in America and Europe by the Edison electric light company, and in Europe by the Deutsche Edison-Gesellschaft. Edison's first commercial lamps were made in two sizes, of 8 and 16 standard candle power, but by 1883 a 25-candle-power lamp was in production. Gösta Bergman provides a useful chart of comparative light intensities (see Table 2).[1]

Table 2   Comparative light intensities

Oil lamp with one wick (could be up to 8)	c.2 candles
Argand lamp	c.10 candles
Gas jet	c.14 candles
Auer gas burner (with mantle)	c.60/70 candles
Arc lamp (6 amps)	c.320 candles
Arc lamp (12 amps)	c.920 candles
Electric filament lamp in 1880s	c.8–25 candles

With these figures in mind, it is understandable that until the output of electric lamps was increased, many theatres operated with a mixture of both gas and electric lighting. In 1893 the Paris Opéra sent a representative to London to study the machinery and lighting resources of the theatres. He reported that the English retained gas-light in the battens and that 'the mingling of the two kinds of lighting, gas and electricity, produces a light that is warmer, somehow more alive, more mobile and that pleases the eye'.[2] He may well have been reporting on stage practice at the Lyceum Theatre, where Henry Irving resisted the introduction of electricity, and had become extremely skilful in colouring and blending light on his gas-lit stage, employing combinations of coloured light much as a painter would use a palette of pigments. He did not content himself with the traditional, very limited set of colour filters but added a large number of new shades to the range of colours. Bergman says that 'he had transparent lacquers applied to the glasses of the limelights and, when electric light came in, to the bulbs of the electric lights, and thus produced effects of colour both of intensity and delicacy up till then unknown'.[3]

The lighting system that was installed in 1898 at the new opera house in Stockholm would seem to represent the very latest contemporary technology and to be similar to that which would have been available, for example, in London, Paris, Moscow and Berlin, and therefore to Craig, Appia, Stanislavski, Meyerhold and Reinhardt at the commencement of their theatre practice. At Stockholm, the permanent lighting installation[4] on stage consisted of nine pairs of wing 'ladder' battens each consisting of three circuits of eight lamps each. There were nine matching overhead battens located behind the hanging borders, each similarly consisting of three circuits of forty lamps each. The colours in the three circuits were white, red and green. In addition, there were extra battens known as 'movable lengths' that could be placed behind ground-rows and set pieces of scenery, and movable upright light 'standards', or 'bunches' for similar use – in all some 600 extra lamps. Thus the total number of lamps in fixed battens amounted to 1512 plus the additional 600 in portable units, but all these incandescent lamps still had a luminous intensity of only 25-candle power – less than half the intensity of the very latest mantle gas burner. For the lighting for special effects, such as moonlight or sunrise, and for increased local intensity of light there were eight electric arc lamps of 9 amps each, complete with polished reflectors; however, a stage technician was needed to operate each of the individual arc lamps. The overhead battens and wing ladders were made out of sheet-metal, the inside of which was painted a reflective white, and iron-wire guards protected the hot bulbs from contact with canvas and other flammable materials. The system was controlled from a lighting switchboard that used both electrical resistance and liquid electrolyte dimmers placed close by the proscenium arch on the left side of the stage.

Although, on account of the quantity of bulbs used, this system offered between a third and a quarter more light than a typical gas installation, the basic principles and theory of stage lighting remained very similar to those that had developed throughout the nineteenth century. However, electricity, principally by means of the arc lamps, which produced an intense white light, offered in its capability for special effects new visions of theatrical wonder ranging from the intense colours of symbolist drama to the erotic fantasy of the speciality female dance. In 1892, the American dancer Loïe Fuller was a considerable success in Paris performing her 'serpentine dance'. This was a fairy drama in which she manipulated lightweight veils of gauze-like material and, in whirling movement, danced in changing, coloured, lights, which the audience enjoyed in a darkened auditorium. Bergman says: 'Loïe Fuller's serpentine dance was a hymn to light, the mystifying light, from which, with literally maniacal interest, she succeeded in drawing new possibilities.'[5]

The mixing of primary colours to create intermediate shades had been used with gas lighting, but the safety of the enclosed electric filament bulb coupled with an increase in intensity on account of the numbers used, encouraged considerable experiment with glass colour filters and opened a new world of coloured light that had never been seen before. Lacquering was possible to achieve intermediate colours, but the heat of the bulbs quickly degraded the colour whereas glass filters, placed some distance in front of the source of heat, lasted much longer. By 1895 an English painter, Alexander W. Rimington, presented the findings of his research in a lecture on what he called the new art of 'colour music':

> In painting, colour has been used only as one of the elements in a picture, although perhaps the greatest source of beauty. We have not yet had pictures in which there is neither form nor subject, but only pure colour. Even the most advanced Impressionism has not carried us that far ... [with] the three great influences of *Time*, *Rhythm*, and *Combination* slow, rapid and varied. Colour thus is freed from the trammels of form, and dealt with for the sake of its own loveliness.[6]

He demonstrated a 'colour organ' – a keyboard that he had constructed, with which he could project changing shades of colour in flowing sequences upon a projection screen. He based his colour music upon an analogy between the twelve-tone musical scale and the colours of the spectrum, where the red colour at one end of the spectrum has a frequency that is half that of the violet colour at the opposite end. Each complete octave on his keyboard produced an equally complete spectrum of colour, whilst the higher or lower octaves represented higher or lower intensities of light. In addition, the keyboard had a swell-pedal that changed the intensity of each individual projected light, and was used to introduce nuances into the colour-music. Rimington went further and developed an instrument consisting of three levers that would each control the intensity of red, yellow, and blue light as they were displayed on the screen, and thereby were capable of creating any colour within the spectrum. He experimented with shutters, diaphragms and different screen surfaces and textures in order to create the appearance of form as well as colour.

The opportunities created by electric light and especially this new concern for changing and dissolving colour seemed to offer a route towards entirely new forms of art. Hubert Herkomer, a painter and early filmmaker, declared in a lecture in 1892 at the Avenue Theatre in London attended by the young Gordon Craig: 'It is through the management of light that we touch the real magic of art.' In Russia the composer Alexander Skriabin tried to realize colour music in association with orchestral work. *Prometheus*, a 'poem of fire' for orchestra, piano, chorus *ad lib*, organ and colour keyboard was composed during the years 1909–10 and was an attempt to transcend the boundaries of music and to create a performance that would combine vision and sound. A special notation was developed for the score to represent the interaction of illumination, colour and sound, which had been worked out using what Skriabin called a *clavier à lumière*. The changing, rhythmical play of colour would, like Rimington's, be projected onto a screen situated behind the orchestra. However, it was not until 1916, at a performance in New York, that the greater light generated by the technology of tungsten filament, gas-filled electric bulbs existed to enable *Prometheus* to be produced according to the instructions of the composer.

The more sensitive theatre artists, such as Irving in London, Stanislavski in Moscow, or David Belasco in New York, combined many of the technical resources of control and colour and used them with a painterly subtlety and care primarily in the interests of pictorialism, or to provide an atmosphere of greater psychological intensity than had been achievable by gas. Nevertheless, the fundamental conflict between the lighting needed for painted static scenery and that needed for the three-dimensional living actor was mercilessly exposed in the rapidly increasing intensity of electric light. In 1899 Adolphe Appia describes the problem:

> The arrangement of painted canvas to represent the setting demands that the lighting be exclusively at its service in order to make the painting visible, a relationship having nothing to do with the active role played by lighting and quite distinctly in conflict with it. The spatial arrangement, because it is in three-dimensions, permits light a little of its active function but only to the detriment of the two-dimensional painted drops. If we introduce the actor onto the stage, the importance of the painting is suddenly completely subordinated to the lighting and the spatial arrangement, because the living form of the actor can have no contact and consequently no direct rapport with what is represented on the canvas.[7]

Gordon Craig's appreciation of the expressive qualities and theatrical potential of lighting developed alongside his experience of these traditional approaches as he worked at the Lyceum Theatre in Irving's company during the early 1890s. For instance, he writes admiringly of the 'lime-light men' of the Lyceum and especially appreciated the way the light they produced, coming from the fly-floor side galleries of the stage house, could reveal form on stage and 'glance' like the bow of a violin upon the scenery. On the other hand, Adolphe Appia, the first, arguably the only, and certainly the most significant, theoretician of lighting in the theatre, had no such personal experience of the stage. His Swiss Calvinist background and upbringing were far removed from the world of professional theatre;

indeed, being allowed to study music first at the Leipzig Conservatory from 1882 to 1883 and then, following an intermission in Paris, at Dresden from 1886 to 1890, was considered a liberal opportunity. It is all the more remarkable therefore not only that his writing and his practice should perceive the falsity of existing practices with such detailed precision, but that he should be able to so thoroughly foresee, appreciate and indeed theorize the opportunities that the technology of electric lighting might offer. His ideas have served as the grounding for the development of subsequent practice, and significantly guided the development of stage-lighting technology through the century.

While at Leipzig, he discovered the music dramas of Richard Wagner, whose *Ring* cycle was given its first complete performance in 1876 at Europe's most technologically advanced theatre, built by Wagner in Bayreuth. The popularity of Wagner throughout Europe and North America developed rapidly – energized by an Englishman, Houston Stewart Chamberlain, and his publication the *Revue Wagnérienne*. Appia formed a friendship with him in 1883, and Chamberlain served to promote and sponsor his passion for Wagner. By the close of the century, most metropolitan cities and universities in Europe and North America had their 'Wagner Circle', or similar organizations of passionate admirers. However, since Wagner was also the first producer of his music-dramas, the Bayreuth productions and their scenographic approach quickly acquired a distinctively canonical status, which survived through the tenancy as artistic director first of his wife Cosima, and then of his son Siegfried, into the 1930s when the music-dramas and the institution at Bayreuth were adopted by Hitler and the German National Socialist Party.

Appia tried, in his early pamphlet *La Mise en Scène du Drame Wagnérien* (Paris 1894), to interpret the fundamental concept of Wagner's *Gesamtkunstwerk* by providing what he thought to be the correct approach to its *mise en scène*. Instead of the full, detailed and locationally illusionistic settings mounted at the *Festspielhaus*, Appia proposed a simple arrangement of spatial forms that would not serve to represent any specific location. The stage setting should merely provide an evocative stage 'place' in which the major emphasis would be upon the movement in space of the actor and the illumination of that actor with what he termed 'living light'. The concept of the stage as 'place' rather than as 'scene' was also fundamental to Craig and it is significant that one of Appia's earliest recollections of scenographic interest should indicate a similar concern. Richard Beacham quotes Appia's 1921 essay that recalls his childhood:

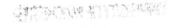

One of my friends at boarding school had seen *Tannhäuser* in Germany and gave me a report of it. I tried to pin him down and inquired whether the characters were really 'in a place' and what this 'place' was like. He didn't understand me. I remember having been rather insistent and having finally asked almost in despair, 'Where were their feet?'[8]

This was, of course, an especially perceptive question since the actors' feet existed on a formal timber stage floor with the conventional lines and marks of traps and grooves, whilst their upper bodies were framed against a perspective illusion; how could the two phenomena ever by reconciled? Appia developed his ideas for staging Wagner by publishing a more substantial and detailed analysis of the falsity of current stage practice, and further developed his theory for the role and use of light in the theatre. Sponsored by Chamberlain, this was translated from the French and published as *Die Musik und die Inszenierung* (Munich 1899). Although further developed in essays over the next quarter century, and significantly influenced by his work with Jacques Dalcroze at Hellerau from 1910 to 1914, this book represents the fundamental account of Appia's theory of the stage and its lighting. The work contained eighteen illustrations of proposed scenographies for Wagner's music-dramas, which, as Lee Simonson says in his foreword to the first translation into English in 1962, 'embodied Appia's aesthetic principles with such finality that they became a revelation of a totally new kind of stage setting and stage lighting, then as strange as the outlines of a new continent seen at dawn and now so familiar'.[9] Fuerst and Hume in their *Twentieth-Century Stage Decoration* (New York, 1929), the first comprehensive survey of new approaches to scenography and *mise en scène*, quite simply take the publication of Appia's work in 1899 as the beginning of the modern period in the theatre.

The starting point for all Appia's work and thinking was his response to Wagner's unification of music with poetry – in Appia's eyes, an achievement of the utmost human and artistic significance. It was, as Beacham says, 'a new type of musical drama in which a work's inner values as expressed through the music were conjoined with its outward meaning as articulated through dialogue and plot'.[10] Nevertheless, Appia had to acknowledge that the physical realization of the music-dramas, even as they had been directed on the *Festspielhaus* stage at Bayreuth by Wagner himself, utterly failed to realize this dramatic potential. For what was to be his final production, Wagner had spared no expense and had sent his scenic artists on an extensive trip of research in order to find a suitable model for the temple of the Holy Grail in *Parsifal* (1882). The Baptistry of the *Duomo* in Sienna was chosen and lovingly re-created on the stage at Bayreuth. But Appia says: '[t]hat Wagner was aware of the value of the visual elements (both scenic and mimetic) is evident in the arrangement of the Festival Theatre at Bayreuth. But strangely enough this otherwise purely idealistic genius did not have an idealistic visual sense.'[11]

Parsifal was the first production that Appia saw at Bayreuth, when he was nineteen (see Figure 6). He describes the effect of this scene on stage:

> In *Parsifal* at Bayreuth when the curtain went up on the scene of the interior of the Grail temple, painted scenery had to be sacrificed to the darkness necessitated by the scene change – imparting a marvellous life to the setting. As the lights started to come up, the illusion was continuously dispelled until finally, in the full glare of the border lights and the footlights, the knights made their entrance into a pasteboard temple.[12]

The extensive costume research and construction that had been undertaken suffered a similar fate in Appia's view:

> Characters in scrupulously historic costumes proudly descend a wooden staircase. In their luxurious and authentic footgear they tread boards cluttered with set pieces, and appear outlined against walls and balustrades which the well-lighted painting indicates to be of marvellously sculptured marble. The costume, in contact with the set pieces and the drops, lighted by light not designed for it, is completely devoid of meaning – a museum piece, nothing more.[13]

Whereas the majority of theatre artists rejected scenic tradition and simply ridiculed some of the more obvious defects, the singular importance of Appia is that he was able to so accurately describe what was happening in that tradition and furthermore to precisely account for its inevitable failure. Appia built his theory of scenography, therefore, from components that were revealed by his profound understanding of existing practice. It is his objective ability to move from rigorous observation and description to reflection and analysis that makes the resulting conclusions and theory so compellingly inevitable:

> Because living light was not used, the audience became accustomed to using its imagination to interpret the flat painted perspectives of the vertical

canvas; it came to enjoy having life presented by means of signs, whose easy manipulation permitted great liberty in the choice of subject matter. And so the real life which only lighting and a three-dimensional setting can give is sacrificed to the desire to behold in *indication* many fascinating and spectacular things.[14]

It is likely, for example, that if Appia had experienced working in the theatre, he might well have found it quite artistically acceptable to place, in potentially interesting contrast, the living performer within a conventionally signified theatrical space.

Unlike Craig, who consistently rejected the primacy of dramatic literature within a hierarchy of theatrical production, Appia did not. He believed that a logical hierarchy should exist, and that theatrical production – the *mise en scène* – should exist as an expressive art in order to create a living realization of a central dramatic action. In the majority of Appia's writings, the source of this dramatic action would be seen to derive from the inspiration of the poet–dramatist. In the new theatre form that Appia proposes, the musician–poet would control all aspects of production – including settings – and he also recommends that a synthesis of all elements should form the unique *mise en scène* for each work. However, Appia cannot conceive of a fundamentally collaborative artistic process of theatre making and therefore, like Craig, proposes the individual artist/director as being responsible for making production in the theatre of the future. Appia's logic is clear:

It is the word-tone poet, then, who possesses the guiding principle which, springing as it does from the original intention, inexorably and of necessity dictates the *mise en scène* without being filtered through the will of the dramatist – and this principle is an integral part of his drama and shares its organic life.[15]

Accordingly, Appia conceives the idea that there should be a necessary and seamless integration between dramatic intention and its physical realization as a *mise en scène*. But this is something altogether more fundamental than a demand for a closer relationship between content and its form. Appia's assertion is that the actual forms and means, including light, of theatrical presentation *become* the content. In this way theatrical production acquires meaning and expressive significance *in its own right*, not simply as a transliteration or interpretation of a pre-existing dramatic idea. Right at the heart of this proposed synthesis of sound, movement, space and light, lies music:

> The word-tone drama is the one dramatic form which dictates most accurately the actor's role in all its proportions. It is therefore the only drama which empowers the actor through his use of the setting to determine the relation of the spatial arrangement to the lighting and to the painting, and thus to control, through his role, the entire visual expression.[16]

The actors should be relieved of their traditional job of 'filling out' and 'making real' the dramatic character from their own personal experiences. The individual actor's reality is the reality of stage presence and not that of a fictional, fully rounded character; the actor should be an expressive medium that responds in sympathy with the living force that emanates from the work of the poet–dramatist.

This was articulated and proposed by Appia at precisely the time when Stanislavski was suggesting quite the reverse. Six years later Craig, in England, wrote his provocative essay 'The Actor and the Über-Marionette' (1905), in which he said that he wanted the fire and passion of the actor on stage, without the personality of the actor, who currently served merely as an instrument for literature and impersonation. He proposed a way forward for the actor, along a route that Appia was to advocate: '[b]ut I see a loophole by which in time the actors can escape from the bondage they are in. They must create for themselves a new form of acting, consisting for the main part of symbolic gesture.'[17] However, a form of acting that asserted its living immediacy must accordingly be located within an environment that would be similarly immediate and equally capable of life. In 1904, in an essay called 'How to Reform our Staging Practices', Appia argued that:

> The plasticity demanded by the actor aims at a completely different effect, for the human body does not seek to create the illusion of reality *since it is itself reality!* What it demands of the scenery is simply that it bring out that reality; which has the natural consequence of completely changing the whole object of the scenery: in one case the desire is to achieve the real appearance of objects; in the other, to give the highest degree of reality to the human body.[18]

In his preface to an unpublished 1918 English edition of *Die Musik und die Inszenierung*, and in the light of his practical experience, Appia refined and extended this concept of a synthesis between music, human action, and light in performance, which he had first articulated in 1899:

Eleven years later, I became acquainted with the Eurhythmics of Jacques-Dalcroze, who was just beginning his experiments; and there I found the answer to my passionate desire for synthesis! By closely following this musical discipline of the body, I discovered the living germ of the dramatic art, in which music is no longer separated from the human body in a splendour which is after all illusory, at least during performance, nor subjugated to it, a dramatic art which will direct the body towards an externalisation in space, and thus make it the primary and supreme means of scenic expression, to which all other elements of production will be subordinated.[19]

The qualities of music and its performance became Appia's dominant metaphors in his analysis of light. Light would become an expressive element in performance – 'what music is to the *partitur*, light is to the presentation'. He would conceive of an organization of stage lighting – the lighting plot – that would begin with the first chords of an overture and would continuously change, blend and harmonize throughout the entire time sequence of the production. Such a conception of lighting would operate beyond illumination, beyond visibility, or even beyond an accompaniment to the drama. Appia conceived of stage lighting as being capable of the deepest and most profound human expression; like the music itself, it would be capable of expressing what belonged to 'the inner essence of all vision'.

What is additionally remarkable in this perception is that when Appia articulated these ideas, the technology of electric lighting was less than twenty years old in the theatre, and, as has been seen, the vacuum bulbs available were each capable of little more than the equivalent of a modern 25-watt bulb. The battens were simply set in parallel rows behind each layer of painted scenery. Dimming was unsophisticated and relied heavily upon the use of liquid-electrolyte-filled cylinders. The overall ambition, quite logically when the tradition of two-dimensional painted scenes is considered, was to produce as close to a shadow-free illumination of the stage as possible. Notwithstanding the early development of electric light technology and his own lack of practical experience, Appia identified the essential qualities of light in the theatre and, by clear implication, the nature of the necessary equipment and lighting installation. He described the principal functioning of light as: '[a] daylight that floods the whole atmosphere, but nevertheless we are always aware of the direction from which it comes'. But he realized that the direction of light could only be sensed by means of shadow, and that accordingly it was the quality of the shadows which would express the quality of light. He logically deduced that in the real world, '[s]hadows are formed by the same light which illuminates the atmosphere'. However, he also appreciated that this 'tremendous effect' could not be achieved artificially. He concluded: 'On stage this task must therefore be divided, so that part of the lighting equipment will be used for general illumination, while the rest will cast shadows by means of exactly focused beams. We shall call them "diffused light" and "living light."'[20] To these two kinds of light he added the idea of projecting images using what today would be called 'gobos' – cut-out shapes, textures and colours placed in front of a light source that would produce a broken, dappled or otherwise textured light when projected onto a screen or onto the stage. Magic Lantern slides had been used in theatre for some time, and although their objective focusing lenses were limited, electric arc lighting provided a powerful source of light. Appia illustrated the value of projected gobos in a forest setting where:

> a few plastically constructed tree trunks blend into the borders, whence coloured illumination, filtered and brought into play in various ways, throws onto the stage light characteristic of the forest, the quality of which leaves to the imagination of the audience the existence of obstacles they have no need to see ... and thus the characters as well as the three-dimensional portions of the setting are immersed in the *atmosphere* suited to them.[21]

In identifying these three kinds of stage light, and the kinds of equipment necessary to create them in the theatre, Appia's conclusions have not been significantly changed to the present day. The catalogues of stage-lighting equipment manufacturers a hundred years later display theatrical luminaires for producing a soft, 'diffused light' – generally the wide-focusing spotlight with a diffusing 'fresnel' lens; luminaires with lenses that will focus light in brighter, more hard-edged pools of 'living light' – spotlights and beam lights; and luminaires that have condensing and lens capabilities to project sharp focused images. Modern research and technological development in the early twenty-first century is constantly trying to produce a single luminaire that will effectively achieve all three of Appia's functions through the sophisticated manipulation of lens, light source and ventilation. Inevitably the technology of the intervening period has made significant improvements to safety, flexibility and light output, but the essential functions and dramatic purposes of theatre light as identified by Appia in 1899 have changed little.

The low light output of early electric bulbs, and therefore, the great quantity of them needed to produce a shadowless 'diffused light', led to experiments with alternative lighting installations. However, it was quite unacceptable for the sources of light – the battens or individual lamps – to be seen by an audience. Within a scenographic convention of two-dimensional painted vertical surfaces this was easily resolved by placing the battens of light behind each surface to the sides of the stage, and behind each border above. However, ridding the theatre of such a scenic convention left the problem of where to locate the lights effectively to produce an even wash of light. The intensity of light produced by the battens was too low to place them further away from the stage, and, of course, they were unacceptable if visible to the audience.

Working in both France and Germany between 1900 and 1910, the Italian designer Mariano Fortuny[22] proposed an entire stage-lighting system and designed its requisite technologies to address this dilemma. Like Appia he rejected conventional lighting solutions, which had simply transferred the conventions of gas lighting to electric power. Focusing upon the large, heavily subsidized opera houses of Germany, he proposed the adoption of the permanent plaster-covered cyclorama (the *Kuppelhorizant*), which would provide a fully masked sky setting to back, sides and top of the stage house. He also designed a temporary cyclorama consisting of a double silk dome, which was constructed in the Théâtre de l'Avenue Bosquet in Paris in 1906, and the following year at the Kroll Opera House in Berlin, and which, when C. Harold Ridge described it in 1928, was still in use at La Scala Opera House in Milan:

> This dome works like the hood of a perambulator, the metal rims being kept in a vertical position until required, when they open out into the shape of a quarter orange with the bottom rib near the stage floor. The silk is kept tight and free of wrinkles by being made double with the space of a foot or so between, and this space is exhausted of air by a power-driven exhaust pump. The effect of this cyclorama is magnificent.[23]

To achieve the full infinity-of-space effect of the cyclorama, however, the wings of the theatre and the overhead flies could not be encumbered with flats or borders that might conceal battens of electric lights.

Although by 1907–8 the introduction of tungsten filament lamps enabled bulbs up to 500 watts to be produced, it was not until gas-filled tungsten filament bulbs replaced vacuum bulbs in 1913–14 that wattages of 750–1000 watts were feasible. Given the distance from concealed lighting positions and the intensity of light required, Fortuny had therefore no alternative but to use electric arc lamps. These provided the intensity needed to light the cyclorama, but could not be dimmed by electrical means and required complicated mechanical masking shutters. In attempting, like Appia, to start from basic principles, Fortuny noted that nature created two kinds of light – direct light and reflected light – and he considered that any system of lighting the stage, therefore, must provide both. To light the cyclorama, the arc lamps were hung high over the stage, and shone directly upon large frames of variously coloured satin that then reflected light either onto the cyclorama or down onto the stage to produce the diffused, shadow-free light that was desired. He tried to create a large range of colour washes, but was inevitably hampered by the cumbersome dimming capability of his lamps. The painted and dyed screens could 'scroll' in front of the lights to facilitate colour change, and patterns of closely spaced black chevrons on the screens provided some dimming effect. As was becoming increasingly fashion-able, he reduced the overall intensity of footlights, preferring to light the acting area of the stage with spotlights located on a bridge over the proscenium arch and to the sides of the stage. The basic principles of Fortuny's system were sound and were to dominate stage-lighting practice until the Second World War. However, the equipment to implement the system that he designed was never fully developed.[24] The arc lamps were costly and cumbersome and they required con-siderable attention, whilst the scrolling tinted reflection screens and dimming shutters needed complicated motors and tracker wires for their operation.

In the summer of 1910, Appia worked with architect Heinrich Tessenow, and with the painter Alexander von Saltzmann, to design Europe's first studio theatre space at Hellerau, an experimental 'garden suburb' community of Dresden. The rectangular space of the performance hall had no proscenium arch and there was no formal demarcation of space between that provided for an audience and that for performance. A removable orchestra pit traversed the space, but when it was covered over, the bare hall was in daily use for Dalcroze's eurhythmic classes and exercises. As we have seen, Dalcroze insisted that eurhythmic work was not an art form in itself, but a path towards art. Performance – certainly anything beyond the sharing of work with friends – would be a by-product of the institute's work, not an end-product. This may have been a significant reason for the unique lighting installation adopted by Appia and Saltzmann at Hellerau, which, when not being used for performance, was invisible and provided a calm, neutral, focused space for class-work and teaching. In an essay, 'Eurhythmics and the Theatre', written in 1911, Appia had written:

> Up to now, only quiet attention has been required of the audience. To encourage this, comfortable seats have been provided in semidarkness, to encourage a state of total passivity – evidently the proper attitude for spectators ... *Eurhythmics will overturn this passivity!* ... Light, no longer forced to illuminate the painted flats, can radiate, carrying form into space, filling it with living colour and the limitless variations of an ever-changing atmosphere.[25]

The interior walls of the space were hung with lightweight canvas (calico) that had been impregnated with cedar oil. This provided a warm, tinted translucency similar to that of roller-blind fabric. Although not referred to by those who wrote of their experience at Hellerau, the fragrant smell of cedar oil must also have been especially memorable. Battens of lights (reported to contain in total 7,000 individual bulbs) were placed behind the hangings and light was reflected from the white painted walls onto the surface of the fabric. Appia's 'diffused light' created an entire environment for performance that was illuminated by the glowing walls of the hall, where no distinction was made between the hangings surrounding the performance space and the surroundings of the audience. Saltzmann said: 'instead of a lighted space, we have a light-producing space. Light is conveyed through the space itself, and the linking of visible light sources is done away with.'[26]

In order to achieve the other form of light, the 'living light', Appia proposed the use of removable spotlights placed in the ceiling of the hall, and the whole installation, both diffusing battens and spotlights, was centrally controlled. Unfortunately, we have no evidence of the precise equipment used either in the indirect battens or for the spotlights, and although there are enthusiastic comments from audience members about the unearthly and ethereal qualities of the light, only the well-known photograph of the descent of Orpheus, and the flight of steps to the rear of the space and the intensity of the light that 'follows' him, provide an indication of the effect that Appia intended (see Figure 13). Nevertheless, it does appear that through these means the entire place of performance at Hellerau could respond to the dramatic action, the emotion, the music, the atmosphere, and indeed to the totality of the living performance. The music achieved a physical embodiment through the eurhythmic movement of the performers, whilst the light could represent the music within the entire space. George Bernard Shaw, who visited Hellerau with Granville Barker in 1913, said:

> The theatre has walls and roof of white linen with the light behind the linen. ... This afternoon we went again and saw the lighting installation – acres of white linen and the multitude of light behind and above it. It needs only a transparent floor with light beneath it to make it capable of anything heavenly.[27]

In the festivals which displayed the work of the Institute, and which took place during the summers of 1912 and 1913, the community-living ideas of Hellerau, Dalcroze's Eurhythmics and Appia's ideas for scenography were seen by most of the leading theatre artists of Europe. Their reactions to the work were consistently enthusiastic, but especial praise was given to the scenes from Gluck's opera *Orpheus and Eurydice*, which seemed to display the synthesis of dramatic action and its physical realization in time and space that Appia had outlined in his *Musik und Inszenierung* of 1899. The radical and enduring nature of his theory at this time may be usefully summarized:

- The performer is a being of three-dimensions, therefore –
- The *mise en scène* should create a 'living space' by creating simple three-dimensional settings.
- Painted scenery is utterly inappropriate – dramatic emotions grow, change and develop; whereas painting is static – therefore representational painting has no place in the *mise en scène*.
- A proper use of light is therefore essential for such a setting, and for the full dramatic exposure of the performer.
- Stage light should consist of atmospheric 'diffused light', which would be complemented with form-revealing 'living light'.
- In addition, both atmosphere and form may also be created by projected images.
- The use of footlights should be abandoned since they represent an utterly non-real angle of light.

The outbreak of the First World War saw the closure of Dalcroze's Institute as the army requisitioned the Hellerau Studio and in so doing curtailed this remarkable series of experiments in performance.

It is important to note Appia's achievement, summarized above, in developing an extremely sophisticated and far-reaching theory of stage lighting between 1899 and 1914, and to recognize that in his practice with Saltzmann and Dalcroze at Hellerau he had realized many of his most significant concepts. Kenneth MacGowan and Robert Edmund Jones wrote their enormously influential *Continental Stagecraft* in 1922, in which they summarized:

> In the 'eighties and 'nineties, when electricity came into the theatre to take the place of gas, light was only illumination. By the first decade of the twentieth century it had become atmosphere. Today it is taking the place of setting in many Continental theatres. Tomorrow it may be part of drama itself.'[28]

For MacGowan and Jones it was Appia who outlined the stages of this progression by not only articulating the theory and practice of stage lighting, but also integrating this within an entire philosophy of live performance.

Appia's achievement at Hellerau, and Bernard Shaw's comment upon it, clearly indicate the desire to represent a form of limitless infinity as a context or background for performance, a representational approach, albeit one that did not rely upon painted landscape backcloth or 'cloud' and 'sky' borders. Fortuny had proposed the cyclorama, and whilst his portable model was never very successful, a deeply curved, hard-surfaced background became an ideal to which many theatres aspired during the 1920s and 1930s. MacGowan and Jones claimed that by 1922 such a sky-dome, or some variant upon it, was to be found in practically every German theatre, where significant municipal and regional subsidy could bear the very high cost of installation. The more affordable variant consisted of a large, neutrally coloured cloth suspended from a curtain track that curved around the sides of the stage. This could be raised from the stage floor to permit scenery to be shifted beneath it, or it could be completely flown out when not required. By the 1920s also, high-powered gas-filled tungsten filament bulbs enabled the manufacture of sophisticated luminaires capable of producing a light that hitherto had required electric arc-light technology. The German electrical manufacturer founded by Max Schwabe in the early 1920s developed a system of colour mixing and cyclorama lighting that effectively defined the technical approach to stage lighting until the middle of the century. Similar equipment was produced elsewhere in Europe and North America, but Schwabe used ground lenses of high optical quality (and cost) in place of the cheaper moulded glass lenses used by other manufacturers.

C. Harold Ridge installed an entire Schwabe lighting system in the Festival Theatre at Cambridge in 1926. The hard-surfaced plaster cyclorama was lit by groups of Schwabe 'horizon' lights located in front of the lighting bridge behind what remained of the original early nineteenth-century proscenium arch. Each luminaire contained a 1000-watt bulb (although by that date, in larger theatres, up to 3000 watts might be used). Ridge describes its working clearly:

> the centre of the lantern is occupied by the lamps themselves, and there is room both above and below for four coloured glass slides and a metal shutter. The glass slides and metal shutter are controlled by tracker wires leading to the interlocking control mechanism.

Modern stage lighting is accustomed to using a wide range of heat resistant Mylar plastic filters to enable the selection of precisely the desired colour. Prior to this plastics technology of the late 1960s, gelatine and celluloid filters were used but in a limited range of colours and with a tendency to fade and crack in the heat generated by the lighting equipment. Schwabe produced glass filters of considerable durability but in a small range of colours, and the Company became strong advocates of a system of colour mixing based upon seven 'standard' colours. Ridge's description of the Schwabe colours and their use is an interesting indication of the thinking about colour in performance at that period:

> Dark blue: This is a peculiarly vivid violet blue which is exceedingly beautiful in itself. It is the most commonly used of all the Schwabe colours, but owing to its density only a small proportion of light passes through, and more lamps fitted with these colours are needed than in the case of the others.
> Middle blue: This is a decidedly greenish blue. It is not very attractive in itself, although used alone it is a useful moonlight colour. Its chief use is in combination with the dark blues to produce a resultant lighter blue.
> Light blue: This is a blueish green, and by itself an unpleasant colour. It is never used alone, but only in combination with the dark blues and, or, middle blues to produce very light summer skies and similar atmospheric effects.
> Daylight blue: It is not necessary to say anything about this colour except that it is ordinary artificial North daylight. It is only used to dilute the other colours or combinations, and these lamps are used less than any other colour in the set.

Green: This is the least satisfactory colour in the Schwabe system. It is a very unpleasant yellowish green and unsuitable for use by itself. It is used principally in conjunction with the blues to produce dark and stormy atmospheric effects, and also neutral greys of a varying tone. ... No glass manufacturer is able to produce the true emerald green glass, and any other medium, such as gelatine, refuses to stand up to the intense heat and light conditions.

Yellow: This is a very perfect and pure colour, and is used by itself or in combinations with the red for ambers and oranges, and in combination with the blues for dawn and sunset atmospheres.

Red: This is also a fairly good colour, though somewhat on the pink side. It is used principally with the blues to produce purple, for warming up the yellow light, and is introduced into other combinations to give depth and warmth.[29]

In this way, coloured lighting effects of very great subtlety were achieved by mixing the primary and their variant colours. Ridge describes the mechanically controlled colour filters that enabled a reduction in the overall number of instruments and, by juxtaposing filters, the mixing of colours from an individual luminaire. However, and especially when using a limited range of intense colours, Ridge noted that as the light source was dimmed in intensity, so the colour changed significantly, becoming more orange and distinctly 'warmer' in tone. Although a sophisticated lighting control board of circuit switching and dimmers was installed at Cambridge, the major 1000 watt colour-mixing luminaires that have been described were also fitted with mechanical dimming by means of shutters, which, although tending to generate great heat, avoided the difficulty of this undesirable colour change.

Although it was not used at Cambridge, Ridge describes a system installed at the Konigliches Schauspielhaus, Dresden, *c.*1916, by the German lighting designer Adolph Linnebach. This interestingly adopted the Schwabe approach of direct lighting onto the cyclorama, but also employed Fortuny's approach to indirect light. Ridge says that the lighting of the acting area was considerably reinforced by light coming from three banks of 'Linnebach' luminaires. These consisted of arc lamps contained in metal housings that were opened both to the back and in front. Magazines of glass colour slides and shutters, connected to the switchboard by tracker wires, allowed the coloured light to be altered or dimmed. The light coming from the back of the lamps impinged directly upon the plaster cyclorama, whilst that coming from the front of the lamps shone onto an angled white surface which reflected indirect light down onto the stage and, according to Ridge, produced a subtle and particularly soft effect. However, as with the Fortuny system, the Linnebach luminaires required a heavy current and of course they could not be electrically dimmed, and they entailed considerable trouble and expense in the maintenance of the arc light.

The Schwabe instruments that hung on the lighting bridge at the Festival Theatre in Cambridge could fill the visible space with shadow free flexible light in any colour, or with the bright 'expressionist' statements of colour that were a feature of Terence Gray's and Ridge's work. However, and with much regret, Ridge and Gray retained the use of footlights at the theatre, since Ridge could find no technical solution that would bring light onto the faces of actors when they moved down stage onto the forestage with its shallow steps that led into the audience. He wrote about the desirability of light coming from front-of-house spotlights located on the fronts of the gallery, but it seems that the equipment available to him at the time could not really be focused with sufficient precision and as far as he was concerned, no light should ever spill over onto the proscenium arch itself. Of course, he also had the conventional problem with the audience being able to see the source of the light of spotlights or – worse still – floodlights that might be in view in the auditorium. All he could suggest was that light for the front of the acting area should come from the sides of the stage from behind the proscenium arch, and from the batten overhead beneath the lighting bridge, and that the footlights should be used very subtly and gently to fill-in the extreme downstage areas.

In addition to the overhead batten, spotlights were hung on the lighting bridge and were also placed upon stands in the wings of the theatre where they could provide the harsh, form-revealing cross-lighting that was a significant feature of new approaches to staging in the 1920s and 1930s. Considerable experiment was also made with the indirect lighting of calico-covered frames that formed part of Gray and Ridge's re-usable 'kit' of scenic screens, forms and units. In this way, Ridge's carefully thought-out installation at Cambridge offered a comprehensive and reasonably affordable (the installation cost £2,000 in 1926) system to realize lighting in the theatre that offered both a diffused, coloured, atmospheric light and the bright, focused 'living light' of individual spotlights.

In many theatres, however, such 'living light' continued to remain the exception: in 1932 the Shakespeare Memorial Theatre in Stratford had only four 1000-watt 'Stelmar' spotlights, and Covent Garden Opera House, when re-fitted in 1934, had but nine of these luminaires.[30] During the early 1930s Frederick Bentham began his career with the UK stage-lighting manufacturer Strand Electric, as a lighting technologist and designer. His early work as a consultant on stage lighting and lighting installations confirms the principles and theory involved:

I had been called in [1933, Questor's Theatre, Ealing] to advise on a lighting installation. ... There had to be a cyclorama, and as masking I adopted the permanent ceiling of the Festival Theatre Cambridge, as described by Harold Ridge, instead of the borders – even for open-air scenes. Along the top of the up-stage edge of this were three circuits of 'home-made' cyclorama floods with gelatine colour filters, while in the cyclorama pit there were three circuits of china sprayed lamps. ... Initially the primary colours were used.[31]

And in the following year he undertook a more impressive consultancy:

Until 1934 Covent Garden opera productions had used traditional painted scenery and someone, and I can only think it was Beecham, decided that they must go modern with a great encompassing cyclorama and all that entailed. The Germans were well used to such techniques but over here any cyclorama used in theatre had been tiny and usually confined to the up-stage area. For the new Covent Garden stage lighting the cyclorama would not just form part of the installation but a major part – 184 kW no less. ... My 'I was there' experience had to do with working the board, which I found myself doing at rehearsals as the 'great expert' on mixing the three primary colours, red, blue and green. The whole of the great Haseit cloth cyclorama was lit on this principle with double wattage blue. The new *Ring* had sets by Gabriel Volkoff and was directed by Dr Earhardt who brought Max Haseit ... along as technical adviser. All had been brought up on the Schwabe seven colour system ... there would be calls from the stalls for yellow cyclorama ... and to a murmur of satisfaction I would bring up the reds and the greens gently to the required level.[32]

The technical sophistication of bulb and luminaire design provided by the Schwabe equipment at Cambridge and at Covent Garden, and by Strand Electric elsewhere, finally enabled the ambitions of the earliest advocates of colour music to be achieved. Colour music also achieved a significant life outside theatrical performance in trade exhibitions, and especially in the huge palatial cinemas that sprang up after the general introduction of sound technology at the end of the

1920s. The internal architecture of the large, typically 'art-deco' cinemas, consisting of cornices, coving, arches and reveals painted in a neutral colour, responded well to concealed coloured light arranged in circuits of the three primary lighting colours, red, green and blue, that would be used to harmonize and accompany live or recorded music. Bentham established a considerable reputation working on this 'colour music' as a prelude to the main feature film, to accompany the cinema organ, and on trade exhibitions. He designed a lighting control (see Figure 19) that resembled, and used, much of the technology of a multiple-console cinema organ – typically accompanying 'pop' classical music such as Debussy's *Soleil* or *Clair de Lune*.

By the time of the outbreak of the Second World War, readily available technology provided the means to achieve Appia's first two ambitions for stage lighting. Reliable, long-lasting and powerful gas-filled tungsten filament bulbs located in compartment battens could provide the shadow-free diffused atmospheric light over the stage. Flood lights, either simple 'biscuit-box' units, or the more sophisticated Schwabe 'horizon floods', could light open backcloths and

Figure 19   Fred Bentham's cinema organ light console (*Sixty Years of Light Work*, London: Strand Lighting, 1992)

cycloramas of varying degrees of completeness. Coloured glass was still preferred for extensive use where high light output produced the greatest heat, but gelatine filters were becoming increasingly effective.

When Jacques Copeau and Louis Jouvet opened their Théâtre du Vieux-Colombier in Paris in 1919, lighting for their 'architectural' stage could not be undertaken on traditional lines, or even those suggested by Fortuny and Appia. There were no flies, no upper stage or lighting bridge to hide battens and no wing spaces to conceal either battens or lights on stands. Furthermore, the permanent stage floor merged into the auditorium space by means of shallow treads that made footlight battens impossible. In the photographs of the theatre there can be seen four octagonal objects hanging from the roof trusses (see Figure 26). These were ingenious luminaires, designed by Louis Jouvet, for projecting a soft coloured light onto the stage. Two were suspended on either side of the stage. Each of the faces of the polygonal boxes held a coloured glass filter. Whilst the lamp inside remained static, the body of the luminaire could be rotated, thus providing a choice of eight different filters for the lamps to shine through. Crude as this arrangement seems by today's standards, it represented a considerable advance on the use of footlights, being capable, as Rudlin notes, of 'picking out the actors' eyes rather than their chins',[33] and went some way towards creating the 'living light' that Appia sought.

David Belasco used electric light and its capabilities to seek a more intense and atmospheric naturalism and developed lighting changes motivated by dramatic psychology. In 1919 he echoed Appia and said: 'Lights are to drama what music is to the lyrics of a song. No other factor that enters into the production of a play is so effective in conveying its mood and feeling. They are as essential to every work of dramatic art as blood is to life.'[34] His approach to stage lighting and to *mise en scène* dominated theatre practice in the USA for the first quarter of the twentieth century – until the influence of new European scenographic ideas began to have an impact during the late 1920s. With his technician Louis Hartmann, they developed 'the baby lens' shortly before the First World War. The advantage of this was that it could be placed where it was needed, required very little manual handling (unlike an arc spotlight) and offered the possibility of increasing or decreasing the light by means of electrical dimmers. The 'baby lens' consisted of a metal tube that was painted black on the inside to avoid reflection. But their real innovation, as their name suggests, was their use of an optical-quality lens to concentrate and focus the light. They were hung above the proscenium and on lighting stands on the side of the stage. By 1930, Hartmann considered that 'the idea of the baby lens was the first decided innovation in modern stage lighting.'[35]

By the late 1920s, therefore, Appia's theory of lighting seems to have been accepted throughout Europe and North America and by the early 1930s was even taking on a populist form in the new sound cinemas. Technology had developed rapidly, especially in the development of new filaments and gas filled bulbs, and was capable of delivering equipment to provide both the shadow-free diffused light and, more slowly, Appia's 'living light', a light that could reveal form and focus attention.

The Century of Light, 2

Light Beams and Images

> I perceive light physically, not only visually. For me, light became a substance.
>
> Josef Svoboda[1]

The third kind of stage light that Adolphe Appia described in *Die Musik und die Inszenierung* was the texturing and breaking up of light beams by 'gobos' and the projection of focused images. He described them as, 'one of the most effective means of decoration, a hyphen between lighting and decor, which renders immaterial all that it touches'.[2] In this chapter I want to examine ways in which light in theatrical performance has gone beyond its function of illumination, of creating atmosphere and even dramatic revelation, and has taken on a material quality in its own right, and, in a variety of ways, has become a collaborator in the creation of performance.

In extensions of Rimington and Skriabin's original concept of colour music, light (especially the beam of light and the projected image) became an important ingredient on the palette of the proposer of abstract, non-representational art, and by the early 1920s, on the stages of the constructed theatre of early revolutionary Soviet artists. In the experiments of Bauhaus artists such as Walter Gropius, Farkas Molnár, Oskar Schlemmer and László Moholy-Nagy during the 1920s, light and the projected image played crucial roles in their examination of plasticity in their space-theatres and abstract-mechanical productions. Projected and filmic images were extensively used by Erwin Piscator at the Berlin *Volksbühne* in the mid-1920s, most frequently to provide images of revolution and actuality, and were planned to surround the audience and to make flexible the internal architecture of the Synthetic Total Theatre of 1926 (unrealized) that Gropius designed for Piscator. In the metropolitan theatres and opera houses of western Europe and America, projected imagery was perceived as offering greater scenic realism, greater atmosphere and a more rapid and magical change of scene. But to achieve all these aims, powerful light sources and optical systems of considerable technical sophistication were required.

The acceleration of electrical and optical technologies that was urged forward by the Second World War created radical innovation in the production and control of light as the new technologies filtered through into the theatre during the 1950s and 1960s. From the 1960s onwards, the insertion into a tubular bulb made of quartz of certain halogens (such as iodine or bromine) enabled the filament temperature to be significantly increased, and so increased the luminous efficiency and output of the lamps. Above all, these halogens lamps could yield a more constant, whiter light than the earlier tungsten spotlights and the tubular bulb was very small compared with the big bulbs of the old spotlights. The smaller filament of the halogen bulb therefore greatly facilitated achieving the optical focus that was required for an intense projected image. This technology enabled scenographers such as Josef Svoboda to treat the beam of light materially, as they might a beam of timber – stage light could achieve presence and material solidity within space by delineating and creating the space of performance itself.

As Appia, Craig and Meyerhold atomized and pondered the consistency and texture of the theatrical experience during the early decades of the twentieth century, they realized that as well as serving to represent the real world, light could also serve to expose the falseness of traditional conventions and to celebrate the only true theatrical reality, which existed at the moment of performance itself. Furthermore, the experience of colour music and its exploitation of abstract, un-delineated colour coincided with attempts by painters to pursue non-representational art. During the period 1910–14, the painter Wassily Kandinsky felt that by dissolving colours into themselves he was able to abandon the more conventional painterly use of lines for the purposes of definition. In consistently stripping away narrative and representational content, he was convinced that colour and form might 'speak' for themselves and become the 'materials' of the artist. In his 'Concerning the Spiritual in Art' (*Über das Geistige in der Kunst*, 1912) he outlined his theoretical understanding of colour and its place within psychology and perception. Also in 1912, in his essay 'On Stage Compositions' (*Über Bühnenkomposition*) in *Der blaue Reiter Almanac*, he attempted to connect music and visual images through a form of non-representational, abstract theatre in which 'musical movements', 'colour movements' and 'dance rhythmical movements' would combine to produce a monumental art of the future, in which light and projections would play a central role. The essay formed a preface to what Kandinsky called a 'stage composition', 'The Yellow Sound' (*Der gelbe Klang*), which was published in the *Der blaue Reiter Almanac* in 1912.[3] 'The Yellow Sound' made use of intangible divisions between music, moving form, and colour. The composition consisted of six 'pictures' that blended into each other, each having a moving programme of symbolic sound and each shaped – entirely without spoken dialogue – with music, a choir singing with and without words, pantomimic movements and dance, changeable 'mobile' scenery, and above all, with coloured light of changing intensity that passed through a range of tonal expressions – from brilliant yellow to grey-black. Kandinsky had moved significantly beyond the earlier experiments of colour music, and in 'The Yellow Sound' the spotlights acted like the solo parts of a choir, throwing beams of light of varying colours in rapid tempo upon the group of yellow giants:

> Beams of light in glaring colours drop in rapid changes from all sides (blue, red, violet, green) and alternate several times. All these beams melt in the middle, where they are mixed. All is motionless. The giants are almost invisible. Suddenly all colours disappear. For a moment everything is black. Then a matt, yellow light filters down over the stage, becoming by degrees increasingly intense, until the whole stage is glaringly lemon yellow.[4]

Although Kandinsky's abstract symbolism is cryptic and quite inaccessible, his ambition for light in performance was remarkably precise, especially considering the technology of contemporary stage lighting. 'The Yellow Sound' remained only a scenario in *Der blaue Reiter*, but the ideas and principles examined by Kandinsky were to remain strong motivations in the making of performance over the next two decades.

The visceral ability of light to identify directly with human sensation and emotion that Kandinsky explored, alongside the assertive modernity of electricity, were inevitably to be the source of considerable interest and experiment by futurist artists. In 1917 at the *Teatro Constanzi* in Rome, Stravinsky's *Feu d'Artifice* was performed by Serge Diaghilev's *Ballets Russes* Company, although no ballet and no actors appeared in the performance. The production was designed by the futurist clothes designer and painter Giacomo Balla, who built an irregular pattern of pyramid-shaped forms on the stage. The pointed tips of these pyramids were covered with a transparent material and were brightly painted with flashes, zigzags and other futurist imagery. The pyramids were lit from within, and the overall scene was illuminated by beams of colour from numerous spotlights, which were invisible to the audience. Balla had also designed and built a control keyboard of switches from which the lighting changes could be operated. The conductor was Ernest Ansermet and although the whole performance lasted little more than five minutes, there were forty-nine lighting cues, which synchronized precisely with the music.

The Theatre Department and its Studio were established at the Bauhaus School of Design, Building and Crafts in Weimar by Walter Gropius and, initially, by Lothar Schreyer in 1921. Oskar Schlemmer took over the theatre work in 1923 and was joined by the two Hungarian designers Farkas Molnár and László Moholy-Nagy before the School moved to Dessau in 1925. The modernist mission of the School was radical and bold and, in its vision of the design process, demanded a holistic commitment from staff and students. Central to this commitment was the need to fully integrate twentieth-century technologies alongside artistic design practice. Gropius recollected in 1961: 'Teachers and students as a working community had to become vital participants of the modern world, seeking a new synthesis of art and modern technology.'[5] The artist and designer should no longer think of themselves as outsiders to everyday living and modern industrial processes of technical production. Confirmed in their utter rejection of past forms, conventions of artistic practice and aesthetic values, the curricula in all departments at the School began with studies that were based on an examination of the biological facts of human perception. The phenomena of form, space and time were investigated in a spirit of unbiased and frank curiosity, in order to arrive at clear working methods that could integrate individual creative work within what was believed to be a common background of perceptual understanding.

Technology would prove to be the mortar that would unite everyone and bind societies together within the 'new faith' of the modernist Utopian vision. Especially during the early days of the Bauhaus, therefore, there was a sense of tremendous social optimism and spiritual exhilaration at the opportunities which new technologies might offer to creative artists, architects and industrial designers. Schlemmer said:

> the possibilities are extraordinary in light of today's technological advance-ments: precision machinery, scientific apparatus of glass and metal, the artificial limbs developed by surgery, the fantastic costumes of the deep-sea diver and the modern soldier, and so forth. ... Wondrous figures of this new sort, personifications of the loftiest concepts and ideas, made of the most exquisite material, will be capable also of embodying symbolically a new faith.[6]

If the figures of the drama were to become creations of the designer and manipulator of these technologies, then Schlemmer argues that it would be probable that the theatre designer would, in future, develop a range of optical phenomena and *then* seek out the poet and dramatist who would provide an appropriate language of words and musical sound. Although the word is not used at this time, the concept of the designer as devisor and creator of theatre, as 'über-scenographer', is clearly established at the Bauhaus. Moholy-Nagy shared Schlemmer's sense of modernist[7] intoxication as the possibi-lities of new technologies are revealed:

> Nothing stands in the way of making use of complex APPARATUS such as film, automobile, elevator, airplane and other machinery, as well as optical instruments, reflecting equipment, and so on. The current demand for dynamic construction will be satisfied in this way, even though it is still only in its first stages.[8]

Although dominated by an overall visual *schema* of architectural construction, as seen in *The Triadic Ballet* (performed in Weimar in 1923), the living, individual human figure remained quite central to Schlemmer's experiments. However, within the projects of the painter Moholy-Nagy, and also evident within the architectural projects of Molnár and Gropius, there was a consistent desire to rid the theatre of domination by dramatic literature and to consider the actor as just one among many of the potential ingredients within the overall plasticity of a constructed theatrical event. The starting point for Moholy-Nagy's artistic work came from his perception that true reality could be found only in the modern industrial world of new technology and the invention of machines:

> To use machinery is to act in the spirit of our century. ... It is the art of Constructivism. ... In it the pure form of nature finds expression – unbroken

colour, the rhythm of space, the balance of form. ... It is independent of picture frame and pedestal. It extends to industry and architecture, objects and relationships. Constructivism is the socialism of seeing.[9]

For Moholy-Nagy the essential 'purity' of expression and form offered by colour and the machine 'will not tolerate the actor with indistinct or splotchy make-up and tattered costuming'.[10] Furthermore, the time-based opportunity offered by lighting and by human responses to the phenomena of colour, as explored by painters such as Kandinsky, led Moholy-Nagy to develop the perception of light as a distinctive force within a new concept of dramaturgy: 'this will constitute the new ACTION OF LIGHT, which by means of modern technology will use the most intensified contrasts to guarantee itself a position of importance equal to that of all other theatre media'.[11] His argument logically extended the abstract painter's view of colour and pigment: if pigment were to assume the primacy of expression as both the subject *and* object of painting then its role, as perceived through light, would be similar in the theatre: 'There is no doubt', he said, 'that ... a direct beam of light could create a very much more intense effect if it could be controlled to the same degree as painting with pigment. And that is indeed the future problem for the visual arts: the creative use of direct light.'[12]

Although lacking the rigorous modernist articulation and the overt social commitment to new technologies of the Bauhaus argument, Craig clearly had very similar interests in the possible use of light as a dramaturgical agent in performance. He had written of the importance of light in his 'screens' projects of 1910–14, as being not only that of illumination and revelation of the form of physical structures, but also important in the creation of new form: 'the relation of light to this scene', he said, 'is akin to that of the bow of the violin, or of the pen to the paper'.[13] The instrument is silent until it resonates with vibration and makes music, and the paper is blank until it is approached by the pen. The idea of a moving spotlight and the beam of a projector were new technologies in performance; they introduced a new aesthetic and a quality of change, movement and plasticity that had not been seen before. In 1910, when Piot visited Craig and saw his plans for lighting the screens he reported back to the manager of the Théâtre de l'art, Jacques Rouché:

The decoration is simplified in that, above all, the changes of light, refracting against the various volumes, give expressiveness to the decor.

By these simplifications one seems to achieve 'une fluctuation musicale du décor' which, in time, links the decor to the changes of the drama. ... It is desirable that the decor, mobile as the sound, elucidates phases of the drama in the same way as the music accompanies and underlines all movements, just as it develops in pace with the drama.[14]

In 1927, Schlemmer gave a lecture-demonstration in Dessau to the 'Circle of Friends of the Bauhaus' and described his own 'screens' scenography and their functioning with light:

since we have no interest in make-believe forests, mountains, lakes, or rooms – we have constructed simple flats of wood and white canvas which can be slid back and forth on a series of parallel tracks and can be used as screens for light projection. By back lighting we can also make them into translucent curtains or wall areas and thereby achieve an illusion of a higher order, created directly from readily available means. We do not want to imitate sunlight and moonlight, morning, noon, evening, and night with our lighting. Rather we let the light function by itself, for what it is: yellow, blue, red, green, violet, and so on. ... Let us rather open our eyes and expose our minds to the pure power of colour and light. If we can do this, we shall be surprised at how well the laws of colour and its mutations can be demonstrated by the use of coloured light in the physical and chemical laboratory of the theatre stage.[15]

Craig consolidated, clarified and extended many aspects of his own screens project in the publication of *Scene* in 1923. In this, he was more precise in articulating the need for light to physically move with the scene as well as to change in colour and intensity. Such movement, he said:

meets the requirements demanded by the modern spirit – the spirit of incessant *change*: the sceneries we have been using for plays for centuries were merely the old stationary sceneries made to alter. That is quite a different thing to a scene which has a changeable nature. This scene also has what I call a face. This face expresses. ... Its shape perceives the light, and in as much as the light changes its position and makes certain other changes, and inasmuch as the scene itself alters its position – the two acting in concert as in a duet, figuring it out together as in a dance – insomuch does it express all the emotions I wish it to express.[16]

Although the language is significantly different, none the less, Craig was self-evidently close to Bauhaus thinking on the theatrical functioning of light. Furthermore, Craig anticipated later scenographers such as Josef Svoboda, who attempted to create *kinetic*, mobile stage pictures which changed in tune with the changing rhythm of the drama, and, as Bergman claimed, 'solved the problem of how, with the aid of light ... to give even the decor a dimension of time'.[17] Seventy years later, Svoboda extended Craig's 1923 *Scene* articulation and clarified his response to the nature and purpose of scenic movement – citing the particular influence of Craig:

> It is perhaps already clear that you can't do static theatre, in which scenery rigidly gazes down on actions played out within its space. After all, what is actually fixed in the stream of life? Is a room in which someone declares love the same as a room in which someone is dying? By the same token, a summer pond with an unending horizon is not transformed solely by the atmosphere of the day, but primarily by the gaze of those who stand on the shores. Gordon Craig once explained it in a note that actually foreshadowed his design drama, *The Stairs* [1907 – usually known as *The Steps*]: 'Have you ever been in love and had the feeling that the street before you suddenly expands, that houses grow, sing, lose themselves, and it seems to you that the street darkens drastically, levitates, and becomes transformed into a cloud? In reality you were walking along an ordinary street – or so everyone claims, but it's a lie, don't believe them, keep faith in your own truth, which is the truth of ecstasy.'[18]

Walter Gropius extended the Bauhaus concern for light into probably his most influential theatre project, the projected designs that he made in 1926 for his 'Synthetic Total Theater' for Piscator. In 1935 at a conference in Rome he presented his designs to an international gathering of writers and directors, saying: 'The contemporary theatre architect should set himself the aim to create a great keyboard for light and space, so objective and adaptable in character that it would respond to any imaginable vision of the stage director.'[19] Although the physical architecture of the building focused upon the large central revolving platform, which could move audience seating in order to create different forms of theatre, it seems clear that for Gropius the real interest in the project lay in the fact that the building itself could become a space of transformation and performance. Projection screens surrounded the interior like wallpaper suspended some distance from the walls – behind the stage and throughout the auditorium. Not only would these serve the experimental aims of designers and directors, but also in the face of the development of cinema, they would enable the theatre to re-assert its living immediacy and encourage the audience to 'shake off its inertia' as it entered the building and experienced the effects of the transformation of space through image and light. To enable this, Gropius planned a complex system of spotlights and multiple film projectors, with front and back projection screens, which between them could transform the walls and the ceiling into moving pictures and which would completely replace the 'cumbersome paraphernalia' of painted scenes.

Notwithstanding the radical and experimental nature of the Bauhaus theatre work, the use of light and the projected image as a representational alternative to traditional scene painting was to remain a frequent priority. Early in the century, Adolph Linnebach developed some sophistication in projecting reasonably complicated scenic images in German opera houses and State theatres. He used a simple metal rectangular casing to house an electric arc lamp, or by the 1920s a gas-filled tungsten filament lamp, and placed a cut-out or 'fretted' image on a stand some distance in front of the lamp housing. The projected image was large and could achieve a reasonable focus by moving the stand backwards and forwards in front of the light source. The distance from the arc light also meant that the 'fretted' image remained relatively cool and this enabled coloured filters, or painted transparencies, to be used. Multiple Linnebach projectors could be used to fill a large back scene with meteorological, marine and simple natural imagery. However, by the close of the 1920s, bulb and optical technology was such that a projected image might fill an entire stage and its cyclorama using photographic diapositive glass slides. It is, however, important to note, especially in the light of the experiments of Appia, Craig and the Bauhaus, that the desire to imitate nature – to project 'realistic' clouds upon a back scene, for example – remained the ambition that controlled the developing design of projection equipment in the theatre. More particularly, the production of opera on the international circuit of theatres still dominated the order books of equipment designers and manufacturers. The mobile, touring nature of both singers and productions of opera necessitated a technical theatre structure that was transferable from theatre to theatre. The portability of rolled canvas and two-dimensional framed scenery, flatly illuminated by a systematic lighting installation, provided this international flexibility. This most traditional of theatre forms therefore tended to retain its equally traditional representational scenographic ambitions until eventually threatened by innovations after the Second World War such as those at Bayreuth and subsequently, during the 1960s, in Prague.

As with most aspects of lighting technology during the late 1920s and through the 1930s, the Schwabe Company led the market and developed techniques and equipment for others to imitate. Although it was not installed at the Festival Theatre, Cambridge, Harold Ridge describes the centrepiece of Schwabe's late 1920s catalogue – the cloud-projector:

> The two-tier cloud machine ... is extensively used in continental opera houses and large theatres. A 3000 watt gas-filled lamp is placed in the centre, and around this are mounted 20 projection attachments, each of which can be fitted with a cloud diapositive. These diapositives are prepared from actual photographs. The clouds are made to move across the cyclorama by slowly rotating the entire apparatus by means of an electric motor. As the images from the objective lenses are reflected onto the cyclorama by means of plane mirrors it is possible to obtain a vertical movement by tilting the mirrors. The tilting movement of each tier of mirrors is worked by two electric motors. By using all three of the electric motors the clouds may be made to move in any direction and it is possible to make one bank of clouds move over the other.[20]

As might be expected from the work that Ridge undertook with Terence Gray at the Festival Theatre in Cambridge, and from his innovative approach to stage lighting that he published in 1928, he included the description of the cloud-projector for completeness rather than out of real conviction. His own view of the artistic value of this machine was that it would be a significant distraction in a 'serious' play and that therefore its use should be limited, at least as far as realism goes, to use in the production of spectacular plays. Such technology, accordingly, found considerable favour not only in the international opera house but also in the spectacular musicals of the 1930s – C. B. Cochran's *White Horse Inn* at the London Coliseum in 1931 had a complete cyclorama lit by Schwabe 'horizon' lights and cloud-projection machinery. But foreshadowing post-war use of large-scale scene projection, Ridge concluded: 'If, however, the machine is used by the scenic artist for purely imaginative designs which aid the atmosphere of the scene, this type of machine can become a valuable servant in the theatre.'[21]

Nevertheless, in the still relatively dim images achieved by scene projectors when they had to compete alongside the light needed to illuminate actors further down stage, many perceived more fundamental problems of representational identity. The intangible, ethereal quality of the projected image seemed to distance and separate it even more destructively from the world of the flesh-and-blood actor than had the painted scenic image. Fuerst and Hume noted in 1929: 'The setting stands at the back of the stage like an illustration of the action, without ever becoming part of it.'[22] However, they did not reject projection out of hand, but believed that if it were to be used, then it should exploit its sense of visual difference and 'seek a new beauty of its own at the side of, and apart from, drama'. However, they added the caution that 'when new scenic means appear so seductive, there is a temptation to exaggerate the importance that projections may have for the *mise en scène* of the future'.[23] The exploitation of scene projection was unlikely to be widespread until lamp and lens technology could provide both the intensity of light and the ability to focus with precision at such great size.

Notwithstanding the slowness of technology to enable scene projection, the 1930s produced some very significant changes in the approach to the use of light on stage. Fuerst and Hume summarized achievement in 1929 and set the scene:

> With the substitution of the high-powered incandescent lamp for the arc came the control from the switchboard of spotlights, floods and other units carrying lamps, ranging from three hundred to three thousand watts, just as formerly the border lights had been controlled. The result was that the old border lights themselves were replaced by high-powered lamps. In some theatres we saw the border light transformed into a steel light bridge capable of carrying any number of spot and floodlights and one or two electricians as well.[24]

The desire for light intensity and the ability to produce sharp, hard-edged beams of light led to considerable technical development in the increasingly used spotlight. Precise dates are not especially relevant, but in 1933 Kliegl Brothers (USA) and Century Lighting (USA) simultaneously produced what were probably the first ellipsoidal spotlights in the 'Klieglight' and the 'Lekolight'. It was well known that the rays from a light source, placed at the first focal point of an elliptical reflector, would converge toward the second focal point, so that consequently it was possible to pass all the rays through a comparatively small colour filter or diapositive slide by placing it close to the second focal point. In its simplest form the luminaire, like its 'baby lens' predecessor, consisted of a tubular casing with a blackened interior surface. A light source (by now an argon gas-filled tungsten filament bulb) was placed at the focal point, with an ellipsoidal highly polished reflector placed behind, and a plano-convex lens set at the front. Such an arrangement produced the distinctive conical, hard-edged beam of light that was rapidly becoming an icon for theatrical performance. Because of its focusing ability, the ellipsoidal spotlight could also operate as the projector of focused images when images painted onto heat-resisting mica sheets or fretted gobos (shortened from 'go-between') were placed at the focal point between the lens and the light source. With a significant boost in the light source produced by halogen bulb technology in the 1960s and more general improvements and variations to lens and mechanical handling, the ellipsoidal spotlight (mirror, or profile spotlight in the UK) remains the basic technology of modern stage lighting and still provides, of course, the 'living light' envisioned by Appia.

Whilst the date of the 'invention' of the ellipsoidal spotlight is not especially important, it is interesting to note that a year earlier, in 1932, a work of stage-lighting theory and practice was published that not only used such luminaires, but relied upon them. Stanley McCandless was a professor at Yale University (1925–64) and was one of the first teachers to offer a course in Stage Lighting. His two major works, A Method of Lighting the Stage (4 editions, 1932–58) and A Syllabus of Stage Lighting (11 editions, 1934–64), provided the first structured, formal 'method' for lighting the stage. His method required that the stage be divided into a series of 'lighting areas'. A lighting area was a small section of the total acting space. McCandless asked that you should imagine a cylindrical space approximately eight to twelve feet (2.5–3.5 metres) in diameter and seven feet (just over 2 metres) tall. Although much would depend upon the specific floor-plan of the setting, he proposed a system using a minimum of six 'lighting area', placing three areas across the front of the stage and three beyond, toward the back of the stage – the wider and the deeper the stage, the more of these 'plains' of lighting areas would be required. McCandless's original theory proposed the use of two lights focusing upon each area, both of which should be placed above, in front of, and to the left and right of the performer at as close to 45 degrees from a central axis as possible. To light all six areas, therefore, a total of twelve luminaires would be needed. McCandless went further and suggested that in lighting each area, one of the two luminaires should be filtered with a warm colour (typically amber or pink) and the other with a cool colour (typically pale blue). Subsequent editions suggested that three luminaires per area should to be used for a thrust stage, and four per area for a theatre-in-the-round stage. Lighting the stage in carefully defined areas like this focused the illumination on the performer's face, and by varying the intensity between the individual lighting areas, served also to focus the audience's attention. Thus the stage would be provided with a thorough, but flexible system of providing key lighting to any area of the stage. This key lighting would then be augmented by 'fill' light that would consist of atmospheric 'washes' of light, being provided by the traditional overhead battens, side-lights and footlights. The key light would establish the highlights; the fill light would control the colour and depth of the shadow areas. The relationship between 'key' and 'fill' was to be established by a difference either in colour or intensity – the key light would tend to be the brighter or the warmer of the two.

In this way the theory and practice of lighting the stage that had been in operation since the introduction of electric lighting was effectively reversed, although the main principles of Appia still held true. Hitherto the diffused, shadow-free general illumination from battens and borders had provided the foundation of stage lighting, within which *occasional* spotlights might be used in order to model and emphasize. In McCandless's method, the systematic use of spotlights, individually focusing upon defined acting areas, provided the basic illumination of the stage, which might then be blended, harmonized and coloured by the battens. It was a system firmly rooted in a belief in the plasticity of the stage and therefore it furthered Appia's ambition. It acknowledged the overall primacy of form and modelling in the role of stage lighting, and that, accordingly, lighting should primarily exist to reveal the actors and their actions within a scenic structure of three-dimensional architectural form. It also responded, through the circuitry used to connect and manipulate the 'pairing' of lights on the acting areas, to the idea that stage lighting should be able to follow the action; that lighting might serve as a continuous score of visual accompaniment within the performance. The remarkable coherence and thoroughness of McCandless's method, coinciding with the development of appropriate technology, has contributed to ensuring that its principles still form the basis of our contemporary approach to lighting.

However, the system, when first proposed by McCandless, made considerable demands upon light-control and dimming facilities. By the early 1930s, it was becoming common for the lighting control board to be separated from the dimmers, which were frequently, and for safety's sake, placed away from the stage in a more fireproof

environment – usually in a basement area. To do this initially necessitated cumbersome mechanical operation with tracker wires and
pulleys, and then by the 1930s and learning much from the technology
of the cinema organ, by using electrical servo-motors to move the
dimmer levers. In 1933 the General Radio Company (USA) developed
a continuously variable transformer, known as the 'Variac', that could
replace the uneven and often jerky operation of the resistance or
electrolyte dimmers. As with older forms of dimming, but with greater
ease, the autotransformer dimmer could be remotely operated. These
developments were simultaneously matched by European companies
and served as the principal form of electrical dimming system until
the introduction of Silicon Controlled Rectifier (SCR) dimming during
the 1960s.

But to achieve the continuity and flow of a stage-lighting score and
the sense of seamless integration within the dramatic action that was
suggested by both Appia and facilitated by McCandless's method,
a lighting-control system was required that could be 'played' like a
musical instrument, with its operator having a clear and uninter-
rupted view of the stage. Fred Bentham's 'colour organ' of the late
1930s (see Figure 19) and its variants seemed to provide the technology and also a suitable mental 'attitude' for an artist/operator
accompanying performance. But its ultimate flexibility was con-
strained by the limitations of the remote servo-controlled autotransformer dimmers stored beneath the stage. Such limitations had proved
less of a problem when the emphasis of stage lighting had relied upon
a limited number of 'colour' circuits arranged in battens, accompanied by a still relatively small number of spotlights. But after
McCandless and also, as Bentham notes, after the Second World War,
'theatre was becoming more and more spotlight and other localised
light based; so who would want primary colours battens?'[25]

Whilst a large number of relevant technologies were initiated
during the 1930s in the field of filament design, luminaire development and increasingly sophisticated lighting control and dimming,
reactionary and extreme political forces in Europe had the effect of
limiting significant innovatory stage practice to the few experimental
theatre companies in the USA. The scenographic experiments of Gray
and Ridge at Cambridge, of Meyerhold in the Soviet Union, of Georg
Grosz, Caspar Neher and Erwin Piscator in Weimar Germany, of the
experimental artists of the Bauhaus, and of Italian Futurism, and
Surrealism in France, all withered as their artists escaped into exile to
the USA, retreated into a politically safer 'classicism' or, like Gray,

abandoned theatre practice altogether. There was, therefore, after the end of the Second World War, a sense of rediscovering the experimental basis of scenography that had been initiated in the 1920s.

A very particular and important rediscovery in connection with lighting and its technology occurred at the *Festspielhaus* in Bayreuth, where its close association with the National Socialist Party necessitated a very thorough and radical re-evaluation of production values. Wolfgang and Wieland Wagner, the grandsons of the composer, were required to re-stage the complete canon of Wagner's music-dramas in a way that disassociated them from their pre-war colonial status as emblems of the *heilige deutsches kunst*, and their exploitation and effective 'ownership' by Hitler. In a series of remarkable productions through the 1950s, Wolfgang and Wieland Wagner not only achieved this 're-birth' of Wagner's work, but also, by example and influence, revolutionized approaches to the staging of opera throughout the world. Appia's collected *mise en scène* for the works had been initially rejected out of hand by Wagner's widow, Cosima, and had consistently been over-ruled and generally derided at Bayreuth up to the outbreak of the War. Furthermore, although Appia's work on *Tristan und Isolde* at La Scala, Milan in 1923 and on the *Ring* cycle at the Opera House in Basel in 1924–5 had been significant and historically important, the lighting technology available at that time was less than adequate to fully realize Appia's ideas. However, in the early 1950s, Bayreuth had access to spotlights of considerable power through the electronic and optical developments of the German company Reich & Vogel, and also to scene projectors that could either dominate the stage with gobo texture, or fill the entire back-scene with powerful and clearly defined imagery.

Ludwig Pani began in the early 1930s as a division of a maker of optical quality lenses, Optischen Werke C. Reichert in Vienna. Building upon associated technologies of illumination and optical definition that the War urged forwards, by the early 1950s they were making scene projectors which had incandescent filament light sources of up to 5000 watts and sophisticated and adaptable systems of objective lenses. Although extremely costly, and therefore very much restricted to large international opera houses and state theatres, the early ambitions of Appia, Linnebach and Gropius were now technically possible. Of equal, if not more importance was that Bayreuth now had the circumstance and the will to realize Appia's vision of a scene that would be fully integrated within the dramatic action of its musical score (see Figure 20). The scenes (like Appia's designs) have

Figure 20   Projection after the Second World War – Wagner at Bayreuth realizing the scenic ambition of Appia, *Rhinegold*, 1952 (*Festspielhaus Bayreuth Bildarchiv*)

little if any pictorial significance in their own right; they provide a context for performance, but also in their inseparable partnership with the dramaturgy of the poetry and its music, they became integral to the performance. The projected scene could now serve, in Appia's terms, as the 'hyphen' that united dramaturgy and its environment. Furthermore, in rendering 'immaterial all that it touches', the projected light had the ability to endow the physical reality of stage and scenic material with movement and change. The intensity of light produced by the Pani projectors was such that the sense of separation and 'difference' of the projected image from other stage lighting noted by Fuerst and Hume could be avoided.

If it is Adolphe Appia who serves to exemplify the fundamental principles of stage lighting in performance, then it is Josef Svoboda who took the idea of movement and change, implicit in a movable beam of projected light, and developed it within his practice of kinetic scenography. In 1993 he wrote, 'If the standard scenographic guide in the '20s was a painted rendering and in the '30s a three-dimensional model, then in the '60s it was a ground plan, lighting scenario, and a filmed record of a kinetic model.'[26] Svoboda's writings, articles

and interviews do not have the sonority, *gravitas* or sometimes her-
metic qualities of Appia nor the elusive possibilities of Craig, nor
the overt political commitment and modernist social agendas of the
Bauhaus. Nevertheless, *The Secret of Theatrical Space* (1993) is an
extremely important collection of theory and principles derived from
his sixty years of scenographic practice that in many ways united
and extended the scenographic energies of the original theorists and
artists. Svoboda's account ranges from anecdote to memoir and reflection, and from scientific precision to poetic stream of consciousness.
Whilst he was always committed to an understanding of scientific
principles and the development of advanced technology within his
scenographic solutions, he also maintained a great respect for the
intuitive solution and was consistently sensitive to the inter-relation of
time, space, movement and light in the theatre – to the holistic sense
of the plasticity of the stage that has been such an over-riding
perception of the twentieth century. He was trained as a carpenter and
then as an architect, but began designing for the stage shortly after the
end of the Second World War. By the time he was 30 in 1950, he
was head of 'artistic-technical operations' at the National Theatre
in Prague. Having developed the technical and optical processes
involved for display in International Trade Fairs, he founded the
experimental Laterna Magika theatre in 1973 to pursue experiments
and to make theatre that integrated filmed and live performance –
experiments that continued ceaselessly in his position as Artistic
Director until his death in 2002.

Implicit in the theory articulated by McCandless was the important
concept of darkness – expressed simply, the theatre space is not one
that is illuminated in an overall general way, but fundamentally a
place of darkness that is energized and brought to life by the
performance of light. The division of the stage into lighting areas that
should be determined by the dramatic action, and the ability to select
or deselect any such area, meant that light should not exist at all until
generated and occasioned by dramatic action. This seemingly ele-
mentary description of the stage and an approach to light lay at the
heart of Svoboda's concept of scenography. He said: 'After all, it's
not a matter of theatre space, but of the space for a production,
therefore production space, and that is fundamentally different from
theatre space.'[27] The power and flexibility of post-war spotlights and
the optical developments that paved the way for scenic projection,
coupled with increasingly sophisticated lighting control, enabled
Svoboda to conceive of the space of production as a distinctive

construct *within* the architectural theatre space; a construct of space-defining light born out of darkness, an abstract spatial composition shaped by light. The stage of a theatre building is a dark space; its sides disappear into the further blackness of the wings and there is no ceiling, and only the floor has a given physical reality (and even that may be scenographically redefined). The entire architectural space is therefore capable of giving birth to production space and its transformation, and from out of this darkness it is light that will create that space. The challenge for the scenographer is to create a space that both serves a production and is defined by the production. 'I'm not interested in making a burning bush or an erupting volcano on stage, in creating an illusion of reality, but in acknowledging the reality of theatrical elements, which can be transformed non-materially into almost anything. I've called them "space in space." '[28] For Svoboda,

Figure 21   Technology and performance: Josef Svoboda used a web of laser beams as scenography for *The Magic Flute*, Bayerische Staatsoper, Munich, 1970; directed by Gunther Rennert (*Šárka Hejnová*)

therefore, light as atmosphere, light presented as the material quality of light beams, and light as the projected image with its possibilities for reflection and refraction, became the fundamental ingredients within the process of scenographic transformation. Although re-articulated and extended by Svoboda into technically sophisticated new effects, these remain, of course, essentially the three qualities of light as described by Appia in 1899.

Scientific investigation, and its ability to generate new technologies, have been a consistent feature of Svoboda's artistic process and therefore of the internal organization of the theatre. The scenic department of the National Theatre in Prague was organized as a collection of research laboratories that examined optical and electrical qualities of stage equipment, and the material qualities of fabrics and plastics in Svoboda's ceaseless experiment with surfaces for receiving, reflecting and transmitting light. When the theatre could not provide the expertise, Svoboda developed relationships with academic and commercial scientific research – for example, in 1970 he worked with Siemens to develop what they called *Lasergrafie*. Between them they created a moving web-like cradle of coloured laser light-beams for use in Günther Rennert's production of *Die Zauberflöte* at the Munich Staatsoper. The seemingly 'solid' needle-like beams of light inter-meshed in space and created apparitions that gave body to the forces and powers of Mozart's work. Svoboda's excitement and commit-ment to *Bühnenlaser* was great until the considerable safety implica-tions of laser technologies became apparent and made significant future development in the theatre impractical.

> This union of art and science is essential and vitally necessary for our time. It provides art with a rational basis and helps us to carry our investigations further. If I need a cylinder of the light on stage with a dispersion of less than one degree at its base, I need to gather an entire scientific and technical team to construct such a cylinder.[29]

In 1959, he created the scenography for a production of *Hamlet* at the National Theatre in Prague. Its requirement for light illustrates Svoboda's concern for not only making production space within the architectural framework of a theatre stage, but also achieving its fullest integration within the dramatic and psychological action of the performance. He described his inspiration as being that of three kinds of light upon a stone and their interplay: the intense, bright illumina-tion of the sun directly striking the stone; the deep, black shadow

Figure 22   *Hamlet*, National Theatre, Prague, 1959 (*Šárka Hejnová*)

beneath the stone; and, at one side, a half-shadow and a softened light reflected from an adjacent stone. These three kinds of light, he said, were the prototypes of any plastic form that could be created by sharp, diffused and reflected light (see Figure 22). The scenic arrangement for *Hamlet* consisted of twelve rectangular screens (very similar to the Craig pattern) that were covered by a black plastic material, which had almost 50 per cent of the reflective quality of a black mirror surface. The screens were lit by spotlights hanging upon the lighting bridge, which traversed the stage directly upstage of the proscenium arch. The actors and all other scenic details were illuminated simultaneously by both direct and reflected light. As a result of this, the range of shadow values was essentially extended, hard contrasts disappeared, and, Svoboda says, forms were fuller – and in the optical sense, more real. He clarified:

> It did not conventionally describe the place of action or even create it. It placed the action in absolute space, which can represent any place and any time. That is, the scene did not picture a concrete place. The movement of the abstract panels not only indicated spatial changes but was also a materialisation of rhythm, by means of which the action progressed. Similar to the function of a film cut, it evoked the psychic state of the characters.[30]

Similarly, at Bayreuth in 1974, light was used to express the duality of love as represented in *Tristan und Isolde*. He wanted the scenography to reflect upon the absolute, ideal nature of love whilst simultaneously being able to recognize its palpably very human, sensuous character. A scenic surface that would both reflect projected light and also transmit the light beyond the surface of the screen was used. In several productions at this period, Svoboda was experimenting with the reflective qualities of tightly stretched thin ropes hanging a few centimetres apart, and which therefore created a semi-transparent 'wall'. He described the effect in *Tristan*:

> The shifting character of light envelops the shimmering environment of the entire story. The scenography of the final scene, for example, in which Tristan waits for Isolde under a tree, was based on thin, densely clustered vertical cords. A mere change in the temperature of the colours projected onto the cord reconfigured the entire space. Tristan and Isolde were suddenly like sunspots, until at the end they became a part of the sun itself.[31]

Alongside Svoboda's use of projected images and the variety of surfaces upon which they were thrown and reflected, there developed a sophisticated extension of McCandless's ambition to focus attention selectively upon the actor. This had been available, albeit quite crudely, since the days of limelight and the early electric arc lamps, where a brilliant 'follow-spot' would sweep across the space, keeping pace with star performers as they moved about the stage. By the 1960s the use of follow-spots had generally died out for drama, and they were principally to be seen in opera, ballet and the variety theatre. However, the technological development of quartz-halogen light sources, and the invention of plastics-based heat-resistant colour filters, enabled the production of extremely powerful moving spot-lights which, unlike their arc light predecessors, could be electrically dimmed and very effectively coloured.

A consistent challenge to the scenographer who uses projected scenic space is that the illumination required in order to illuminate the actors can frequently dilute the power and intensity of the projected image – rather like watching a television screen in bright daylight. Typically, the old follow-spots had been located right at the very back of the auditorium, shining over the heads of the audience onto the front of the stage – hence the need for the brightest light source available. Svoboda and his team developed movable spotlights that could be placed throughout the theatre, most especially high on either side of the stage as well as at various positions in the auditorium. His scenography for the Prokofiev *Romeo and Juliet* (National Theatre, Prague, 1971) was black and heavily punctuated with beams of back-light that framed the action. A seemingly floating colonnade of exquisitely proportioned Renaissance arches traversed the stage, covered in a dark surface that received the dim projected image of a texture similar to highly magnified fabric. As the tragedy progressed, the texture grew in size as though magnification was being increased – in Prokofiev's ballet, the dramatic action 'zooms in' more closely on the detail of the tragedy. Were the acting spaces of the stage to have been lit sufficiently to see the performers, all this would have been lost. Accordingly, therefore, each actor was 'followed' imperceptibly by two or three subtly coloured, soft-beamed spotlights whose intensity and colouring could change as needed. Highly skilled stage technicians were needed to operate the spotlights with sensitivity and subtlety as they 'picked up' performers with light as they entered the scene.

The quartz-halogen technology of the 1960s had an important additional effect in that it finally enabled the literal treatment of light as a material quality. Light beams of such intensity could be created that their resulting form could present a solidity to match a solid material, but with the ability to transform in intensity and trans-lucency. Svoboda may well be remembered by future generations primarily for his continued experiment with a scenographic 'wall' of light and associated technologies. Using low-voltage luminaires that produced parallel beams of brilliant white light, he projected into space a hollow vertical cylinder of light for *Tristan und Isolde* in Cologne in 1969. For the five productions of Verdi's *Sicilian Vespers* that he worked on with John Dexter from 1969 to 1984, he developed the purest form of his wall of light (see Figure 23). The battens

Figure 23   Josef Svoboda, '*La contra-luce* Svoboda', Verdi, *Sicilian Vespers*, London Coliseum, 1984; directed by John Dexter (*Šárka Hejnová*)

of luminaires were suspended high over the stage and shone almost vertically down, but at a small 'back-light' angle onto the stage. Their intensity was such that light not only achieved the material quality of a wall, but also and primarily achieved the aim of becoming a potent dramatic force within the drama. Impurities, dust and residual smoke in the atmosphere enhanced the visibility of the beams of light. Svoboda said that as *Sicilian Vespers* progressed from its first production in Hamburg to its last version in Amsterdam, the wall of light became harder to achieve as the air became cleaner and more 'conditioned', and smoking disappeared from theatres. To some effect, the spraying of ionized water droplets was used to create an atmospheric haze, and when the effect was no longer required a reverse in polarity would cause the droplets to lose their suspension and fall. Svoboda adopted the name given to the effect in Italy, and remarked with playful sadness in 1999 that '*la contra-luce Svoboda* was never the same when people stopped smoking'.[32]

Svoboda was convinced of the need for transformation and of the ongoing role of technology within the theatre and, like the Bauhaus artists, believed that science and technology were an inescapable condition of modern living that must be reflected in both the process and the end product of art. The challenge for him, as indeed for the Bauhaus or any contemporary artist, was to inject the true essence of life into the work: 'theatre *ought* to be a place of magic. Nothing from life can be transferred intact into the theatre; we must always create a theatrical reality and then fill it with the dynamics of life.'[33] Use of every modern technology available in order to create a facsimile representation of a tree, a house, an office, or a prison will have little effect in the theatre. Even placing the 'thing itself' onto a stage, much as the late nineteenth century had done in order to combat the effect of electric light by putting real motor cars into their scenes, will have little effect. The dislocation from a real-world context into the framed situation of an observed stage scenography will remove any life or significance from the object. During the twentieth century, the focusing and form-revealing quality of a beam of light and the changing atmosphere of coloured light have drawn attention to the fundamental, time-based nature of live performance, and the fact that drama may only be expressed through forms of action. It is therefore the *action* of light within a scenography that may enable life and energy. Through its action, scenography becomes performance. A blue length of cloth may, through the action of performance, become a river, just as, through action, six actors may become an entire army. The texture, quality and colour of the blue cloth may well achieve a theatrical reality, but it is the way in which the fabric *performs*, its role within the overall plasticity of the stage, that may endow it with what Svoboda called the 'dynamics of life'.

Before the Second World War, the mechanical control of dimmers and switching at the lighting control board was limited to the ingenious, but ultimately limited, physical control of the lighting-board operator. Electro-mechanical control through the use of servo-motors allowed the creation of more complex lighting 'states' in which each 'state' might involve the control of many individual lights according, for example, to the method suggested by McCandless. Lighting control boards (or desks, as they became called as they became smaller) of the late 1950s and through the 1960s offered rows of dimmer levers and matching switches. Each 'row' of levers and switches could be used to prepare a lighting state. When required, a single 'master' dimmer lever at the end of the row was used to implement the lighting change in performance. Multiple rows of such levers and controls enabled several such states to be prepared in advance. Inevitably, the system required a dextrous operator with a careful written account of each state, and lighting rehearsals could be slow as the operator recorded the written notation of the light that had been created. Furthermore, the number of lights, or their paired and patched equivalents, was limited to the number of circuits available to each row of controls – although the physical re-patching of lights into other circuits could vary the lights used. In practice, however, technology such as this had the tendency of treating stage lighting as a series of fixed conditions or states, with individual variations and 'specials' made to accommodate specific dramatic situations. The idea of light as a genuine accompaniment, a continuously moving and transforming lighting 'score' that Appia anticipated, was hard to achieve until methods could be found to record numerous 'states' or conditions of lighting and to be able to instantly play back the recorded lighting – better still, to allow the operator to play the entire lighting installation as a giant instrument. Recording notation to magnetic tape was reliable, but difficult to play back in any other than a straightforwardly linear way. With the advent of digital recording to computer disks, lighting control in the theatre had access to an infinitely more flexible and sophisticated means of storing and playing back complex lighting in performance.

However, the ever-increasing exploitation of electronic technologies in the design and operation of lighting control systems tended to further remove the lighting operator from close contact with the performance. Until the 1960s, and later in many old theatre buildings, the lighting control board had typically been located at the side of the stage and was frequently raised high onto a platform behind the proscenium arch. As new theatres were built and modifications were carried out to existing buildings, lighting control was placed at the rear of the auditorium alongside stage management and sound control, all with a reasonably unobstructed view of the stage. But the combination of functions, the inevitable noise and the need for air conditioning and filtration for increasingly complex electronic installations required the use of heavy, double-glazed glass between the auditorium and the control facility. Just as technology created the need for technicians to be isolated in an air-conditioned and sound-proof environment distant from the stage, so technology has more recently been used to bring the operators back into more direct contact with performance. Small and reasonably discrete 'slave' units may be operated from anywhere; the use of mini-disk and computer-manipulated sound has banished the loud magnetic 'clunk' of the tape-recorder and enabled sound to be similarly operated from within the auditorium space.

As the light source and flexibility of the contemporary data projector increases, then it will undoubtedly replace the need for large, extremely cumbersome and expensive scene projectors. Furthermore, the optical challenge of creating the desired image when the projector may need to be sited at an acute angle to the screen, which previously was solved by photographic manipulation in the darkroom and optically at the projector, may now be undertaken as the image is generated, or processed in the computer with far greater accuracy. Accordingly some of the fundamental qualities of change, movement and transformation that have been identified by theatre artists throughout the twentieth century as being the crucial contributions of light and atmospheric colour may be explored and will inevitably accompany this method of creating scenographic imagery.

8 The Scene as the Architecture of Performance

> I wish to remove the *Pictorial Scene* but to leave in its place the *Architectonic Scene*.
>
> Edward Gordon Craig[1]

A considerable feature of the struggle to find an alternative scenographic identity and a new aesthetic for the theatre during the twentieth century has been centred upon finding ways of integrating scenic space and the place of performance – the architecture of the theatre. The fictional space of the play conjured by traditional representational painted scenery – the sitting-room of Hedda Gabler, or the castle of Elsinore – has confronted a developing concern for the material reality of the scenic materials used to create such a fiction. In the tension between spatial illusion and its material reality, the space occupied by the stage has become, and continues to be, a contested and ambiguous place: a place that exists to, in some way, 'realize' a dramatic text; or, a place that is the canvas of its own art. As Gay McAuley says: 'The specificity of theatre is not to be found in its relationship to the dramatic ... but in that it consists essentially of the interaction between performers and spectators in a given space.'[2] Furthermore, the ongoing questioning and re-appraisal of the relationship between performer and spectator has consistently generated debates about the nature of stage architecture and the physical placement of theatre. If the scene should no longer be considered as illusionistic and pictorial, if it should no longer be an ambition to provide the audience with a 'voyeur-like' perspective into a space that, through conventional means, pretends to be other than itself, then what are the alternatives to the proscenium-arch architecture of the picture stage? As the century progressed, why did solutions from the ancient history of theatre seem more attractive and efficacious to new performance than contemporary architectural, modernist design? And as an extension to this, why have so many contemporary theatre artists rejected *any* formal theatre architecture and sought to locate new performance elsewhere than in a theatre, especially in the old, the damaged and the alternative? Why has it proved to be so (increasingly) hard to design a new theatre building?

Early histories of the theatre, that is work written in the first half of the twentieth century, had consistently 'discovered' in antiquity, in the medieval theatre, and in the theatre of the Renaissance, that there had existed an inseparable connection and interaction between the architectural arrangement of audience space and the acting space, and that to achieve this the scenic arrangement in those theatres – the stage setting and its associated technologies – had been an integral part of the whole architectural arrangement. Such a marriage of architectural form and performative function has consistently proved to be deeply attractive, since it seemed to have harmonized into one structure the contemporary style of acting, the conventions of representation, and the dominant dramaturgy of narrative alongside the political location and social function of theatre. With a growing awareness of this complex synergy, the avant-garde and modernist artist of the early twentieth century understandably perceived the theatre architecture of the preceding century as no longer being capable of representing the values of a machine age. Certainly following the First World War, such theatre structures represented a corrupted and a despised vision of society; the ornate and gilded picture frame was considered utterly inappropriate for modern dramatic material, whilst the large size of the buildings and stages that had been driven by pictorial, materialist ambitions, were seen to demean and humiliate the practice of the actor.

But modernity itself appeared to offer alternatives that were in themselves unsatisfactory if not deeply flawed, and they seemed to pay little attention to the histories of theatre that were being written and the discoveries that they were making. In the early twenty-first century, many theatre artists believe that 'contemporary' theatres built in the 1950s and 1960s have failed to reflect upon the important interactive relationships between spectator and performer that theatre history, and increasingly studies in the anthropology of performance, have indicated as being fundamental. For example, the 'democratic' neutrality of modernist auditoriums, whilst providing more rigorously for health and safety, and offering more equitable viewing and hearing for the audience, have consistently failed to encourage a meaningful locating of theatre within cultural life, and the equally neutral stage spaces have offered little sympathy with the practices of acting. This chapter will examine a series of attempts over the period that have sought new ways of integrating the place (architecture) of performance with the space (stage) of performance, and will examine the technologies that have facilitated and occasionally hindered this search.

Richard Wagner designed his theatre at Bayreuth, which opened in 1876, as an opera house solely for the purpose of staging his music-dramas. He had a practical agenda of 'improvements' to the universal dominant form of the Italianate galleried, horseshoe theatre. But he had no agenda of radical change; his ambition was fundamentally to make the 'game' of absorption more effective and acceptable for his audience. As Peter Brook argues:

> At every moment we keep this double vision: we are in this place where people are playing a game, and we're watching them performing. ... The peculiarity, over several centuries, of what we call the *théâtre à l'italienne* is that the audience is invited – although this never works completely – to enter into a different game, which is pretending that they themselves and their world have completely disappeared and this other world on the stage is absolutely real.[3]

In order to create an enhanced picture-frame stage, Wagner totally removed the ornate gilded and decorated proscenium arch, allowing the termination of the walls and ceiling of the auditorium to form the frame of an opening onto the stage. He further increased the quality of separation of space by removing the traditional wide orchestra pit with its distracting and glittering lights on music-stands, and he placed the orchestra beneath the stage within what might be thought of as a large wooden horn flattened into a long, thin opening at the front of the stage – thereby creating an 'invisible orchestra'. He also removed the obvious social hierarchy implicit in a galleried audience and replaced it with the single span of a fan-shaped steeply raked auditorium. Wagner's design for the *Festspielhaus* was therefore an elegant and effective purification of the picture-frame stage; it rid the theatre of surplus decorative elements and the nineteenth-century social pretensions that an opera theatre should look something like a palace or cathedral, and focused instead upon practical functionality.

In this way it may be considered as the first truly modern theatre. So effective have Wagner's rationalizing approach and his improvements been, that the basic form of the *Festspielhaus* has served as the paradigm for the theatre architect for over a hundred years. The *Festspielhaus* created a *sense* of integration between audience and stage through its openness and its functionality, whilst it still retained the neutrality of the stage house as a 'box of tricks' to amaze and surprise an audience. In this way, of course, it may be thought of as the architectural conclusion to Loutherbourg's late eighteenth-century ambition for a theatre of amazement and emotional transport. The rejection of this over-riding theatrical ambition by many artists in the early years of the twentieth century led to more radical architectural propositions concerning the nature of the place and of the scene, and of ways in which these may be (re)united.

At the Arena Goldoni School in Florence during the years 1912–14, Gordon Craig began to extend his examination of the architectonic qualities of scenic structure. Like many during the twentieth century, he developed a powerful and emotional attachment for the theatre structures of Greek antiquity. In the 'Argument' that he wrote for *Scene* in 1923 he considered the Greek to be the '*1st Drama*' and said:

> One place – one time – one action.
> (Unity of *place*, time, and action – not of *scene*, time, and action.)
> Open air: ... Dance – Song – Speech – Masks – Architecture combine in this Drama.[4]

> The whole Theatre was of stone – *the whole Theatre was the Scene*. One part of it held spectators, the other actors; but all of it was Scene – the Place for the Drama. ... Their Scene then was a *genuine* thing. A work of architecture. Unalterable except for trifling pieces here and there ...[5]

The building in Florence in which he worked served as a provocation to Craig and one that he used as the basis for several architectural propositions. The Arena Goldoni, as Craig found it, had a curved, open-air auditorium that was backed by a colonnaded 'gallery'. Two high arched entrances served in the positions of the *parados* to either side and provided entrances to the semicircular orchestra space. However, the scenic space on its raised stage was effectively a covered, traditional proscenium arch stage, off which were the rooms used by Craig as workshops and as the publication offices of his journal *The Mask*. The frontispiece that he drew for *The Theatre Advancing* (1921) shows an interesting response to the Arena Goldoni

Design for a Theatre open to the air, the sun and moon.

Figure 24   'Design for a theatre open to the air, the sun and moon';
frontispiece to Gordon Craig's *Theatre Advancing* (London: Constable, 1921)

and reflects both his interests in the theatre of antiquity and his
desire to recreate an 'architectonic' scenic space (see Figure 24).
It shows a semicircular audience space similar to that of the Arena and
of a small Graeco-Roman auditorium, a forestage that descends by
shallow steps into a classical orchestra, and a stage house that blends
some of the permanence of his understanding of the *skene* of antiquity
with the possibilities for movement, lighting and change suggested in
his work on the screens project. His ambition that such a theatre
should be completely freed from the illusionistic emphasis of the
immediate past is indicated in the frontispiece title: 'Design for a
Theatre open to the air, the sun and moon'.

Shortly before he opened the School in Florence, he had responded
favourably to the comment that his 'screens' of 1910 were more
of a 'place' than a 'scene': that the stage as 'scene' seemed false
whereas the stage as 'place' rang true. His focus of attention upon

this important distinction has had reverberations ever since. Some years earlier, in 1907, he had attended a performance of Bach's oratorio *St Matthew Passion* in Amsterdam and had conceived the idea of creating a theatre and stage for its performance. In his response to the *Passion*, he thought that

> something might be added ... but very little ... nothing like one of those Reinhardt performances, with everybody shouting and waving their arms in the air and people catching hold of a man and dragging him away and putting him on a cross. All that would be simply futile.[6]

In his experiments and the stage models that he built, and which occupied much of his time at the Arena Goldoni, he sought to create an art of movement in space, and to create a place of performance that was somehow comparable with, and reflective of, that produced by the progressive movement of Bach's music. Increasingly his studies in theatre history urged him to examine the important relationship between space and place. He was especially interested in the seamless inter-relationship between the structural formalities of the scenic space and the audience space, which he believed had been achieved in medieval liturgical drama, in the street drama of the *commedia dell'arte* and in the formal architecture of Andrea Palladio at the *Teatro Olimpico*, in Vicenza (1580) and of Andrea Scamozzi at nearby Sabbionetta (1588). The unchanging streets of the *Olimpico* set within their architectural sculpted scenic façade, and the formal single perspective of Sabbionetta's scene, seemed to define places for the activity of performance – not for any particular play, but for plays in general. Craig naturally appreciated the similarity of this architecture to that of the Elizabethan public playhouse and wanted to examine its contemporary potential.

Inspired by drawings that he had made of the interior of the tiny Romanesque church of San Nicolao in the town of Giornico in the Italian-speaking Swiss canton of Ticino in August 1910, he built a model of a permanent structure that comprised many different 'places', all interlinked by the possibilities of movement (of light and of actors) between the spaces. The result focused upon a high, bridge-like balcony that crossed the 'nave' above steps that led down into a below-stage basement crypt. Over and beyond the balcony he added a flight of steps receding high into the distance. Craig's original model was almost twelve feet (3.5 metres) tall, but was destroyed when the Italian army requisitioned the Arena Goldoni in 1914. Another model, slightly smaller at eight feet (2.5 metres) tall, survived in small

Figure 25   Gordon Craig model for a proposed production of J. S. Bach, *St Matthew Passion*; reconstructed by Edward Craig *c.*1968 (*London, V&A Theatre Museum*)

sections and was extensively rebuilt and interpreted in drawings by Craig's son Edward during the 1960s (see Figure 25). This is the surviving model.

Craig extravagantly proposed that a church should be requisitioned, modified and used solely for the annual performance of the Bach oratorio. At first sight therefore, the idea and its model really do seem to present an absurd proposition. Furthermore, its subsequent interpretation by Edward Craig (who remembered working with his father on the model when he was eight years old) suggested a choir of hundreds and great orchestral forces – indeed very much in the spirit of a spectacular Reinhardt-like production that Craig had consciously rejected in 1907. Critical judgement of Craig's *Passion* project has nevertheless relied almost exclusively upon this possibly questionable interpretation by Edward Craig. In particular we should note that Craig's inspiration in Giornico was a tiny church of exquisite human scale that is now used, ironically, primarily for musical performances. Setting this original inspiration alongside what we should think of as merely an act of interpretation, alerts us to the importance of Craig's original scenographic ambition.

Beneath this huge, deceptive model, which does not readily communicate a sense of human scale, lies an important principle of twentieth-century scenography. Craig's proposition created a number of architectural spaces: flights of steps leading to (and from) a high and distant eternity; smaller, intimate spaces for human interaction; platforms for declaration and more intimate interaction with an audience; and an interior basement 'cellarage' of mystery and atmosphere. As in all Craig scenes, stage architecture and the scene were to be brought to life by the atmosphere and movement of light, enabling performance and the new technologies of controlling and colouring light to create spaces that would be simultaneously neutral and eternal, but might also become as particular and intimate as the garden of Gethsemane. Although the proposition was clearly derivative of the twelfth-century Romanesque architecture at Giornico and, in the balcony-like central bridge, of the scenographic and architectural qualities of the Elizabethan public playhouse, Craig had created an essentially modern architectural stage. Some of the physical structure and much of its underlying philosophy are similar to those of countless experiments and achievements in stage architecture that have taken place, throughout the twentieth century, in theatres all over Europe and America.

Jacques Copeau and Louis Jouvet visited Craig in 1914 and were impressed with the *Passion* project. The architectural formality of Craig's stage alongside its underlying simplicity accorded closely with Copeau's fundamental dislike of stage scenery. He told an American audience in 1917: 'What is the new Theatre, the new movement in theatre? It is scenery, that is all. And I am most of all against scenery.'[8] The huge model and long discussions with Craig were extremely important to Copeau and Jouvet in their concern for finding a way to integrate the architectural and the scenic. 'There is,' Craig told Copeau, 'there must exist, as there does for every one of the

fine arts – and we will discover it one day – a new material, the very
material of the stage, which is not words, painting, architecture ...
but technically, *specifiquement* of the stage.'[9] By the end of Copeau's
visit to Florence, he and Craig had decided to share a proposed French
patent for the development of such a 'material' – in practice a 'kit' of
scenic parts that would comprise a collection of three-dimensional
units which, like building bricks, might be formed and re-formed to
make any number of architectural backgrounds and stages. Copeau
discussed and experimented with Jouvet for several years to develop
such a system, but the practical problems of weight, and the technical
issues of linking the units together, prevented real progress.

At the conclusion of the First World War, Copeau and Jouvet
returned to the Vieux Colombier theatre in Paris (Figure 26) and
completed the structural changes that had begun when they originally
took over the building known as the Théâtre de l'Athénée in 1912.

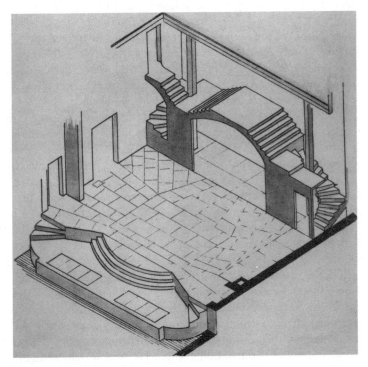

Figure 26   Théâtre du Vieux Colombier, 1919 (photograph from Leon
Moussinac, *The New Movement in the Theatre*, London: Batsford, 1931)

Their ambition was that *décor* would be replaced by an architectural stage, which by itself, by its presence, would already be a statement of action, and which would be capable of materializing dramatic action within its physical form. The basic structure of the Vieux-Colombier stage was completely exposed: it was built of concrete and was uncompromising in its construction. Copeau not only made it plain that there would be no romantic 'treading of the boards' in his theatre, but was also announcing to potential playwrights that his stage would have no truck with illusion, and was made out of real twentieth-century materials. Although the theatre did not have a strong vertical emphasis, the design of the stage very closely echoed the spaces and the floor arrangement of Craig's *St Matthew Passion* model with its raised, arched central bridge, and the steps to either side. The stage platform was low and it met the audience in a series of shallow formal steps. Small additions were made to modify the architecture for specific plays – properties, furniture, a balustrade or curtain, etc. The most significant addition, in 1920 for their production of Molière's *Les Fourberies de Scapin*, was the simple wooden platform placed in the centre of the open stage – the *tréteau nu* – that became so closely identified with Copeau's work in the theatre and, perhaps more importantly, exemplified his approach at his theatre school in Burgundy, which became the focus of his energy when he closed the Paris theatre in 1924.

Copeau and Jouvet chose not to pursue the three-dimensional unit system of scene-changing that had been considered in their discussions with Craig, and their eventual work at the Vieux-Colombier preferred the permanent concrete of their stage architecture, enlivened by sparse furniture and properties. Nevertheless, the idea of some form of 'kit' of scenic parts set within a formal architectural framework for the stage was a significant scenographic energy throughout the century, ever since Craig's successful attempt to patent his 'screens' in 1910. The work of Terence Gray and Harold Ridge at the Festival Theatre in Cambridge from 1926 to 1933 came close to realizing the Copeau/Jouvet/Craig project. Gray was rich, a 'gentleman archaeologist', and he had no formal theatre training. He left no book of theory (although his extended programme notes and articles in the *Festival Review* include important statements of theory), and in 1933 he gave up the theatre and moved to Tain-l'Hermitage in France, where he grew and sold an outstanding wine. He was widely admired by his predominantly undergraduate audience but his seemingly iconoclastic amateurism appears to have angered most of the theatrical establishment. Perhaps in consequence his seven years of achievement in Cambridge have been unjustifiably overlooked, and his memory and achievements have been wrongly set aside in histories of the theatre in favour of Soviet, German and American work. As Richard Allen Cave argues:

> To read these ... accounts and reviews of plays staged at the Festival between 1926 and 1933 is to be aware of how consciously Gray worked to be part of an international movement. ... He set himself to explore the possibilities of Theatre in the spirit of free enquiry and that included testing innovations in technique that he learned about from abroad. It is significant that Gray was one of the few British practitioners whose work was included in Fuerst and Hume's *Twentieth-Century Stage Decoration* of 1929 and the only one to be illustrated in some detail.[10]

Throughout all his work, Gray showed scant regard for the sanctity of the play-text – including those of Shakespeare – preferring to consider dramatic literature as an opportunity to initialize creativity and make theatre art: 'the producer's aim is not to interpret any author's text but to create an independent work of theatre-art'.[11] His practice at Cambridge seems to anticipate Grotowski's relationship with the dramatic text:

> [a]nd the same for the director. ... One structures the montage so that this confrontation can take place. We eliminate those parts of the text which have no importance for us, those parts with which we can neither agree nor disagree. Within the montage one finds certain words that function vis-à-vis our own experiences.[12]

For example, in Gray's production of *The Merchant of Venice* (1932) when his Portia embarked (somewhat listlessly) upon the speech 'The quality of mercy is not strained ...' the entire court relapsed into attitudes of extreme boredom whilst the judge whiled away the time playing with a yo-yo. Wooden cut-out figures representing minor characters in the play were used by Gray to boost the slender casting resources of the small company, and their lines were declaimed off stage by an actor speaking through a megaphone.

Gray and Ridge converted the Georgian Theatre Royal, Barnwell, built in 1814, into a remarkable building in which they systematically aimed, as Cave suggests, 'to graft Edward Gordon Craig's ideal of an Art Theatre on to an efficient repertory house where streamlined preparation of productions was an absolute necessity'.[13] Gray had a very clear concept of the role of the director and the designer, and of the art of the theatre that he sought to establish:

> The producer is an independent artist, using other artists and coordinating their arts into a whole, which is a composite art of the theatre. The author contributes a framework, ideas, dialogue, the designer contributes line and colour and architectural form, the actors contribute sound and movement by means of the human body in speech and action, and the whole is designed and built up by the producer into what should be a work of theatre-art.[14]

The proscenium arch and proscenium doors were torn down to effectively make what would today be called an 'end-stage'. Behind the remains of the proscenium pediment a lighting bridge traversed

Figure 27   Doria Paston, designs for *Richard III*, Terence Gray – Festival Theatre, Cambridge, 1928

the stage. The stage floor was equipped with a 15 foot (a little under 5 metres) hand-operated wooden revolving platform set within a new stage whose front, like that at the Vieux-Colombier, was formally stepped down into the auditorium. A smooth, plaster-surfaced cyclo-rama some 40 feet (a little under 13 metres) high surrounded the acting area and removed the need for side and upper masking. Black and silver reversible curtains hung on tracks that followed the path of the cyclorama and could be rapidly reversed. The down-stage wing spaces made little attempt to hide or disguise additional machinery, the prompter, stage manager and waiting actors.

The stage architecture for the productions by Gray and his designer Doria Paston consisted of plain-surfaced levels, ramps, steps and columns, similar to designs by Appia for 'living spaces', which could be quickly changed for rehearsal in the two-weekly repertory pattern of performance. Very little colour or texture was applied, and the surfaces of the units were frequently painted with aluminium paint to take and reflect the sophisticated lighting experiments of Harold Ridge. Although plays from the modern repertoire (including Ibsen and Chekhov) were performed with a startling defiance of realistic illusion and location, Gray's work at the Festival is most noted for his staging of Shakespeare and classic drama. Norman Marshall, who worked as Assistant Director at the Festival Theatre quotes Gray:

> We are the theatre theatrical. We don't want the wisest or the most foolish member of our audience to play a visual make-believe or ever to forget that the stage is only the stage. And what should the stage be? We think the stage should be a raised platform designed to give the greatest mutual relations of the actors playing their part in each play, and accordingly for each play there should be a specially designed raised platform, the levels and angles of which fulfil a function in emphasising the dramatic relation. Beyond this platform all that is called for is a background against which the actors can be seen, and such objects architectural or otherwise as may be designed to emphasise some aspect of the play.[15]

Gray and Ridge were well aware of and understood recent scenic and architectural experiments and developments throughout con-tinental Europe. Their work in Cambridge was most frequently likened (at least in scenographic externals) to that of Leopold Jessner (1878–1945) and his scenographer Emil Pirchan (1884–1957) at the Berlin Staatstheater from 1919 to 1925. Jessner's production of *Richard III* in 1919 typified his scenography and indicates the similarity of approach to that of Gray and Ridge. Pirchan's stage was a single flight of functional, undecorated steps leading to the back wall of the theatre. Richard's rise to power was indicated by his movement up the levels and by an increasing intensity of the colour red in both lighting and costume. At the end of the play, Richard was forced into a descent of the steps by the white-clad Richmond. On Richard's death, the white had washed away all traces of red. Steps and levels were frequently employed in this way to indicate power, dominance or oppression and were used to such a degree that the term *Jessner-treppen* (Jessner steps) came into use to describe such an approach. Intense colour provided by lighting was used in a similarly pro-grammatic manner – Othello's moods served as motivation for the entire cyclorama to become green with jealousy or red with rage. Marshall says:

> The criticism of Jessner by Kenneth MacGowan and Robert Edmond Jones in *Continental Stagecraft*[16] [1923] might with equal justice be applied to Terence Gray. 'Jessner appears to worship the obvious, to believe that the theatre is a place of ABC impressions and reactions. He is daring enough in his technique but not in his ideas. He flings out symbols right and left, but they are symbols of the primer. He directs in words of one syllable.'[17]

This may have been Marshall's view, but even in faded photograph and written description, Gray's architectural scenography can still excite and provoke. His production of Shakespeare's *Henry VIII* (1931) was performed on a permanent setting of considerable beauty and simplicity, which consisted of an 'aluminium' painted ramp that followed the perimeter of the stage revolve and rose steeply in a gentle curve high above the stage. The actors were dressed in formalized costumes reminiscent of the court figures in a pack of playing cards, and made most of their entrances from above down this ramp. Marshall continues the description:

> The constantly changing lighting, glowing on the aluminium, was of extraordinary beauty and effectiveness, heightening the different moods of the play like an accompaniment of incidental music. Until the end of the play Wolsey wore stilt-like *cothurnoi* [sic] beneath his robes which made him tower above the other characters. ... Gray ... emphasised its [the epilogue's] ludicrous insincerity by using a baby which was a lifelike caricature of what Queen Elizabeth might have looked like at that age and by producing the scene somewhat as it might be done in a Crazy Show at the Palladium, with the stage revolving madly, until finally with a shout the company tossed the baby into the audience.[18]

The production was received on its first night with a pandemonium in the audience, compounded of cries of rage and shouts of delight. The shock of shifting reactions resulting from a radical re-ordering of theatre expectations and architecture has provoked some of the century's most extreme responses. And Gray was always very precise in his ambition to provoke: 'I seek the unexpected reaction, the unanticipated pleasure, the irresponsible wrath, the readjustment of values.'[19]

Copeau, Jessner and Gray were no strangers to twentieth-century technologies: Copeau was proud of the uncompromising qualities of his concrete stage; Jessner was amongst the first to use the intensity of light and colour made possible by high-power gas-filled tungsten bulbs; and, as we have seen, Harold Ridge designed the most technically sophisticated lighting installation at the Festival Theatre, and used newly invented aluminium paints to reflect and respond to coloured light. But in even more radical ways, twentieth-century technologies served to inspire new solutions to fill the void of rejection. Perhaps nowhere was the rejection of past forms more systematic and structured in its study and response than at the Bauhaus during the 1920s.

The Staatliches Bauhaus was created in 1919 in Weimar by the architect Walter Gropius, who articulated the radical and comprehensive extent of the Bauhaus agenda: 'The aim of the Bauhaus was to find a new and powerful working correlation of all the processes of artistic creation to culminate finally in a new cultural equilibrium of our visual environment.'[20] Since rejection of the past was axiomatic, forms and styles could not be derived from existing work, and the artists and designers had to begin their work with a radical analysis of the principles and qualities underlying their art, and find solutions more relevant to the modern world. Working with and integrating new technologies into new theories of design was accordingly a fundamental approach that united all experiments and teaching at the Bauhaus. Formally, the Bauhaus operated as a college, but it preferred to think of itself as a learning community whose work would break down the significant distinction that had been created by nineteenth-century industrialization, between the designing artist and the constructing craftsman. The attempt to integrate social function and artistic form initiated the dominant styles of modernist product design, interior decoration and urban architecture. It also introduced the idea that new technologies allied with this 'function-determined' architecture might provide the diversity of theatre spaces that the future would require. The adaptable and multi-functional theatre building to which many theatre artists and architects still aspire began in this Bauhaus conjunction. Gropius sought the 'flexible building, capable of transforming and refreshing the mind by its spatial impact alone' that he had identified in his 'brief to the architect'.[21] The holistic ambition to integrate scenography and architecture alongside new technologies that would together serve, in turn, to inspire new dramaturgy is central to this vision of the future. Gropius concluded:

> Thus the Playhouse itself, made to dissolve into the shifting, illusionary space of the imagination, would become the scene of action itself. Such a theatre would stimulate the conception and fantasy of playwright and stage director alike; for if it is true that the mind can transform the body, it is equally true that structure can transform the mind.[22]

The experiments in performance led by Oskar Schlemmer at the theatre department of the Bauhaus were small in scale, intense and very much based within *atelier* studio spaces, whereas architectural thinking at the Bauhaus responded to the speed, intensity and mass of modern society and in consequence tended to seek solutions in the large building complex and high-rise urban living spaces. However, in 1926, Gropius designed a 'total theatre' for the director Erwin Piscator (see Figure 28) in which he tried to facilitate what he believed were the three fundamental forms of theatre: the arena stage (theatre-in-the-round), the thrust stage and the proscenium stage. To achieve this he created a central revolving platform that contained seats, and to one side of this, a circular area of performance space. Turning the revolve would move the off-centre performance space to one side (to form a thrust stage) and to the centre (to provide a central arena stage). The acting area set on the revolving platform could be replaced with audience seats in order to create a unified audience in front of a proscenium stage space. Surrounding the audience and to the rear of the proscenium stage, screens were set between pillars. Through these means, as has been considered in an earlier chapter, film projection would be used to transform the whole of the theatre building, not only the scenic stage space. Also surrounding the entire audience was a platform that could be used to enable performance to take place throughout the building. Engineering technologies of hydraulic movement and sophisticated image projection would therefore provide the means to unify the scene of dramatic action and the spectators – to physically and holistically embed the dramatic action within the space of the architecture. Piscator never achieved the funds

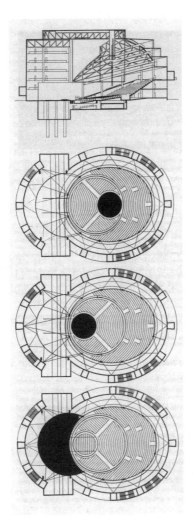

Figure 28   Walter Gropius: cross-section and plans for his Total Theatre Project, 1926 (*Bauhaus-Archiv, Berlin*)

to realize Gropius's planned theatre, although its plans and details were published and were to prove especially influential during the period of theatre building that followed the Second World War.

Meyerhold's ambitions for new performance space were not dissimilar, especially in their assumption about the role that new technologies would play:

> What kind of theatre do we envisage for the presentation of the new spectacle? ... The only design suitable for a performance created by the combined efforts of actors and spectators is the amphitheatre, where there is no division of the audience into separate classes dependent on social standing and financial resources. ... Also, we must destroy the box stage once and for all, for only then can we hope to achieve a truly dynamic spectacle. By making the stage machinery sufficiently flexible to present a series of rapidly changing scenes, we shall be able to abolish the tedious unity of place and compression of the action into four or five unwieldy acts. The new stage will have no proscenium arch and will be equipped with a series of platforms which can be moved horizontally and vertically to facilitate transformation scenes and the manipulation of kinetic constructions.[23]

Building was far advanced on Meyerhold's new theatre by 1937–8, but owing to the increasingly intransigent political situation within Stalin's dictatorship, it was never completed.

Although not formally a member of the Bauhaus group, the Austrian designer and architect Frederick Kiesler (1896–1966) shared and extended the design values of Meyerhold and Gropius. Kiesler appreciated the fundamental problems in locating performance that occur following such complete rejection of past forms, and he foresaw new functions for theatre:

> The elements of the new dramatic style are still to be worked out. They are not yet classified. Drama, poetry, and scenic formation have no natural milieu. Public, space, and players are artificially assembled. The new aesthetic has not yet attained the unity of expression. ... We have no contemporary theatre.[24]

Between 1916 and 1924 he designed (but never built) a theatre which was planned to seat some 100,000 people. In 1930, Kiesler described what he called this 'Endless Theatre':

> The whole structure is encased in double shells of steel and opaque welded glass. The stage is an endless spiral. The various levels are connected with elevators and platforms. Seating platforms, stage and elevator platforms are suspended and spanned above each other in space. The structure is an elastic building system of cables and platforms developed from bridge building. The drama can expand and develop freely in space.[25]

From the Bauhaus and the work of men such as Gropius and Kiesler, the environmental theatre learned to reject conventional theatre spaces and to seek in the event itself organic, dynamic and ultimately architectural articulations of physical space.

The Bauhaus artists dispersed during the 1930s, with Walter Gropius, Mies van der Rohe, László Moholy-Nagy and other Bauhaus artists travelling into exile; many went to the USA where they established influential institutes and university departments of architecture and design training. However, unlike the subsequent countless blocks of modernist urban housing and office complexes, few theatres were built that reflected the large-scale ambitions of modernist architects and designers like Gropius, Kiesler, or the American Norman Bel Geddes. Nevertheless, the idea of using sophisticated engineering to physically move the audience and/or sections of performance space has inspired numerous adaptable and convertible theatres, and the energy of ideas that Gropius's total theatre vision represented has been and continues to be an important solution to the challenge of linking scenic and architectural space.

During the 1960s and 1970s, and especially throughout Europe and North America, many theatres were built that used engineering and electronic technologies in order to try to create a functional and flexible theatre architecture. Many were urged by civic authorities, who wanted increased value for money – by combining theatre functions with those of the concert hall, civic auditorium or even the sports facility. To achieve this it became necessary to move large sections of staging and audience seating. An industrial development of the hovercraft industry was the air pallet – 'pads' supported on compressed air that were able to lift and facilitate the movement of large units. Few of these theatres, however, have achieved the full ambitions of their original artistic directors and architects, and, like the Vivian Beaumont Theatre at the Lincoln Center in New York, they have tended to remain set in one theatre 'form' and have subsequently been re-modelled to a more 'permanent' condition. Rejecting and abandoning the need of the traditional proscenium theatre to hide lighting equipment, the designers have used comprehensive grids to span entire theatre spaces to allow the suspended lighting equipment to serve differing theatre forms. But the full achievement of the flexibility of basic architectural form conceived by Bauhaus-inspired architects has remained something of an architectural chimera. Engineering and electronic technologies can find ways of moving and rearranging large sections of an audience, and can also rearrange spaces and stages of performance, but the architect has found it much harder to create and then rearrange the 'dramatic atmosphere' of, say, a thrust stage, and replace it with the atmosphere and dramatic energy of a theatre-in-the-round. The true dynamic 'energy' of a place of performance is clearly more than can be expressed by the physical rearrangement of audience space and performance space. Nevertheless, the modernist principles of functionality and their associated technologies have endured. Gropius justified this approach by appealing to a logical derivation from structural, constructive and functional imperatives – things which, like the framed image on the stage, can be measured and controlled. The specialized disciplines which the modern era has produced (particularly relating to technical know-how and quantifiable knowledge) have seized upon this culture of logic so that, for example, listening and seeing have become 'acoustics' and 'visibility', although their application has done little to effect an understanding of the dramatic energy of a successful place of performance.

The understandings gained from studies of the anthropology of performance and of past theatres and their audiences have together demonstrated strong interconnections between architecture, performance convention and scenographic approach. Iain Mackintosh has examined in some detail[26] the internal structural dynamics of traditional 'Italianate' theatre architectures to attempt an explanation of, for example, why actors prefer to perform in old theatres, rather than newly designed, recent buildings. Why does the interaction with an audience generally prove to be more lively and responsive in an old building? The precise location and densities of audience arrangement, the interaction of the audience amongst themselves, the social hierarchies that auditoriums have reflected, the precise relationship between the performer and the audience in terms of height and distance, all defy modernist ergonomic analysis, and yet their importance to both audience and performer is unquestionable. The real significance of such study, and therefore the real challenge to the contemporary architect, has been to recognize that the architecture of a successful place of performance reflects and represents a social construct – a product of the combined sensibilities of theatre artists, their audiences and shared community values. If modernist architectural forms were to achieve real flexibility, then they had not only to provide places of performance – the typically bifurcated space for audience and for actors – but also to find ways for the architecture to reflect the social assumptions and connotations of the performance event. The technical management of visibility, sightlines, acoustics, health and safety regulation, aesthetic neutrality and an ambition to offer a 'democratic' theatre experience to as many of the audience as possible, have alone not been able to create a truly twentieth-century theatre architecture.[27] The challenge to the theatre architect and planner has been and continues to be considerable, especially within an increasingly pluralistic, multicultural society in which audiences have similarly pluralistic expectations of the theatre experience. Exposure to globalized media, and an expanding cultural diversity that has accelerated throughout the century, have inevitably made it unlikely that (other than on quite a small community basis) large urban groupings of society might 'prefer' and therefore select one form of theatre architecture.

Since the late 1960s, an alternative to high-cost (and frequently unsatisfactory) theatre architecture has been the flexible, multi-form studio theatre whose small audience capacity has enabled performances to be created for pluralistic, increasingly 'niche' audiences. The theatre artists of the early twentieth century all demanded schools, workshops, 'little theatres', laboratories, study sites, or *ateliers*. The need for continuous, focused experiment has, along with rejection of the past, been one of the most unifying features of the entire period. The agenda of the *atelier* has dominated the institution of theatre and the increasing diversity of performance practices; it has created theatre training and the disciplines of Theatre Studies and it has inflected and in some cases defined theatrical practice. One solution to the integration of scenography within the place of performance, therefore, has been the dominance of the studio performance space as an architectural form, although a studio theatre's defining neutrality evades the fundamental problem by providing not an ultimate solution, but one that will be changed by the scenographer with each production.

The theory and principles of the *atelier* form were established in the work of Appia and Dalcroze at the Hellerau Studio (see Figure 13). The importance of this work and the ideas that were generated may be thought of as creating an alternative model that parallels the mainstream architectural model of Wagner's *Festspielhaus*. The fullest, direct articulation of Appia's ideas on the topic was written in his 'Theatrical Experiences and Personal Investigations' (1921). In this, and stemming very directly from work at Hellerau in the years immediately preceding the First World War, he theorized the concept of what he called the 'study site':

> The designs I first produced for Dalcroze[28] were still in essence oriented towards a spectacle presented to the eyes of others; they therefore only partly encompassed the auditorium. Today I have reached extreme conclu-

sions with regard to the hierarchic principle of stage production. Reaching beyond theatre, it will serve all living art. I imagine a rectangular, empty and unadorned hall equipped with complete lighting installations. On either side are large annexes for storing sections of three-dimensional units. These would be built with lines and proportions appropriate to the human body and broken up into segments that could be joined together to form every possible arrangement of levels, whether horizontal, vertical or sloping. They would be combined with curtains, folding screens, etc., and everything would be covered with canvas of a uniform type. . . . This would be called the 'study site'.[29]

The suggestion of a formal 'kit' of scenic units covered in a neutral material and brought to life by the use of sophisticated lighting technologies closely mirrors contemporary ideas of Craig in Florence, Copeau and Jouvet in Paris, and, somewhat later, the successful application of this approach by Gray and Ridge in Cambridge.

Although quite revolutionary in 1921, Appia's basic architecture seems to describe the ubiquitous studio performance space of the theatre complex, arts centre or educational campus of the early twenty-first century. But Appia's later theory pushes the idea beyond the practical request for a neutral empty space that may be adapted into many theatre forms by the use of platforms, units and rostra. He wanted to move beyond what he described as a theatre that was 'in essence oriented towards a spectacle presented to the eyes of others'. He sought to locate an understanding of the 'study site' alongside his more complex and uncompromising conviction of the living nature of true art. Although the site might be temporarily fitted with platforms to accommodate an audience, his real ambition for the space was that it should no longer reflect the traditional bifurcated distinction made between the act of performance and its reception by a formally identified and spatially located audience: 'A moment of living art with no one viewing it except the performers themselves exists fully, and with more dignity than when reflected in the eyes of passive onlookers.'[30] To illustrate the distinction that he attempted, he contrasted the experience of a dance made by a young girl, happy in the fields, with the experiences of one who may observe and listen to her performance. Or again, he invited a comparison between the experiences of participating in singing the first great chorus of Bach's *St Matthew Passion*, and being an audience listening to a choir sing it. In other words Appia's ultimate living work of art reflected the experience of direct and engaged participation. Appia's 'study site' represents an inter-active, sympathetic environmental scenography – a place – that enables, welcomes and locates performance. His choice of the word 'study' was appropriate and significant. He concluded:

> The obstacle to living art is the audience. We are in it, and it in us! Therefore the very concept of an audience, the expression of passivity, must be neutralised through an effort to overcome this passivity. Yet to forgo everything that suggests and maintains passivity in our time would mean the abolition of three quarters of our public life! So we must mark time for the moment and allow our attitude to work from within. Then we shall understand how and why art is such a supreme instructor.[31]

Appia's study site therefore presented two approaches: one of which culminated in the modern high-tech studio theatre, a studio that is a carefully arranged 'warehouse' of theatre-making technologies, and that makes no claim to enduring architectural or scenographic personality. The Cottesloe theatre within the building complex of London's Royal National Theatre marked an institutional establishment of the form in 1977, and since that time has served as an exemplar of architectural design and possibilities. Location and budget have inevitably created many variations, but generally such studio theatres have become focal points for the application of advanced technologies of electronics, computer control, and more recently, high-tensile stretched steel rope grid systems that create a 'trampoline' mesh over the entire space both to enable access to technology and to protect the audience from technology. By the early twenty-first century these studios have become highly functional spaces for the making of almost any form of theatre – ballet, opera, musicals, and small-scale drama.

But Appia's other concern for the study site has had a less clear-cut trajectory of development and change. This approach concerned the building of a space that not only would provide for the interaction of actors and audience but would also find ways to include the audience within the framework of its scenographic identity – within its environment of performance. Theatre making, in Appia's view, was therefore about making a theatre for the entire event, rather than a highly conceived and constructed scenography placed before a supposedly neutral and disengaged audience. The bare *atelier* studio space, where no architectural distinction is made between audience space and performance space, has led to experiments in environmental scenography, in which the whole of the available space may be selected and converted into a performance-specific environment, in variants of what Schechner (quoting Michael Kirby) called 'nonmatrixed performance' where 'traditional distinctions between art and life no longer function at the root of aesthetics'.[32] In performance a space may serve as audience seating (life), but may be surrendered by the audience to become a part of stage setting (art): the selection (and its controlling aesthetic) being created by and through the act of performance.

During the 1960s, Jerzy Grotowski's Laboratory Theatre explored the scenographic qualities of their 'study site' place of performance. The production of Juliusz Slowacki's *Kordian* (1962) created an intense encounter between audience and performer within an environmental scenography. The action was located in a mental hospital and the performance was made in a basement cellar that contained metal-framed bunk beds. The audience sat on and between the beds, on which the actors also played; all else was removed to create a ritualistic experience in which spectators and performers together could achieve a form of 'collective introspection' on the ideas of the play. The basement was the architecture of the studio, but, by selection, became the basement space of a mental hospital; the beds implicated the audience within the action by serving as seats and as hospital beds.

But this 'environmental' concern for a thematic and physical linking of audience and performance space has also encouraged a desire to find alternative spaces and sites of performance where the 'found' location and its architecture have an atmosphere and prior history that could replace, or at least become integrated within, individual production scenography. Is this closer to Appia's concern for removing the barrier between the act of watching and the act of participation? It may be, since he considered that the passivity of an audience, the lack of real engagement as it sat and observed, was the most damaging quality that was embedded in traditional theatre architecture. The implications of Appia's thinking are undoubtedly more concerned with the need to redefine the social activity of engagement with performance, to redefine the nature of spectatorship and to relocate performance within society, than to proscribe a particular architectural form. Nevertheless, experiment with architectural form has frequently been the result of attempts to find new engagements with an audience. The scenographies of Ariane Mnouchkine and the company of the Théâtre du Soleil have continually reinvented actor–audience relationships. The production *1789* (1970) was staged as a fairground, employing the multiple and simultaneous framing of five fixed stages and a continuously flowing movement of actors, puppets and audience within the fair, initially in a basketball court in Milan, at the Roundhouse (a disused railway-engine turning shed) in London, and in the building that would become the Company's base, the Cartoucherie (an old gun-cartridge factory), in Paris. Victoria Nes Kirby described the production for the *Drama Review* in considerable detail:

> Before the performance, the space is brightly lit, and the hall gives an impression of enormous spaciousness and simplicity. Nothing is hidden from the audience. We can see performers (of whom there are about forty) applying make-up in front of a long table and bench under the 'control tower'. More costume racks, tables and benches, trunks and lockers are located at the two far ends of the hall. The audience is free to roam about, talk to members of the company, or find a place to watch the performance. The majority of the spectators seat themselves in the raked grandstand until this area is filled. Those remaining, and those who perhaps know that the space inside the stages is available to the audience, begin drifting, searching for a stair or a cross-bar to perch on.[33]

The Company's Technical Director Guy-Claude François said:

> Every production possesses its own characteristics, and it's precisely for that reason that we have no fixed criteria in terms of scenography. Only three years ago, we had certain ideas, we wanted a multi-purpose hall. Now our thinking is rather that each production requires a different form of scenography, even (almost) a form of architecture.[34]

From that time onwards, the practice of changing the performance 'architecture' for each new production became a significant feature of the Company's work at the Cartoucherie until the 1990s. A split-focus staging was created for *Mephisto* (1979) that simultaneously presented the official Nazi stage of the State Theatre, and the alternative Hamburg cabaret stage. The audience sat on benches whose back-rests could be moved to allow them to take either viewpoint. The two other architectural 'sides' contained a fresco of Prussian militarism confronting, across the audience, the steel-mesh grating of a concentration camp. For *L'Indiade* (1987), Asian screens filtered the light through the roof skylight windows into a white space that had a stage made of (seemingly) marble and terracotta tiles. *Les Atrides* (1990–2) required the audience to enter the place of performance, which had qualities of beaten earth, hot stone and faded planking, through an archaeological excavation. Essentially, although the internal architecture was re-configured, these spaces were all bare, but they were not empty. Mnouchkine said: 'Like Peter Brook, I work on the concept of the empty space. ... I like purity, but I hate austerity. I think an actor needs a magnificent empty space.'[35] These scenographies gave significance, resonance and in many cases, magnificence to the austere bareness of the Cartoucherie space, and served more as indicators of the Company's experimentation with theatre form and with finding new narrative strategies for live performance, than as scenic interpretations of dramatic material.

The durability of Appia's understanding and his concern to deconstruct the traditional relationship between the performer as aesthetic object and the spectator as a form of 'mirror' to the performer's internal, spiritual search is especially reflected in the work of Grotowski, and continues in the work of contemporary performance artists and many contemporary site-specific scenographies. Grotowski focused Appia's scenographic and architectural concern into a provocation for all theatre artists:

> For a moment the actor finds himself outside the semi-engagement and conflict which characterises us in our daily life. Did he do this for the spectator? The expression 'for the spectator' implies a certain coquetry, a certain falseness, a bargaining with oneself. One should rather say 'in relation to' the spectator or, perhaps, instead of him. It is precisely here that the provocation lies.[36]

For Grotowski, the function of the scenographer would be to realize this 'in relation to' so that the 'instead of' might become possible. He said, 'our productions are detailed investigations of the actor–audience relationship. That is, we consider the personal and scenic technique of the actor as the core of theatre art.'[37] The function of scenography for Grotowski at this stage in his development of performance was therefore to design this relationship, and, as Appia implied, this should be a relationship that is more intense than the physical location of actors and audience. Peter Brook talks of the importance of building an audience:

> Any audience is a chaotic mixture. This is not a bad thing: the bigger the mixture, the more vital the audience. But we cannot expect all these people with so little in common suddenly to enter into a shared event. A process is necessary. The aim of this process is to make the 'inner' and the 'outer' merge, to convert a 'show' into an 'experience'.[38]

The bareness of Grotowski's scenographies were, of course, aesthetically carefully controlled – size, shape, contour and, especially, surface and texture – but the 'performativity' of his spaces was established in the careful and deliberate 'process' of building the audience in and around the spaces, which we shall examine later. Brook's artistic collaborator Marie-Hélène Estienne described a good place of performance:

> There's a strong silence – which is not necessarily just a physical silence – a kind of gentleness, an openness to different possibilities, a listening quality. It's not a church, but one feels that it could be, it has a certain tranquillity. It's a place where one can open oneself, reflect in peace, take risks without being too hurried. It still imposes a certain rigour, but not too strongly.[39]

Although the neutral studio space has remained a dominant architectural form, most theatre artists still believe that a good space of performance cannot be entirely neutral, for an impersonal sterility gives no food to the imagination. A similar pragmatism and responsiveness to found space and material marks the development of

Figure 29 Centre International de Création Théâtral (CICT), Bouffes du Nord theatre, Paris (*photograph by Jean-Guy Lecat*)

Brook's Centre International de Recherche Théâtral (CIRT), which became the Centre International de Création Théâtral (CICT) when they moved into their home base, the *Bouffes du Nord* in Paris, which they acquired in 1971. The *Bouffes* was built in 1876 in a less than fashionable district and never really succeeded as a variety or a dramatic theatre, having a number of different companies and managers. It finally closed its doors in 1952 and continued its process of structural decay. A raised stage no longer existed and Brook and the CICT removed the original decaying stalls seating from the pit of the high circular volume of the auditorium and replaced it with raked bench seating that followed the curve of the large acting space – a space that was not separated from the audience by height or colour and stretched to the back of the original stage house. Over the performance space, the original architecture of the high proscenium arch has been stripped of framing, beyond which lies the bare stage house. Much has been written about this theatre and its use.[40] In the context of this discussion, however, it is important to note the constant reference by directors and actors to its atmosphere, its richness of colour and texture, the energy that the architectural space of the theatre generates, and the balance between neutrality and personality that the theatre offers. 'The Bouffes', Brook says, 'is black velvet in a superior version – a nothingness which is full of life'[41] – the 'magnificent empty space' that Mnouchkine sought. Jean-Claude Carrière, an actor who has collaborated at the CICT since its inception, said of *La Tragédie de Carmen* (1981):

> Over the course of a rehearsal one senses what kinds of speech come across better than others, and the space has an influence on the text which one senses only in an intuitive, empirical way. It has likes and dislikes, and one must be attentive, one must listen to the demands of the space. It imposes a certain kind of speech, a certain kind of acting, a certain kind of mise en scène which are in harmony with the spirit of the place.[42]

Brook's first response to the architectural 'spirit' of the building in 1974 is therefore significant:

> Suddenly the door opened and there was the Bouffes – a majestic volume with light streaming down through the dome and the dusty air on to what looked, at ground level, like a bomb site. There was a heap of rubbish in the middle of the space with wires hanging everywhere, evidence of destruction in progress. I was immediately certain that this was the right place for us. Even in its suffering condition there was an elegance to the proportions, a

dignity to the atmosphere. It was clearly a theatre, but it looked nothing like it must have done previously: the 'cultural' skin of architectural finish had been cauterised away. All the stalls seats were missing, except a few that had been smashed up and thrown to one side. It seemed obvious that all we had to do was sweep away the rubble and find a means to sit people at the ground level. ... And the walls could also stay as they were – covered in pockmarks, flayed raw by time, weather and human destruction.[43]

Theatre artists who have chosen to make places of performance in old, derelict buildings and warehouses, places that have multi-layered histories of associations and meanings, have frequently been accused of pretentiousness or a misplaced 'colonizing' nostalgia. None more so than Brook as the Centre has set about re-creating the qualities of the *Bouffes* in other cities: 'the architectural equivalent of the intentionally worn look of a Ralph Lauren jacket' (Michael Kimmelman, *New York Times*, 25 October 1987) and '$5 million to turn theatre into a dump' (*Weekly World News*, October 1987). Brook's 'defence' makes an important distinction between a neutral, and therefore dead, space (as in a modern studio theatre) and a living space that enables performance:

One day, the *Bouffes* and the Majestic [the New York theatre adopted by Brook for the Company's tour in 1987] will be out of date. But if they still continue to be living spaces it is because they are 'open' or 'undefined'. In being anachronisms, they are not of yesterday, today or tomorrow. They are 'alive' because of their colour, their texture, their proportions and, above all, their humanity. They are open to many types of work, because they make no statement. This is what 'chameleon' means.[44]

When making productions in such a building, it is the architecture of the place of performance that becomes transformed into the scene of performance – it is the spatial qualities, such as the colour and texture of the floor and of the rear wall beyond, that are modified and 'designed' to accommodate the performance. In other words, each performance asks that the architecture be inflected in order to create the scene – rather than introducing stage scenery into the architecture. Brook's collaborator Jean-Guy Lecat says: 'Our work is singular in that we use the 'space of the place' as the 'space of the show'.[45] For example, in *La Tragédie de Hamlet* (2003) the scenographer is not locating the play in some theatrical Elsinore of battlement, throne room and chamber, but rather attempting to design the actual performance of the play – creating a place for the play's energy, for its mood, for its atmosphere; converting the architecture of the *Bouffes* into a place of the play, of *Hamlet*. Chloe Obolensky's scenography for *The Cherry Orchard* in 1981 illustrates the principle in more detail:

> A rolled-up carpet became a raised path or a fallen tree along which the characters walked; the other carpets became a lawn when characters lounged upon them. The salon of Act 3 was once again demarcated by screens, but this time with the ballroom beyond on the large space of the old stage. This infection of the entire space with the life of the play, the sharing of the play's world with ours, took on a tragic force when the carpets were stripped at the end, leaving the bare stage inhabited only by the servant Firs (who had been forgotten in the rush to move out). As the family left, never to return, the doors of the theatre all around the audience were slammed and audibly 'locked' in turn. This was the first time the theatre had been used as a whole environment implicated in the universe of the drama.[46]

In this way, the architecture of the theatre building and of the performance space, which are frequently considered to be passive, neutral, mute, inanimate, and subordinate things into which theatre artists project their ideas, are in fact things that need to be constantly brought back to life and into a fresh perspective, just like the text of the play. If it is a theatre's 'function' to bring people together into an audience and provide the pathway towards a sense of communion, it is impossible to imagine a space in which this can happen being satisfactorily achieved at the level of architectural technicalities, of sight lines, seating angles and fire exits.

The open air, public theatres of the English Renaissance have served as powerful sources of inspiration within the twentieth-century desire to integrate (or re-integrate) the scene and the architecture of the theatre, in the attempt, as Obolensky said in the context of the *Bouffes du Nord*, to build a theatre space that may be 'a whole environment implicated in the universe of the drama'. William Poel's experiments in minimal staging with the Elizabethan Stage Society during the 1880s and 1890s were the first that tried to engage seriously with the performance practices and structure of the staging of Shakespeare's plays in ways that went beyond a mere 'picturesque' concern for the theatre of the past. These coincided with the discovery and early analysis of the Johannes de Witt/Arend van Buchell drawing of the Swan Theatre of 1594 at the University of Utrecht, in 1888.[47] The importance of this image, notwithstanding concerns over its reliability and provenance, cannot be over-estimated since it is the only image of the interior of an Elizabethan amphitheatre. It very clearly is a drawing of a theatre architecture that served, simultaneously, as a stage setting, and its relationship with Shakespeare studies and practice has been profound. Although it is not an image of the theatre in which Shakespeare worked, De Witt's appended description assures us that it is the same in all significant ways. More recent scholarship by Andrew Gurr and John Orrell[48] associated with the building of 'Shakespeare's Globe' on the Bankside in London (see Illustration 30), alongside the archaeological examinations by Simon Blatherwick of the Rose and Globe theatres in 1989, has suggested that there were significant differences in size and internal structure between the theatres. But notwithstanding this refinement of understanding, and beginning from the period of Poel in the late nineteenth century, the very *idea* of the Elizabethan amphitheatre stage has continuously offered a compelling (if at times a perilously nostalgic) example of how it was believed theatre *ought* to be. Indeed, the iconic status of this theatre has tended to increase as scholarship and archaeology have revealed layers of meaning in documents and manuscripts – including the clear evidence that the acting companies did all

Figure 30   Shakespeare's Globe, London (*photograph by Christopher Baugh*)

they could to leave these theatres in favour of the more socially refined, indoor 'private' theatres.

Speaking of the Globe, Bernard Beckerman claimed it as 'the symbol of an entire art'.[49] On the one hand, the enduring theatrical importance of Shakespeare has created the understandable desire to situate his plays, as Mulryne and Shewring say, 'once more in conditions (spatial, visual and acoustic) akin to those he held in his mind's eye while writing'.[50] On the other hand, the buildings as theatrical icons seem to serve as powerful symbols of a healthy theatre culture. They signify a theatre structure that was accessible to all classes of society; they housed companies that were owned, managed and directed by practising theatre artists; the work of writing and making plays seems to have been integrated within a practice of stage-craft and rehearsal; it seems to have been a place that made no attempt to escape from the reality of its audience, which was always self-evident – the orientation of the stages, for example, meant that the light of the sun shone upon the audience rather than on the actor; there were discrete places designated for the audience and for actors, but the architecture and its decoration seem to have been treated overall within a unified aesthetic; as a structure with a distinctive decorative style, it clearly described itself as a place of playing and artifice: its timber structure was painted to fool the eye,[51] for example, and the ceiling over the stage was a painted simulacrum of the astrological heavens, and even the form of the building acquired a metaphoric status within its own society – as a 'globe', a 'wooden O' that embraced, contained and reflected the whole of society. In short, the image and 'presence' of the Elizabethan playhouse has served to reflect many of the important social and artistic qualities to which theatre architecture has aspired throughout the twentieth century, and furthermore, that seem to have existed during each of the great historical periods of intense and significant theatrical activity.

The influence of this theatre during the twentieth century has, of course, been of two distinct kinds. First, there have been the attempts to reconstruct, as authentically as contemporary scholarship would permit, an Elizabethan amphitheatre; and secondly, there have been theatres designed and architectural scenographies made that have drawn significant influence from the Elizabethan form, whilst not pretending to an authentic reconstruction. Reconstructions have been few, and until 1997 when Shakespeare's Globe began to present work, have been of little more than academic or tourist interest.[52] However, the completion of the Globe reconstruction and subsequent performances have offered a revealing illustration of the efficacy in performance and the impressive scenographic impact of such an integration of architecture and scenography. Perhaps in response to the late nineteenth-century Puritanism of Poel's 'back to basics' approach, production at the reconstructed Globe has surprised by its sheer sense of spectacle. The reality in performance seems a very long way from the 'bare boards and a passion' image of Shakespeare's stagecraft, which has dominated thinking until quite recently in theatre history. The architecture does not retire gracefully to play a supporting role in the background. There is no direct lighting playing upon the stage – naturally no artificial light, but neither is there the sun. Light falls on (a better word is 'bathes') everything on the stage with a great equality; it is unedited, and therefore a very democratic light; and intriguingly, it is a stage without shadows. Certainly, in almost all situations where we could be thought of as audience or onlookers, controlled light has become an inevitable adjunct to the act of spectatorship. In the theatre, this lack of 'light focus' makes the actor part of a remarkably intricate tapestry of colours and textures produced by the richly painted and sculptured architecture. The architecture is therefore a constant participant in everything that takes place upon the stage; the auditorium with its standing pit and the surrounding galleries becomes an exemplification and metaphor for the world, the 'polis', the 'commonwealth', and for humanity.

The scenographic role of costume is significantly expanded in this theatre, as it needs to be in order to make the actor dramatically distinguishable within the vibrant complexity of the surrounding visual context. Elements of stage clothing – a crown, a huge ruff, or a cloak – re-acquire the iconic status that they seem to have held within the scenography of the original stagecraft. Philip Henslowe's inventory of March 1598 of his theatre's possessions lists items such as:

> Item, i rocke, i cage, i tombe, i Hell mought; Item, viii viserdes; Tamberlynes brydell; Item, Cupedes bowe, & quiver; the clothe of the Sone & Mone; Item, i paire of rowghte gloves; Item, i poopes miter; Item, iii Imperial crownes; i playne crowne; Item, i gostes crown; i crown with a sone.[53]

Properties, scenic units and costume accessories were used over and over again in a manner hitherto unimaginable in contemporary theatre of the late twentieth century. They were stock items – perhaps another reading of the scenic 'kit' proposed by Craig, Copeau and Gray – and served as emblems or hieroglyphics to theatrical reality rather than imitations of it. The architectural stage and its context generated this coded imagery – imagery that provided a sophisticated meta-language upon which the plays relied for their theatrical effectiveness. These items would have been instantly recognizable and have served to focus attention and to aid the actors in their quest for attention and recognition within the even and unmediated light of the stage. Extended practice at the Globe is beginning to reveal significant parallels with scenography in other theatre cultures, especially those of the Japanese Nō and Kabuki, which have integrated their performance rhetoric alongside their scenographic rhetoric within the architectural framework of a distinctive theatre building.

A number of theatres have been designed and a great many scenographies made that have been influenced by the Elizabethan form. Most significantly in architectural terms, of course, the form has inspired the development of the thrust stage, either as part of the flexible possibilities of an adaptable, multi-functional theatre or, more successfully, as a form in its own right. The Festival Theatre (1957) designed by Tanya Moiseiwitch and Tyrone Guthrie in Stratford, Ontario, followed experimental seasons in a canvas-covered theatre. Its permanent stage architecture interpreted the formal entrances, inner, below and upper stage of the Elizabethan form, while its audience sat in a single, steeply tiered amphitheatre similar to that of an amphitheatre of antiquity. Although this essential stage architecture remains in Stratford, Ontario, its successor, the Guthrie Theater in Minneapolis (1963), attempted a more flexible, changeable formality at the back of its thrust stage to serve a wider repertoire of plays than in Ontario. After several seasons, however, this was abandoned in favour of more production-specific scenography. The Festival Theatre in Chichester (1963) also began with an architectural stage not unlike that designed by Jouvet for the Vieux-Colombier in 1919, with an upper level that overhung the rear section of the stage, with a formal stair and landings that led down to the stage platform. However, as in Minneapolis, the repertoire of plays caused this to be abandoned. The Crucible Theatre in Sheffield (1971) is undoubtedly the finest example of a thrust stage. Tanya Moiseiwitch served as consultant, and the lessons of Ontario and Mineapolis were incorporated. It has the fairest distribution of audience seating around the thrust and it more carefully balances the size of the stage with the size and volume of the audience. Although a formal and semi-permanent 'scenic wall' to the rear of the thrust was considered, it was never constructed. The Swan Theatre of the Royal Shakespeare Company in

Stratford-upon-Avon (1986) recaptures some of the essential qualities of Elizabethan and Jacobean theatre architecture. It is a warm, wooden space surrounded on three sides by galleries so that the walls appear to be 'papered' with audience. There is no permanent stage setting, although, perhaps significantly, designs for productions have a tendency to make architectural stages that seem to grow organically from the dominantly 'wooden' aesthetic of the theatre architecture.[54]

The desire to achieve a close integration between 'place' and 'space' that began this examination remains a strong energy within contemporary scenography and the design of theatre architecture. Modern architects seek to understand the complex working of past performance architectures in the building of new theatres. Beginning in 1980, the architect Tim Foster designed the Tricycle Theatre in Kilburn, London, closely based upon the form and dimensions of the surviving Georgian Theatre in Richmond, North Yorkshire, of 1789. It was re-built following a fire in 1987, but the efficacy of its design had been tested through seven years of performance. It was precisely 'Georgian' in form; at the Tricycle, however, the galleries were interpreted in brightly coloured scaffolding with stretched canvas 'box' fronts, and the powerful acting area of the forestage was re-instated to thrust forward into the sloping pit. By the end of the decade and through the 1990s, this small-scale, late eighteenth-century form became known as a 'courtyard' theatre and became the iconic 'modern' theatre of its period. Fundamentally traditional theatre architectures, such as the *Bouffes du Nord* and the Memorial Theatre in Stratford-upon-Avon have been consistently re-designed and re-structured to reflect this search for dramatic intensity, and they have usually involved an examination of the spatial qualities of the relationship between forestage and audience in order to (re)create the 'liminal' tension of a good place for playing. Places of performance that have been created within alternative, non-theatrical architectures such as the Cartoucherie, and in the countless warehouses and disused industrial buildings, serve to indicate the importance and variety within this energy, which looks for the precise and fundamental relationships between the architecture and the scenography of performance.

9 Some Rejections of Technology in Theatre and Performance

> The Theatre of the Future necessarily embraces all that has to do with the theatre of the past. ... Without an intimate and affectionate study of the theatre of the ancients it would not be possible for man to create a new theatre.
>
> Edward Gordon Craig, prospectus for *The Mask*, 1907

For the proposer of theatrical change during the early years of the twentieth century, the current state of affairs, frequently referred to by revolutionary artists (somewhat optimistically) as 'the past', presented itself fundamentally as a theatre of material gluttony. Indeed, an identifying feature of all avant-garde art from the 1880s onwards in its acts of rejection was a profound sense of hostility to the material and spiritual excess of its contemporary civilization. At the same time, the use of new technologies in the theatre, and the introduction of their associated production values, frequently represented a major capital expense. These technologies required a considerable increase in the technical infrastructure of the theatre and a parallel development of new skills amongst the technical staff. Both of these were seen to detract from the real relationship that it was felt should properly exist between actor, audience and theatre architecture. Furthermore, the theatre of the late nineteenth century throughout the western world had developed into a large, interconnected, commercial institution in which many hundreds of people were needed to staff the opera houses and major producing theatres. The stage, increasingly filled with extravagant and extensive scenery, required so much technology, and so many staff to manage the scenery, that new plays were being

180

written to serve and exploit the technical possibilities, such as the series of sensation melodramas associated with the designer Bruce 'Sensation' Smith at Drury Lane theatre,[1] which, with the introduction of its hydraulic stage machinery in 1902, became the acknowledged home of such dramas. Old plays from the repertoire were cut, changed and mangled in order to suit new scenographic opportunities. The classic plays of antiquity and of Shakespeare were presented as little more than glittering *tableaux vivants*, with the words of the text functioning as little more than 'sub-titles' to animated pictures. Since the furnishings of the stage were expensive, cumbersome and time-consuming to produce, artistic decisions had to be made many months before the performance and certainly before the actors had begun rehearsal. The sheer, well-upholstered *weight* of the contemporary theatre in all its complexity was therefore seen by the forward-thinking artist as an accumulation of traditions and practices that totally clouded the vision of the way in which performance *ought* to relate to artists and audience. The political and social efficacy that theatre-going might once have possessed, was seen to have disappeared beneath all the surface decoration of its increasingly technological means of presentation.

It is none the less, and especially in the light of ground-breaking scientific discovery before the First World War, something of a paradox that the new art movements, with the significant exceptions of Italian Futurism and the Bauhaus theatre architects, may be defined by relationships with the distant past and with the primitive, rather than with newer, early twentieth-century technical manifestations of modernism. On the other hand, there were close parallels between these avant-garde approaches to re-functioning art, and the dominant scientific methodology of reducing structural complexity to atomic and sub-atomic investigation. As science focused increasingly upon first principles, so new theatre artists discarded the 'upholstery' of scenery and convention and chose to examine, for example, the unadorned actor upon the simplest of bare stages – the *tréteau nu* retained by Copeau after he left the Vieux-Colombier theatre. In the writing of Gordon Craig, rejection of the past (and as far as he was concerned that also included most of the present) was complete because, in his view, its practice ignored the fundamental qualities of performance. However, he articulated a future that could receive considerable energy and inspiration from more distant 'pasts': pasts such as those of Greek antiquity, or of the *commedia dell'arte* and the Italian Renaissance, that he believed to have followed the path of

Figure 31   Piet Breughel, *A Village Wedding*, detail showing a booth stage in use (*The Fitzwilliam Museum, Cambridge*)

'purity' within their theatres. The curriculum of the theatre school that Craig opened at the Arena Goldoni in Florence in 1912 served as a programmatic rediscovery of fundamental forms and as the laboratory for their investigation and analysis.

For the arts, especially those of the easel and of architecture, past and non-western cultures were not a new study. Indeed they had provided inspiration and stylistic interest for several centuries. The middle years of the eighteenth century witnessed a revival of interest in pre-Renaissance gothic forms, and the architectural and decorative neo-classicism of the Adam brothers in the 1760s closely followed the archaeology of Pompeii and Herculaneum. Applied and decorative arts reflected the contemporary taste for images of the *commedia dell'arte*, in the paintings of Watteau, or in the china figurines of Staffordshire and Dresden, and for the aesthetic styles of an oriental 'chinoiserie'. During the nineteenth century a nostalgic medievalism supported the establishment of a developmental sense of British history, and provided a powerful aesthetic influence throughout all the applied arts. Nineteenth-century international exhibitions in metropolitan centres increasingly displayed 'ethnographic arts' from colonial countries. The *Exposition Internationale* in Paris in 1900 provided a vast display of folk art and 'primitive' art forms from all around the world that proved to be extremely influential on many avant-garde artists. Alexander Golovin, who was to become Meyerhold's principal scenographer during the period before the 1917 Revolution, took a significant role in designing the pavilion at the *Exposition* which displayed Russian folk arts and crafts. However, what distinguishes the avant-garde adoption of the past was the more general desire to get beneath the surface appeal of the iconography: to examine, for example, the practice and the dramaturgy of the *commedia dell'arte* in performance rather than simply to admire and emulate the spectacular costumes and masks. The rejection of the present and the attempt to focus attention upon primal, irreducible elements – the actor, the space and people who observe – forged significant relationships with original theatre cultures both within the European past and from within non-western theatre practice. The energies and inspiration that scenography has found within twentieth-century atavism, and the ways in which it has developed (and frequently tested) the relationship between theatre and its technologies, make an important contribution to an examination of scenography and its developing identity during the twentieth century.

Theatres of antiquity, and non-western forms of performance that were believed to have retained ancient forms – Dionysian rituals, shamanistic performance, Kathakali and Balinese dance-drama – offered (and to many still offer) a route towards a more profound and elemental artistic integrity. New ideas of unity and 'purity' were already apparent in architecture and applied decorative arts by the end of the nineteenth century, for example in the practice of the Arts and Crafts Movement, and in the work of the artists and designers William Morris, Alice Comyns Carr, Charles René Mackintosh and the architect Edward Lutyens. Whilst the new drama and its dominant mode of naturalism was urged forward by writers such as Zola, Strindberg, Ibsen and Chekhov, it is perhaps not surprising that the new movements within theatre practice should initially be movements of designers and directors. The earliest ideas of Craig, Appia and Meyerhold aspired to re-create seemingly straightforward, unforced, organic and efficacious relationships between the community that encouraged and supported public performance, the artistic role and social status of the players, and the architecture constructed to reflect

and to contain the performance event. The supposedly natural sym-
biosis represented by these relationships was believed to have been
lost, indeed to have been actively destroyed, by the bourgeois commercial theatre of the late nineteenth century. Of course, in losing its
sense of purpose and social function, theatre had also lost its sense of
true style and a proper scenographic aesthetic. Early revolutions in
theatre and performance were therefore as much about questioning
the utility and social value of theatre, as about replacing outdated
aesthetics and scenic styles.

Locating the value and worth of performance within society and
within the human spirit were concerns as vital for Craig, Appia and
Meyerhold as was their desire to rid the stage of late nineteenth-
century pictorialism. Early anthropological theorists such as James G.
Frazer in *The Golden Bough: A History of Myth and Religion* (1922)
had identified profound social utility and efficacy in performance
rituals of ancient cultures. It was understood that subsequent acts of
'civilization' had served to embellish, codify and extend performed
ritual into sophisticated and complex forms that eventually clouded
and destroyed their original human and societal values. This is
Meyerhold's understanding of this anthropological process:

> Drama proceeded from the dynamic to the static pole. Drama was born 'of
> the spirit of music, out of the dynamic energy of the choric dithyramb'. The
> Dionysian art of the choric drama arose from the ecstasy of the sacrificial
> ritual. Then there began the separation of the elements of the primordial
> drama. The dithyramb emerged as a distinct form of the lyric. Attention
> became focused on the hero protagonist; his tragic fate became the centre
> of the drama. The spectator was transformed from participants in the
> sacred ritual into an onlooker of the festive 'spectacle'. The chorus became
> separated both from the populace which occupied the orchestra and from
> the hero; it became a distinct element which illustrated the peripeteia of the
> hero's fate. Thus the theatre as 'spectacle' came into being.

He explained what he saw as the logical conclusion to this process:

> The spectator experienced *passively* that which was presented on the stage.
> There arose that magic barrier which even today, in the form of footlights,
> divides the theatre into two opposed camps, the performers and the on-
> lookers; no artery exists to unite these two separate bodies and preserve the
> unbroken circulation of creative energy. The orchestra kept the spectator
> close to the action; when it was replaced by footlights the spectator became
> isolated. In the theatre as spectacle the stage resembles a stern, remote
> iconostasis which repels the desire to merge into a single festive throng.[2]

Craig expressed the scenic and architectural effect of this progression more forcefully, and colourfully, when he wrote: 'Once upon a time, stage scenery was architecture. A little later it became imitation architecture; still later it became imitation artificial architecture. Then it lost its head, went quite mad, and has been in a lunatic asylum ever since.'[3] The desire to restore value and a genuine sense of social worth and purpose to performance, although differently expressed, was a strong theme throughout early theatre revolution. The revolutionary and social aspects of early avant-garde performance and the enduring links to anthropological primitivism were clear when Richard Schechner told a much later generation of theatre artists in 1971 that 'the ambition to make theatre into ritual is nothing other than our wish to make performance efficacious, to use [theatrical] events to change people'.[4]

It has been consistently understood that access to this spiritual purity and its social efficacy might be regained through scholarship and anthropological investigation, and it is significant that around the turn of the nineteenth into the twentieth century, some foundational works of scholarship and theatre history were being written. For example, the first serious scenic history appeared in the work of W. J. Lawrence,[5] the volumes of E. K. Chambers's *The Medieval Stage* (vol. 1, 1903) began to be published, and the practical experiments of William Poel with the Elizabethan Stage Society, coinciding with the discovery of the De Witt/Arend van Buchell drawing of the 1594 Swan Theatre at the University of Utrecht in 1888, offered significant insights into early staging and the performance practices of Shakespearean theatre. In addition to increasingly sophisticated archaeology, new and important translations of the work of Greek and Roman dramatists assisted in heightening interest in the staging practices of antiquity.[6] In both these instances, the results of scholarship began to reveal a theatre in which the staging and performance were inextricably implicated within their community and, moreover, where scene design and architecture were aesthetically united.

A parallel route to an understanding of this anthropological view of theatre offered itself through exposure to, and study of, non-western theatre cultures. Japanese actors visited western Europe, and by the year 1910, had performed in most of the major capital cities. W. B. Yeats consciously assimilated what he believed to be the dramaturgy and some of the stylistic practices of the Nō theatre in his experiments at the Abbey Theatre in Dublin, and his adoption of Craig's screens in 1910–11 accorded with this understanding. Meyerhold experimented in his *Dom Juan* at the Alexandrinsky Theatre in Petersburg in 1910 with the formal stage personnel, the *kurogo*, of Japanese theatre, seeing in this a gesture of theatricality that the Japanese had preserved from original performance practice. Elizabeth Hauptmann had made German translations of Arthur Waley's English version of *The No-Plays of* Japan during 1928–9. These introduced Brecht to Japanese drama, whose dramaturgy and stage rhetoric suffuses his subsequent *lehrstücke*.[7] Balinese dance theatre had been performed at international exhibitions and served to inspire a significant number of theatre, ballet, and dance initiatives. Antonin Artaud attended the Balinese dance-drama performance at the Paris *Exposition Coloniale* in 1931, and saw in it an exemplar of the rigorous psycho-physical discipline and expression to which he aspired:

> Nothing is left to chance or personal initiative … everything is thus regulated and impersonal; not a movement of the muscles, not the rolling of an eye but seem to belong to a kind of reflective mathematics which controls everything and by means of which everything happens.[8]

Figure 32   Villagers in a trance in a barong performance in Bali (James R. Brandon, *Theatre in Southeast Asia*, Cambridge, MA: Harvard University Press, 1967)

The Balinese dance was filmed by anthropologists Margaret Mead and Gregory Bateson in their *Trance and Dance in Bali* (1938) and seemed to epitomize many of the values and qualities that expressionists and surrealists had been working towards, but in a seemingly authentic mythic and timeless ritual form. The film suggested that whilst non-literate ritual performance could be entertainment, at the same time the performance could be something more, in that it seemed to form an integral part of community life, part of an extended cycle of playing which reflected the life experiences of its society. The attraction of non-western theatre and performance has been founded upon the assumption that its contemporary practices, which may be documented and studied, have changed little over the centuries, and that the performers and theatre artists have maintained the traditions and relationships within their society that have been progressively erased in commercial western cultures.

But Artaud's response to the Balinese theatre also represents a strong tendency throughout the twentieth century towards a western, colonial appropriation of the exotic and the different, and towards finding in such a confrontation what the colonizing spectator wants to find. Liberation from the need to describe the physical location precisely as indicated by the dramatist has allowed western scenography to range widely over the world in search of startling scenic and costume metaphor – warrior cultures from East Asia or the South Seas have 'decorated' productions of *Macbeth*, Afro-Caribbean cultures have similarly served *The Tempest*, peasants from central European countries have peopled Elizabethan comedy, and aboriginal folk cultures have provided rich iconographies for the staging of the classical repertoire.

This approach remains a significant feature of contemporary scenography. However, in the 'theatre laboratories' and studios of the 1960s, models from outside the European cultural heritage began to be applied in more than a superficial way, seeking perhaps the 'kind of reflective mathematics which controls everything' of which Artaud spoke. Ritual forms were consciously analysed in terms of their reciprocal effects on both actor and onlooker. Grotowski, whose own work during the 1960s involved a rigorous and reflective discipline of psycho-physical practice, comments on Artaud's confrontation with non-western performance culture:

His description of Balinese theatre, however suggestive it may be for the imagination, is really one big misreading. Artaud deciphered as 'cosmic signs' and 'gestures evoking superior powers' elements of the performance which were concrete expressions, specific theatrical letters in an alphabet of signs universally understood by the Balinese. The Balinese performance for Artaud was like a crystal ball for a fortune-teller.[9]

Much avant-garde performance throughout the twentieth century has shared a commitment to some form of quasi-mystical therapeutic purpose, whether in the German or Soviet expressionist form of emotional inspiration that 'transfigured' its audience so that they 'rose up the new men'; or in Artaud's and Grotowski's 'exorcism', intended to strip away the constraints of civilization, restoring natural relationships to the spiritual universe. The line between receiving useful understanding and practical inspiration for the theatre artist from non-western cultures, and an intercultural experience of significance for the spectator, and being a tourist in search of performed and scenographic exotica, remains fine and an ongoing source of contention. Early in the twentieth century, some artists were aware of the need to use their source cultures carefully and with respect. Craig announced the launch of his journal *The Mask* in 1908:

> The object of the publication is to bring before an intelligent public many ancient and modern aspects of the Theatre's Art which have too long been disregarded or forgotten. Not to attempt to assist in the so-called reform of the modern theatre – for reform is now too late; not to advance theories which have not already been tested, but to announce the existence of a vitality which already begins to reveal itself in a beautiful and definite form based upon an ancient and noble tradition.

And Meyerhold cautioned in 1914:

> How do we aim to restore the traditions of the past in the present? Not simply by repeating the devices of the past – this we leave to the Ancient Theatre. There is a difference between mere reconstruction and free composition based on the study and selection of traditional techniques.[10]

The newspaper *Pravda*, 4: 17 (February 1918), comments:

> before the Revolution several masters of the theatre were turning to the popular theatres of the preceding epochs with increasing frequency. They saw true theatrical achievements in them and wanted to proceed from them. How otherwise can Meyerhold's longing for the Italian popular theatre of the Commedia dell'Arte be explained? The awareness that our period had completely lost all true principles of theatrical action compelled Meyerhold to

turn to the Italian popular comedy in order to find these principles, to take from it everything that is eternal in theatre and transplant it to our soil.[11]

However, to identify peoples and the art forms of their cultures as 'the primitive' assumed a privileged spectator; one who awarded value and significance to primitive art and life in so far as it appeared to be the opposite of present-day industrial urban, and increasingly mechanized civilization. Therefore if present-day performance was considered to be too materialistic, driven by a passion for new technologies, generally too rational and sophisticated, then forms of aboriginal performance and theatre could be understood as representing the naive, the irrational and, importantly, the untarnished. European political ideologies have exploited this reading of the primitive, as Christopher Innes says, 'as a left-wing ideal of precapitalist economic and social relations in the 1960s – or, interchangeably, as the Fascist ideal of blood and folk in the 1930s'. In this way, Innes suggests, the twentieth century has frequently made the 'primitive' synonymous with the Utopian and therefore in actuality represents little *real* progress from the late nineteenth century when 'the Victorians, labelling people as primitive (with connotations of dark, cruel, backward, childlike) affirmed their own moral superiority and right to imperial conquest'.[12]

At the conclusion of the First World War, the rejection of the past and the search for a new purity was even more potent, tragic and urgent. The immediate past – the war – was understandably identified as a culmination of a thoroughly corrupt set of nineteenth-century values and ideals. In Amsterdam, an internationally recognized group of architects known as the 'Amsterdam School' published a monthly journal, *Wendingen* (literally 'Turnings'), that devoted issues in 1919 to masks, dance, and modern theatre architecture. This group, with its conviction that in the wake of such political and social trauma a new day was dawning, along with the organization *Kunst aan het Volk* created the International Theatre Exhibition that was held in Amsterdam in January 1922. *Wendingen* had attracted international interest on account of its inventive typography and graphic design as well as its provocative content, and was able to invite and attract an international representation of forward-thinking theatre artists. What was displayed in Hendricus Wijdeveld's spectacular 'total' museum design for the exhibition included designs and models of work by Appia, Craig, Robert Edmond Jones, Alfred Roller, Louis Jouvet, Ernst Stern and Léon Bakst; in fact all who might offer glimpses of theatrical futures, many of whom had been inspired by the 'primitive' and utopian past.[13] In *Wendingen* of March 1919, Wijdeveld's aspirations for the emergence of new dance typify this atavistic desire:

> Thus too flows the flourishing new dance into the great sea of modern art, where the waters continually rise and rise, until they will overflow their banks and inundate all people in a purifying path of spiritual pleasure. Thus the dance will once again take its place among the arts, together heralding a new era, and with the word, and with music, and with architecture and all plastic arts, it will contribute to the great people's stage, the theatre, where celebrations of joy, where ceremonies of sadness, where the consecration of humanity in an offering to art will take place, and where finally, instead of the fading bow of the churches, will flourish once again a sublime ritual.[14]

Wijdeveld's ambitions echo the social and spiritual ambitions of Emile Jacques Dalcroze and his system of Eurhythmics, and the less formalized, but none the less fervent aspirations of Isadora Duncan. The revival of the arts of movement and dance were especially significant since they represented forms that seemed, in their shedding of verbal language and culturally specific clothing, to offer pathways from the past that might lead towards new, more universally harmonious futures. Alongside Craig and Copeau, Wijdeveld contributed a lecture to a series that coincided with the exhibition in Amsterdam and in this he centralized the role of architecture and the place of performance: 'the theatre is the place where all the other arts – and people! – come together and therefore the most beautiful task of the modern architect [is] the construction of the theatre'. He emphasized the idea of synthesis: 'in the drama of the future the word will not be dominant, but word, gesture, rhythm, dance – all equal, altogether forming one great unity'.[15]

Throughout the examination of the state of theatre at the close of the nineteenth century, amongst the key issues that were of concern to the avant-garde artist, most involved the extravagance and the complexity of the contemporary theatre, and the limitations on the human imagination that these imposed. By definition therefore, rejection of the contemporary theatre implied a move towards simpler, leaner, sparer alternatives. Similarly for many, the fundamental attraction of pre-Renaissance and non-western models of performance was that they not only seemed to offer admirable paradigms of community relationships between theatre and performers, but also satisfied the fundamental desire to work with simpler, less extravagant, and more essential resources. But some theatre artists have pursued the rejection of past and existing forms and conventions, over and above the primary role of 'clearing the ground'. For some, absence of resource has become an act of purification: a positive necessity for the making of new theatre. Inspiration may well be derived from an acquaintance and respect for pre-Renaissance and non-western models, but the 'poverty' achieved may primarily serve as a crucial scenographic and performance aesthetic in its own right. Scenographic minimalism has proved to be a significant feature in the search for new theatrical identity.

Throughout the twentieth century, not only technologies and scenographies of the immediate past, but also contemporary technologies and scenographic approaches have been seen as clouding the issue of 'real' theatre and have produced an obscuring and, as Peter Brook called it, a 'deadly' richness. The often quoted opening lines of Brook's first lecture, 'The Deadly Theatre' have ricocheted through rehearsal rooms and design studios ever since their delivery in the mid-1960s: 'I can take any empty space and call it a bare stage. A man walks across this empty space whilst someone else is watching him, and this is all that is needed for an act of theatre to be engaged.' Several days after hearing Brook give his lecture in 1964 in Manchester, my scenography tutor announced to the class that the next exercise would be devoted to considering the challenge of designing a bare stage. Attempting to imbue the poverty of bareness with a rich, but sparse and minimal eloquence has been a consistent challenge to the theatre and its artists ever since Craig patented his idea for scenic 'screens' in 1910. In the lectures, Brook proposed three alternative approaches to the 'richness' of contemporary deadly theatre: a Holy Theatre, a Rough Theatre and an Immediate Theatre; although in the published version of the lectures he stressed their important interconnections and their metaphoric status as ideas: 'two of them mixing together within one evening, within one act. Sometimes within one single moment, the four of them, Holy, Rough, Immediate and Deadly intertwine.'[16]

During the early 1960s, Grotowski abandoned his existing 'deadly' theatre and its processes of production in a desire to find greater meaning and a more intense efficacy in and through the act of performance. He called his theatre a 'poor' theatre: poor in traditional resources but potentially rich in spiritual intent and significance. Grotowski and Ludwik Flaszen established the Theatre Laboratory in Opole in 1959, and moved it to the larger university town of Wroclaw in 1965. It received funding from the state through the municipalities of both towns, and during the late 1960s it had the status of an Institute for Research into Acting. The laboratory existed in a bare studio place where the space for performance was 'constructed' for each production, adopting a range of scenographic approaches that were determined by the work in hand. Grotowski's approach to the placing of performance was distinctive and represents an important and enduring attitude towards scenography during the latter half of the twentieth century. It is worth considering an instance of this approach in some detail.

In 1968 the Laboratory made its first visit to Britain, and in October, they performed their re-working of Calderón's *The Constant Prince* in Manchester. The studio used by the Company had been designed by Stephen Joseph in 1963 and offered a performance space of approximately thirty feet by forty feet (10 by 14 metres). It was bare and functional and its walls were painted a very dark, elephant grey-green, and it had a high-pitched 'gothic' roof dating from the building's days as a Protestant chapel in the nineteenth century. At one end an 'upper stage' provided a small gallery whilst at the other, a raised control box had good vision over the space. The floor was covered with a mid-grey 'TV Studio' smooth plastic Vinyl surface. A small, self-selected crew of young teachers and a few students volunteered to work as 'fit-up' crew and scenic technicians. The Laboratory brought with them only the crew needed to actually run the performance. Ludwik Flaszen described the function of the scenography: 'the arrangement of stage and audience resembles something between an arena and an operating-theatre. One may think of what one sees below in terms of some cruel sport in an ancient Roman arena or a surgical operation as portrayed in Rembrandt's "Anatomy of Dr Tulp".'[17] The scenography for *The Constant Prince* consisted of a four-sided palisade of untreated smooth timber planks approximately eight feet (2.5 metres) high surrounding a central long rectangular performance space (see Figure 33). The performance therefore took place in the round, with an audience that consisted of precisely 80 people sitting in two rows on all four sides of the acting space. This was an accommodation by Grotowski, whose initial wish had been for 40 people only, since that was the precise number that could fill a single row of sitting spaces above the sides of the enclosure. Towards one end of the enclosed acting space there was a low rostrum, about six feet by three feet six inches (1.8 by 1.1 metres) and just under eighteen inches (0.5 metres) high. This too was made from untreated timber. Scaffolding was raised to provide for the two

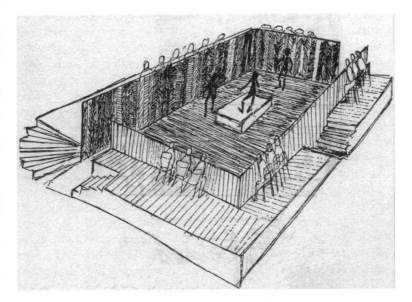

Figure 33   Grotowski, *The Constant Prince* (1968), sketch of the scenic arrangement (*Jerzy Gurawski*)

rows of audience benches on each side so that the top of the palisade also served as the front rail for the audience, who could, if they chose, lean forward onto the palisade to look down into the space. Gaps made in the short end sections of the palisade permitted two diagonally opposed entrances. However, the actors principally used the entrance at the far (gallery) end of the studio whilst Grotowski sat on a chair at the other (control box) end, outside the palisade, looking (peeping) into the space of performance.

The bareness and 'poverty' of both architectural and scenic resource seemed (at that time in the late 1960s) to be self-evident. Yet equally self-evident from the relationship between Grotowski, his actors, and us his scenic technicians, was the care and deep aesthetic attention that was paid to ensuring that this 'empty stage' acquired the powerful eloquence that it had in performance. 'Eloquence' is a word customarily used to account for the fluency, force and appropriateness of speech; how can a space be eloquent? The scenic architecture did, nevertheless, 'speak', and explored a wide range and variety of human responses. Grotowski rejected the use of the studio floor in its grey, linoleum neutrality – 'it must be wood'. A rented wooden floor was installed, but its varnished protective surface was as offensive as the grey linoleum beneath. The proper material and textural relationship with the body of the actor must be created – 'it must be virgin wood' Grotowski told us. Sanding the entire floor harmonized its surface with the palisade and the rostrum, and created a surface that almost dazzled in its cleanliness. To anyone walking through the studio door, the smell of untreated wood was intense. The gentle and repetitive creak of the steps and platforms as the audience filed silently into the place of performance gave the sense that its members were combining to become part of a machine; that they were being initiated into a physical construct that reflected a process that had happened before, and now would happen again. Lighting came from only two sources: two huge (by contemporary studio standards) movie lights with soft-focus lenses were placed on floor-stands by each of the two entrances, and were raised to a height of about ten feet (3 metres). The angle of their wide beams of light bounced off the sanded wooden floor. These luminaires were extremely evident to the audience: they were large and obtrusive, their light was bright and uncoloured and they were controlled from a single, portable dimmer switch operated by a technician sitting next to Grotowski. However, in order to bring the entire space and its bareness into a focused state of performance, another 'performance' had to take place – that of constructing the audience.

The outer doorway to the studio building had been closed and, effectively, guarded by two of Grotowski's crew, formally dressed in dark suits and wearing black ties. They didn't speak neither did they smile. The audience waited outside. They nodded and uttered a very quiet 'good evening' as the audience eventually passed through the outer doors of the building. Their behaviour and presence, standing on either side of the corridor as the audience of precisely eighty people entered the building, quietened and focused the attention of the people as they mounted the stairs to the studio above. The smell of the wood, sound, light, heat and smell from the two powerful movie lights formed the syntax of experience and the focus of attention as the audience was created in the studio. The lamps had evidently been burning for some time before the audience came in and their heat and the smell contributed to a powerful impression of 'earlier' events – we experienced an intense sense that something would happen that had happened before. The anticipation of performance was made to be acute through both the making of such a bare space and the conscious making of an audience (in 1968, few people had sufficient knowledge of Grotowski to harbour much intellectual anticipation). The poverty of the bareness was, of course, aesthetically carefully controlled – size, shape, contour and, especially, surface and texture – but the performativity of the space was established in the careful and deliberate building of the audience in and around it. The 'poverty' proved to be experientially extremely rich and seemed to expand in possibility throughout the performance.[18]

If the careful construction of such an 'empty space' of performance can generate significance and 'speak' to its audience, then what does it say? Traditionally, scenography 'talks' about the dramatic events that are enacted within the space. Expressed as polarities these might be, on the one hand, the total description of the physical location of the dramatic events, and on the other, an abstracted metaphor for the dramatic action that takes place within. To one extent, of course, Grotowski's construction is also a machine for performance: it provides the mechanical necessities of spatial area and extent, limits of playing, ways in and out of the space; a physical relationship with the audience and, in this instance, a raised rostrum to enable focus and emphasis, but it is significantly different from the constructed machines of performance of Meyerhold or of Caspar Neher. Grotowski's construction is also, as Craig remarked about his screens, very much a 'place' rather than a 'scene'. Even during the act of performance, it remained a place; it did not take on any of the locational qualities of the dramatic space of the action. The palisade never *became* the walls of a room or dungeon; the rostrum never *became* a potential platform in the castle nor stood in for a piece of furniture. It seems that Grotowski's 'place' was speaking to its audience in its own voice; in ways that asserted its 'placeness' rather than, for example, speaking about its ability to become, through performance, whatever the actors might have wished – as, for example, through performance the pillars on the Elizabethan stage may become trees in a forest, or pillars in the Roman Forum. Much as the space was unique to *The Constant Prince*, it did not exist to *service* the play; it retained its own unique identity – both providing for performance whilst resting alongside performance.

But Craig clearly asserts that the stage space formed by his screens creates a 'place' if it seems *real*, and a 'scene' if it seems *false*. Did the poverty of Grotowski's constructed place contribute significantly to the reality of experience? How did the space contribute to maintaining the audience's attention upon the immediate reality of the event – illustrating Neher's statement quoted earlier: '[a] picture is never realistic, the stage is always realistic. That's why I maintain that the "realistic stage picture" is a nonsense'? Initially, the experiential impact on entering the space was extremely vivid and strong – colour, texture, smell, sound – all these qualities made the audience aware of the identity of *this* space, its difference and specificity, and in particular of the compound qualities of its materials. The entering people were made aware of the particularity and precision of its arrangement, and the purposeful way in which Grotowski's assistants directed the audience. The accuracy of the audience placement and their relationship with the top of the palisade was precise: an encounter was being constructed in which a significant thing would be enacted; it could not be otherwise because of the deep sense of purpose, the silence and the bareness of the light. The strangeness and artificiality that Grotowski describes are as intentional as the focus upon the encounter: 'the more we become absorbed in what is hidden inside us, in the excess, in the exposure, in the self-penetration, the more rigid must be the external discipline; that is to say the form, the artificial reality, the ideogram, the sign'.[19] The light was non-dramatic light in that it seemed to represent nothing other than itself, it did not try to represent night or sunrise, nor in performance was it used dramatically to highlight an actor or an action. Furthermore, it was a consistent and constant physical ingredient within the perception of the audience – the audience watched the light lighting the space and, lighting the audience, the light was shared.

In performance the actors treated the space and its limits much as acrobats might treat their apparatus; for example, when Ryszard Cieslak cried in agony and licked the floor, the floor and its texture of untreated wood framed and served him much as the surface of an apparatus might frame and serve the gymnast. Significantly, Grotowski uses this metaphor to describe the work of the actor: 'The important thing is to use the role as a trampoline, an instrument with which to study what is hidden behind our everyday mask – the innermost core of our personality – in order to sacrifice it, expose it.'[20] Each maintained his or her individual integrity as an 'instrument' of performance: demonstrating the great skill of the actors and the significant reality of the place in which they made their performance.

This minimalism is a poverty of means; a radical reduction of resource, and an implicit and considered rejection of technologies, that leads to a concentration of experience that is focused upon the immediate reality of that resource. Grotowski transferred the atavistic hunger for a foundational and primal theatre into a twentieth-century scientific analysis and an exploitation of minimal materials – the floor, the texture, and the light. This was an analysis, of course, that precisely matched the primacy of focus upon the activity of acting – the voice, its resonance in and through the body, the journey of the actor into a daring internal space.

In rejecting the institutional richness of the Royal Shakespeare Company in the early 1970s, Peter Brook initially went one stage further and rejected even the bareness of the *atelier* studio in order to seek and to examine the qualities of the 'good' space for performance. In 1971 his Paris-based group – the Centre International de Recherche Théâtral (CIRT) – spent three months in Iran making a production of Ted Hughes's *Orghast in Persepolis*, which was performed in front of the royal tombs of the ancient Persian Kings Darius, Xerxes and Artaxerxes. After considering the building of a 'designed' cube setting of considerable technical sophistication that would have required actors to be suspended on crane structures, the group eventually allowed the site itself to determine its places of performance. Brook said: 'the best we can do in designing and lighting a set turns out to be: nothing at all. ... It's not a process of building, but of destroying obstacles that stand in the way of the latent form.'[21] The processes of exploring the 'latent form' and of performing at the site were ultimately marred by the diplomatic and political complexities of that period in Iranian history, but the making of a place of performance within a found environment and the associated work that CIRT undertook touring in villages, confirmed the need to re-assess the nature of the architecture of theatre and of scenography.

At the end of 1972, CIRT began their tour of villages in Nigeria, but now, instead of being a European avant-garde theatre company in search of 'authentic' settings in Iran in which to make their performances, here the aim was a constant contact with people who in most cases had never seen Western theatre before, and the spaces that the company created for performance were an essential part of this openness to chance. 'There were no pre-conceptions, no recipes for success: it was as if Africa itself was a vast potential theatre.'[22] Although a number of open-air courtyards and built stages were used, most memorably the company unrolled a large blue carpet that served as space of performance and as the delineation of the architectural parameters of the theatre. Brook describes the 'reality' of that carpet as it made theatre space:

Sitting around the carpet on the same ground as the actors in the same light and time is a form of reality, but the imaginative world jointly created on this basis has a different – virtual – quality, and both the real and the virtual qualities coexist. This harks back to Meyerhold, who emphasised that theatre is theatre: it is not pretending that the image we are looking at really exists. At every moment we keep this double vision: we are in this place where people are playing a game, and we're watching them performing.[23]

But making a theatre that worked in performance was more than simply unrolling the carpet. Brook and the company were developing the pragmatic ability to observe and to 'listen' to the found environment and to realize that a good site of performance represented a shared energy between what was 'given' by the environment – its colours, its shapes, its smells, its atmosphere, its history – and what might be created within the space – the imposed practices of performance and the scenography of material, properties, light and sound:

The physical spaces for performance consisted of not more than the carpet and the ways people gathered spontaneously around it: they had only a provisional form, whose success was determined to a great extent by chance factors and flows of energy between the group and the public. Nevertheless, the 'simple pragmatism' with which Brook says the spaces were selected was being conditioned by accumulated experience – a far from simple *intuition* of what syntheses of forms, materials, social conditions, climate and time could open the pathways of communication.[24]

According to many twentieth-century histories of theatre, technologies that were introduced in the late Renaissance were generally associated with social extravagance and forms of deceit – the painted perspective of flat scenes, the magical appearance of deities, and the hidden machinery needed to manipulate them. The machinery of this scenic deceit necessitated the construction of a proscenium that both framed the perspective and disguised its own inner working, and located the act of performance as being 'elsewhere' than within the immediately experienced world of its audience. The costs of such mechanized display required significant patronage either from status as court theatres, or from rich box-office patrons. And the 'jewel in the casket', as Carlson calls the architecture of the Renaissance theatre auditorium,[25] increasingly became a glittering display of wealth and privilege that reflected the political hierarchy and the social aspirations of its ruling class. By this declension, technology has been thought of as having progressively removed the theatre from its fundamental artistic and social roots as a meeting place of actors and audience. There have been, of course, some very significant exceptions within this trajectory, but by the early years of the twentieth century this questionable relationship between theatre and technology was very clear. Accordingly, pre-Renaissance forms such as the touring-booth stage of curtained enclosure and bare fit-up platform of the *commedia dell'arte* had acquired many of the essential qualities of performance that CIRT tried to rediscover through its 'carpet' experiments. The appeal of such forms also seemed to align themselves with critical theories of theatre anthropology such as Mikhail Bakhtin's articulation of the 'carnivalesque', which proposed artistic forms that embodied the anarchic, the grotesque, and the inherently revolutionary energies of the Saturnalia of ancient Rome and medieval popular carnivals as alternatives to what Bakhtin calls the 'limited and reduced aesthetic stereotypes of modern times'.[26]

In order to examine, and in many cases to revive, some of the qualities of these past forms, artists have turned to forms of pantomime and the dramaturgy of *commedia*. Jacques Copeau worked extensively with *commedia* scenarios, and his *tréteau nu* became both his 'carpet' – his practical scenography – and a powerful exemplary statement of actor training based on improvization. The study and staging of *commedia* would, it was believed, reveal the power of what Meyerhold considered the 'primordial elements' of the theatre: the power of the mask, gesture, movement and plot. During his 'Doctor Dappertutto' period between 1908 and 1917, he said:

> Drama in reading is primarily dialogue, argument and taut dialectic. Drama on the stage is primarily action, a taut struggle. The words are, so to speak, the mere overtones of the action. They should burst spontaneously from the actor gripped in the elemental progress of the dramatic struggle.[27]

The *commedia* scenarios and the 'patter' of the charlatan cabotin would provide the textual 'overtones' that would free the contemporary actors to release the elemental qualities in their performance. The actor would be 'overjoyed at the simplicity, the refined grace, the extreme artistry of the old yet eternally new tricks of the *histrions, mimi, atellanae, joculatores* and *minstrelli*' and, Meyerhold concludes: 'The cult of cabotinage, which I am sure will reappear with the restoration of the theatre of the past, will help the modern actor to rediscover the basic laws of theatricality.'[28]

The received impression of the *commedia dell'arte* as its historiography has been progressively documented through the twentieth century has served as a powerful artistic focus in the rejection of technology and its associated scenographic forms.[29] That impression presupposed a form of theatre that focused upon the skills of the actor and furthermore positioned those skills right at the heart of its dramaturgy – acting was not thought of as being merely the medium for the interpretation of dramatic literature. *Commedia* therefore seemed to place the ownership of the theatre in the hands of the theatre artists themselves. In doing this, it seemed to reject the institutionalizing thrust of the Renaissance theatre with its formal architecture and the social hierarchy that this reflected; and, by implication, the superstructure of commercial and literary management that could stifle theatrical creativity. By contrast, *commedia* seemed to offer an image of theatre-making as a collective collaboration of artists and in so doing it served to reflect for the twentieth century not only artistic proposals for creative ensemble work, but also the predominating democratic thrust of the century.

Historically, theatre technologies have come to represent powerful divisions between artists and their audience – the proscenium arch and the enclosed secrecy of the stage house clearly reflect this division. It may not be by chance that access to the backstage areas of a theatre has been hotly contested, nor coincidence that the door between the stage and the auditorium should be traditionally called the 'pass door'. The desire to reject these divisions, to abandon formal theatre and to make performance elsewhere in the community has been a powerful energy of recent decades. For example, the company Welfare State International (founded by John Fox in 1968) was initially associated with large-scale outdoor, spectacular community events, taking its work out of theatres and art galleries and finding places to perform in the landscapes of open spaces and in the street. The Company created a collective of artists who worked to make performances within a community; work that in content and in process opposed the traditional structures of theatre architecture, scenography, audience relationship and artistic hierarchy. While the traditional *commedia dell'arte* were companies of actors who created theatre out of their acting skills, Welfare State International has become a '*commedia*'-like company of artists who make art out of a wide range of the skills of performers, sculptors, poets, pyrotechnicians, engineers, musicians, and painters. The company has made community carnivals and participatory festivals, site-specific performances, lantern processions, and spectacular shows of water and of fire. An important aspect of the work has always been to serve as a resource of advice, skills and expertise for others.

Although the means are quite different, the company seemed to have a similarly '*commedia*'-like relationship with its communities in generating work that was carnivalesque, liberating and politically provocative, whilst being simultaneously beautiful and magical. Though not formally rejecting technology, the work represents a fundamental reappraisal of the relationship between it and art. Alternative technologies and skills such as withy sculpture, lantern making and pyrotechnology have featured strongly in their work, and they consistently break down the barriers between engineering and the arts. In rejecting theatres and galleries, they have naturally rejected the formal, repetitive spatial arrangement of 'performance' and spectator. Relationships have been defined by the nature of performance, which may move and change, expand or contract; the spectator may sit, stand, or walk with the action. The scenography of Welfare State may well be concerned with creating a 'place' for an action, but that place may change or be spread over a considerable area and the spectators may observe it from a distance, or be within it as an active peripatetic participant. The significance of this is that as well as the revival of old, alternative skills-based technologies, Welfare State has not rejected newer technologies. In the context of this discussion, therefore, the important consideration is the consistent rejection not specifically of the technologies themselves, but of the artistic hierarchies and divisions that technologies have historically signified in theatre and performance, and the subsequent attempts to redefine scenography and performance *outside* the hierarchies that are represented by formal theatre architectures.

The themes that have been considered in this chapter are a part of the history of scenography and performance in the twentieth century and are also matters of experiment and concern today. Artists examine and work with models of practice and theatre training from other cultures in attempts to find new meaning and resonance for both artist and audience. The instinct to reject all previous resources as somehow representing residues of past approaches is strong; whilst simultaneously there is continued respect for earlier forms such as the *commedia* and Renaissance stagecraft as objects of study and revelation. The complex technology of theatre architecture may be rejected for *atelier* simplicity and poverty; but that too may be rejected in favour of landscape and alternative sites of performance.

In turn, landscape has become more than a location of performance by becoming, in some instances, fundamental to the making of new dramaturgies. In this way new paradigms of performance have emerged that, whilst they may include the theatre, also represent significant challenges to it.

10 New Technologies and Shifting Paradigms

During the last decades of the twentieth century, new technologies have had quite far-reaching effects upon the development of theatrical practice and performance. Although, as we have seen, the technologies of stage lighting had made a steady progress from the beginning of the century, those technologies associated with sound and sound reproduction did not have significant effects within theatre and performance until the decades following the Second World War. The implications, for both the theory and practice of theatre, of new sound technologies, digital processes and the computer interface since the 1970s are significant, and these technologies continue to have considerable effects both upon 'traditional' theatrical presentation and within the development of new forms of performance practice. This chapter will therefore explore the diversity of effects and opportunities that new technologies have offered, and are offering, to theatre and performance.

Although the invention and commercial exploitation of the recording phonograph and the electric light bulb happened at around the same time, the processes of playing recorded sound found little application in the theatre; whereas electric light, however primitive and dim it might have been when first seen in the theatre during the 1880s, could nevertheless be perfectly appreciated by the human eye – the light perceived was the *thing itself*, not an imitation or a reproduction of light. Of course the objective function of the light, over and above the illumination of the stage space, might have been to represent a sunrise, sunset or moonlight, for example. But such conventions of representation, especially of effects of meteorology, have had a long history of codified simulation in performance, beginning with iconic representations of the sun and the moon in outdoor medieval performance. In the open-air amphitheatres and indoor private theatres of the Renaissance and the seventeenth century, 'dark lanterns' were used on the candle-lit stage to indicate night-time. The painter Gainsborough was amazed at Loutherbourg's effects of lighting meteorology at Drury Lane theatre, but asked Garrick to spare a thought for the safety of the eyes of the audience on account of the brightness. The first reported use of lime-light in a theatre suggests that it may have been used in the London theatre of the 1830s to simulate moonlight pouring through high windows. By the 1880s, the interaction between painted scene and gas lighting had developed an extremely sophisticated and flexible, albeit conventional, scenic syntax of lighting effects.

However, the new technologies of sound, initially the recordings made on the wax-cylinder phonograph, involved imitation and reproduction of a kind that was previously unknown. When the phonograph was used to replicate a sound effect, the resulting sound could be compared instantly both with the knowledge or memory of the original, and especially with preceding theatrical technologies for making sound. For example, the thunder-sheet of metal suspended backstage could very effectively replicate the sound of thunder when properly manipulated by a stage technician. Even more, the almost literal 'surround sound' quality of a 'thunder-run' such as that still in existence high up in the Theatre Royal in Bristol (1766) employed stone cannon-balls that trundled and 'thundered' slowly down sloping wooden guttering. The surviving eighteenth- and nineteenth-century wind-machines and rain-machines attest to the sophistication and ingenuity of early sound-effect technologies and indicate a history of alarmingly life-like sound mimesis in the theatre. As early as 1786, William Pyne reported the spectacular accuracy and ingenuity of the technologies used by Loutherbourg to replicate the sounds of waves and thunder, claiming that in his work on the *Eidophusikon* he had created a new art form, which Pyne called 'the picturesque of sound'.[1]

Not until the mechanical and electrical reproduction of sound had achieved an acceptable realism, therefore, did audio-technologies become used to any great extent in theatre and performance – although the term 'acceptable realism' must inevitably remain relative to both period and circumstance. For example, the sound of recorded music and dialogue, which became familiar to audiences from the beginning of the 1930s with the introduction of sound motion pictures, provided the technology of sound amplification that was also used in the theatre. But this, albeit imperfectly reproduced music was more acceptable in the theatre than a similar quality reproduction of a sound effect such as meteorology or off-stage effects. The moving sound film, by contrast, created a complete reproduction of sound and vision through its technology – the entire experience was a mechanical simulation. Whilst recorded music in the theatre may have served to introduce a mood or to serve as a background to dramatic action, a mechanically and imperfectly reproduced sound effect could be compared alongside the immediate flesh-and-blood reality of the actors on stage, and was usually found to be lacking – an imperfectly reproduced sound of a motor car approaching, or a thunder storm, was much less acceptable than similarly reproduced background music. During the 1940s and 1950s the technical director in the theatre would generally spurn sound-effects recordings, whilst proudly using the twin-turntable 'panatrope' with tone-arms, which could be accurately calibrated to play music on cue.

The first significant book to treat the subject in Britain, Frank Napier's *Noises Off*, published in several editions between 1936 and 1948, makes a clear distinction between music as sound effect and 'noises off', and treats it as axiomatic that the latter are better produced by mechanical devices rather than by using electronic means.[2] 'Live' sound effects – the 'thunder-sheet', the coconut shells that in skilful hands could replicate the sound of horses hooves, the canvas-covered 'wind-machine', and the metal drainpipe of dried peas that could very effectively simulate rain – were therefore only slowly replaced by sound-effects shellac records during the 1950s, and then more rapidly by the hi-fidelity of 33 rpm vinyl recordings. Notwithstanding this improved recorded quality by the 1960s, there were still many cases where the creative stage technician would, wherever possible, prefer to create sound from other means rather than use pre-recorded sequences. Even the improved fidelity of sound-reproduction equipment was challenged by attempts to reproduce 'explosive' sounds such as gunshots and sudden cracks of thunder. Furthermore, effects recordings were, by definition, prescriptive and rarely seemed to fit the dramatic situation precisely. 'Background' music was increasingly provided by recordings, but music has a long history as an adjunct to performance, and the theatre orchestra, even when reduced to two or three players, continued to frame and accompany dramatic theatre until the early 1960s.

As a result of radio and sound amplification techniques developed for military applications during the Second World War, the magnetic tape-recorder became available and was commercially exploited from the period 1948–50. However, it was not until quite late in the 1950s that good-quality amplification and loudspeaker systems enabled the *Ferrograph* and similar tape-recorders such as the *Vortexion* to be used in the theatre. The absolute reliability and cueing accuracy of the *Ferrograph*, alongside the boost given to amplification and loud-speaker design by the development for cinema and for home use of hi-fi and stereophonic sound during the 1960s, very much invented the art of sound design in the theatre.

Whilst the domestic market kept pressure upon the electronics industries to continually improve sound recording and the quality of reproduction, the same market that produced high-quality sound within the home began to be reflected in an increasing dissatisfaction with the quality of sound in the theatre. By the late 1960s this began to manifest itself as the beginning of a consumer preference for the recorded over the live experience. In this respect, the high-quality, stereophonic 'original cast recording' of musical theatre was becom-ing a serious challenge to the audience experience in live theatre: the voices and diction of the cast in the theatre were not as clear as on the recording; the orchestra in the theatre was usually much smaller and did not have the instrumental and tonal balance that had been provided in the recording studio; the live member of the audience in the theatre may well, for example, have been sitting close by the percussion section in the orchestra pit; and, of course the original 'stars' who were featured on the recording might no longer be performing in the theatre. By the 1980s, for many of the large-scale musicals that aspired to long runs and extended replication inter-nationally, it became increasingly desirable and more effective to isolate the musicians away from the stage so that very little truly live sound from instruments could be heard by the audience. Through such isolation, sophisticated electronic engineering could create a sound-balanced reproduction to be broadcast 'live' using carefully focused loudspeakers situated throughout the auditorium, producing a sound that could now compare favourably with the orchestral quality of the 'original cast album'. Musicians' trade unions through-out the world have fought bitter campaigns to protect their members in orchestra pits as, in this way, it has became more effective for some theatre managements to re-conceive of theatre musicians as live operators of carefully amplified and balanced musical synthesis.

Whereas the creation of 'sound effects' and atmospheric back-ground moods had been the prime objectives of the application of sound technology in the theatre during the 1960s, sound 'reinforcement' quickly began during the early 1970s to become a major priority. Instead of focusing upon the recording and playback of specific sounds, the sound designer began, both in musical theatre and quickly in the dramatic theatre, to become concerned with the creation of a 'soundscape' – in many ways an audio equivalent of Appia's concept of the lighting score – the creation and constant modulation of the entire auditory experience of a performance. Initially this 'reinforcement' involved the use of carefully placed, on-stage hidden microphones whose signals could be mixed as the actors moved about the stage, or the use of 'rifle' microphones, which, as their name implies, could be accurately 'aimed' and their reception focused by an operator to pick up a very small area of sound. By the late 1970s and increasingly through the 1980s, however, tiny radio microphones secreted within the costume close to the mouth transmitted the sound of performers to off-stage receivers, where the voices could be processed, blended and mixed into the soundscape of the overall performance. The effects of this technology have been interesting, and for the musical theatre, quite far-reaching: an actor may genuinely whisper and be heard by everyone in the auditorium; the sound may be processed, whereby effects of echo, presence and modulation may be electronically added to the voice; actors, and especially singers, may perform wherever they wish throughout the stage and the auditorium without the need to 'project' their voice from traditionally dominant places on the stage; and, of course, actor–singers with very 'small' voices may now feature in large-scale musical theatre; and it is consequently more easy to replace an actor whilst remaining generally true to the sound of the original cast.

During the final decade of the twentieth century, sound design was also liberated from the mechanical editing, cutting and rearranging of sections of magnetic recording tape in order to prepare a 'show-tape' of sound scenography. Digital recording on mini-disks, CD-ROMs and computer hard-disks, alongside computer-generated 'sampling' and sound synthesis, have almost entirely replaced the technologies of tape-recording. In addition to a more sophisticated range of 'sonic arts' available to the theatre sound artist, the computer interface allows for far more complex manipulation and playback than had been possible with any of the earlier sound-reproduction technologies that relied upon 'mechanical' forms of operation.

As suggested above, the musical theatre has been a particular and significant beneficiary of these new technologies. A distant descendent of the court masque, and more recently of the *opéra comique*, the *féerie*, and the musical revue, the stage musical has, throughout history, always been hungry to utilize new technologies and display extravagant scenography. For Inigo Jones at the Stuart court during the early seventeenth century, the scene-change exemplified the process of authority and power that could, for example, transform a world of political disharmony, horror and darkness into a world of princely light and social harmony. This transformation could not be hidden, it must be undertaken with seemingly effortless ease before the eyes of the spectator. During the nineteenth century, the stage was consistently used to demonstrate the very latest applications of scientific invention. Furthermore, this public display of technology was important to the development and support of the industrial pre-eminence and colonial authority of the western world.

During the 1930s the impresario C. B. Cochran employed the narrative potential of advanced Schwabe image-projection systems; and Emile Littler proudly used the celebratory spectacle of the triple revolving stage at the London Coliseum. In the same period the powerful, silent majesty of the hydraulic stages of Drury Lane theatre were used in the musical fantasies of Sigmund Romberg and Ivor Novello. However, by the 1960s the stage spectacle, with some significant exceptions such as *West Side Story* (1957) and *Oh, What a Lovely War!* (1963), began to pale in contrast with the spectacle now achievable in the film musical, especially through the new cinema formats of Cinemascope and Todd-AO; even the original Cecil Beaton scenography of *My Fair Lady* (1956, New York; 1958, London) looked distinctly jaded in comparison with the film version (1964). The theatre version of *South Pacific* (1949), although extremely popular, could not compete alongside the Todd-AO film of 1958 to present its story of the healing power of love within the spectacular landscape and human horror of the Pacific theatre of war. Although there have been subsequent stage productions, *The Sound of Music* (1965) was conceived from the outset as a film that could exploit spectacular mountain landscapes and the vertiginous angles of the aerial camera. Similarly conceived as film spectacle, *Mary Poppins* (1964) and *Chitty Chitty Bang Bang* (1968) were both enormously successful and popular, although significantly the live theatre has within very recent years developed the technologies to present them on stage. In 1968, following performances in several 'off Broadway' venues, the musical *Hair!* opened on Broadway as, among other objectives, a conscious reaction against the increasingly technical sophistication of musical theatre on the New York stage and of current film musicals. It was conceived and written by Gerome Ragni and James Rado, who said that they were 'aware of the traditional Broadway format, but we wanted to create something new, something different, something that translated to the stage'.[3]

However, the compound effects of the new technologies of lighting control, sound recording and reproduction, and of the computer and its operating interface during the latter quarter of the century, have together made significant contributions to the quite remarkable transformation of large-scale musical spectacle in the theatre – whose effective rebirth interestingly coincided with IBM's invention of the Personal Computer during the late 1970s. Musical spectacle such as *Evita* (1978), *Cats* (1982), *Les Misérables* (1985), *The Phantom of the Opera* (1986), and *Miss Saigon* (1989) represent this rebirth. Although greatly differing in their specific applications of technologies, they share particular technology-aided qualities that became central to their dramaturgy: the automated control of the movement of scenic elements; the computer-stored and computed-controlled memory of lighting states and cues; and the carefully managed and controlled soundscape of the music and performance. These have combined to create a form of narrative dramaturgy that is propelled forwards by technical effect, and that generates an enhanced intensity of emotional experience in the theatre. But most significantly for the re-birthed success of the form, they have produced an experience that may be 'saved' and that has now become fully recoverable, and one that may therefore be replicated in other theatres and in other countries with a hitherto unheard-of fidelity. Technologies combine to facilitate an account of the production, a *modell-buch* to archive the performance, and one which has enabled the production to become a highly marketable and exportable commodity. With less reliance upon the vocal qualities of the original 'stars', star names become less important to the original success and longevity of a production, and the audience 'experience' of the original can therefore be reproduced year after year. The commodified music-theatre product may be globalized and made available in urban centres throughout the world and can take its place alongside other 'international' consumer products and experiences. Baz Kershaw notes that, 'as corporate capitalism spreads across the globe the established estate of theatre is transformed into a playground for the newly privileged, a quick stop-over site on the tourist and heritage map'.[4]

The theme and narrative of musical spectacle has traditionally relied heavily upon stories of almost 'folk-tale' simplicity: stories that rely upon traditional assumptions of right and wrong, good and evil. This fundamental simplicity of theme remains, although new and seemingly more relevant narratives and their 'high-tech' presentation seem to provide true engagement with real and sophisticated worlds: for example, with the political charisma of a South American dictator, in *Evita*; with the revolutionary rhetoric and barricades of nineteenth-century Paris, in *Les Misérables*; with the darker aspects of nineteenth-century sexuality, in *Phantom of the Opera*; with the intercultural issues of contemporary war in East Asia, in *Miss Saigon*; or with the sophisticated perceptions of a great poet's response to the feline world, in *Cats*. Furthermore, the capability of new technologies has enabled the theatre to focus more precisely upon the emotional 'experience' at the very centre of these narratives. The ability of the computerized theatre, as a newly endowed *Gesamtkunstwerk*, to operate with such intensity on this emotional level has generated a new, popular and strikingly populist form. For example, until sophisticated computer control, the movement and mechanics of stage scenery, however skilful in operation, was apparent to the audience – scenery was lifted, pushed or pulled. New control systems, involving miniaturized hydraulics and below-stage tracking, have enabled scenes to have a far greater complexity of manoeuvres, and to return to the theatre spectacle the gasp of surprise and delight that has historically always accompanied the visual scene-change. John Napier's 'helicopter' effect in *Miss Saigon* (1989) not only created such a gasp of awe, but it became the visualization and the emblem of the entire production through the logo that appeared on posters, mugs and clothing. Similarly in *Les Misérables*, the complex integration of technological resources that enabled the construction and manoeuvre of John Napier's vast street barricade has become an emotional 'effect' that is as repeatable as a straightforward lighting or sound effect. To achieve this, the modern musical frequently requires the closure of its theatre for several weeks or even months prior to its opening so that the entire stage can be re-built to house the complex mechanisms of movement and control.

Through such means the stage musical has become a kind of 'people's masque', in that all the wonders of technology may be orchestrated within dramatic parables that, like the Stuart court Masque, celebrate the supposed tastes and desired virtues of its target spectators, in this instance, an international globalized 'tourist' audience. Similarly, like the struggle for supremacy in the control of the Masque during the early 1630s between writer Ben Jonson and scenographer Inigo Jones, the battle has frequently been engaged, in what critics during the 1980s called the 'designers' theatre', between increasingly spectacular effects and the textual plausibility and the value of dramatic incident. Loutherbourg, arguably the first to define by his practice the name 'scenographer', was greeted by a familiar press response on his first 'solo' production, *The Wonders of Derbyshire* (1779): 'As an exhibition of scenes, this surpasses anything we have ever seen: as a Pantomime we think it absolutely the most contemptible.'[5]

Technologies of light and latterly of sound have always been able to operate very successfully on a directly emotional level – colour, music etc. But digital recording and computer control have allowed a quite remarkable multi-media combination of these resources alongside those of scenic manipulation. Since human emotion and predictable responses may be quickly and repeatedly generated, musicals such as *Les Misérables* may be thought of as operating in a way like high-class theatrical courtesans carefully guiding their 'customers' through a roller-coaster sequence of intense emotional experiences, with just enough narrative (and frequently scenographic) 'foreplay' to situate the high points of emotion. As popular masques, and ironically facilitated by the latest technologies, these musicals offer pre-packaged hope and confidence in the durability of human emotion, in a world seemingly de-humanized by increasingly 'invisible' solid-state electronic technology. In this way, new technologies have therefore helped to manufacture, to maintain, and to replicate the modern, international popular musical.

But in providing the control systems to bring together complex aspects of scenography alongside live performance, new technologies have, and are having, wide-ranging effects upon and within an equally wide range of forms of theatre and new performance, and indeed have a very significant role within what Erika Fischer-Lichte has called the 're-theatricalization' process that has been such a significant artistic ambition and attitude throughout the twentieth century.[6] As we have seen, early artists such as Appia, Craig, and Meyerhold all acknowledged the theatrical eloquence contained within the interaction of light and sound, and within the movement of scene. The work of Svoboda has illustrated ways in which the beam of light and the reflected and refracted projected image could acquire a material reality and substance in performance. The ability that more recent computer technologies have of being able to programme precisely controllable movement to light, sound and scene has done much to enable scenography to explore its own vocabulary and, through the duration of movement, to become a performer within performance.

In so doing, new technologies and their scenographic applications have participated significantly in the generation of a new 'poetics' of performance that has in turn enabled new forms and new paradigms of what has been called postdramatic theatre. 'Postdramatic'[7] is a useful term that embraces a wide range of contemporary performance practice and is generally used to refer to works that have been created from the perceptual elements and materials of theatre and which serve their own artistic purposes, not primarily those of the structuring device of pre-existing dramatic texts. As the examination of the ambitions of modernist theatre artists in earlier chapters has indicated, the achievement of such a postdramatic state in performance has been very much a unifying feature throughout the last century. The desire to explore a theatre practice that transcends the interpretation of dramatic literature links the ambitions of Craig, Appia, Meyerhold and Grotowski. Towards the end of the twentieth century, new technologies provided an additional impetus to the exploration of new postdramatic performance forms. At one postdramatic extreme may be the non-interpreted happening, what Michael Kirby called 'non-matrixed performance';[8] in other words a performance or an event that is presentational rather than representational. At another extreme are the complex performance structures of theatre makers such as Robert Wilson, Tadeusz Kantor and Heiner Müller, who might be thought of as representing a first wave of postdramatic theatre, whilst groups and artists such as the Wooster Group, Jan Fabre, Jan Lauwers and the Needcompany, and Forced Entertainment became dominant during the late 1980s and 1990s. Together these artists, and the attitudes they represent, may be thought of as what Christopher Balme called 'the main protagonists of postdramatic theatre'.[9]

The performances made by these artists have rightly challenged definitions of theatre and have frequently occupied and straddled the boundaries between performance art, installation and theatre. Technologically sophisticated and evocative uses of sound, film and video have been introduced into contemporary theatre and the work frequently relies upon the 'density' and focused precision of image within a multi-framed performance. Robert Wilson builds his work from visual imagery that begins as a storyboard series of sketches, to which are added, through collaboration in workshops, movement, costumes, words and music. The result is not a dramatic text or musical score, but a 'visual book' from which the entire production – the performance text – is built, in which, in many instances, the individual scene has the quality of a living painting. Although there are important distinctions and individual differences, theatre pieces by Wilson, the Wooster Group and Forced Entertainment are constructed as assemblages of juxtaposed elements using found materials, films and videos, dance and movement, and multi-track scoring. In many pieces there has been an architectonic approach to scene design where the physical boundaries between performer space and audience space, and between actor and spectator have shifted and blurred, or where performance and spectatorial space have been contiguous. The recorded and televised image with its potential for dislocating the real time of performance has been a significant feature of several artists, and is especially apparent in the work of the Wooster Group. The cross-disciplinary conceptual work of artists such as Jan Fabre quite rightly defies formal categorization: theatre and its components of spectacle, space, audience and duration may feature significantly, but then again, they may not. For artists such as Fabre, the concept and its resonance may pick and choose in order to make performance from amongst the totality of artistic resources available. Overall, however, the work of these artists favours, as Balme suggests, 'the visual image over the written word, collage and montage instead of linear structure, a reliance on metonymic rather than metaphoric representation, and a redefinition of the performer's function in terms of being and materiality rather than appearance and mimetic imitation'.[10]

The storyboards of Robert Wilson[11] indicate the enduring power of traditional graphic representation. Nevertheless, the most apparent application of computing technology within theatre and performance has, in general terms, been the power of control. During the late 1990s, this quality of control has extended into the rehearsal space and the studio and has begun to have an impact upon traditional practices within theatre-making. Scenographers have begun to re-evaluate the 'control' that they might have over the future 'world' that they and their collaborators plan. Virtual modelling within a computer environment greatly facilitates the preparatory work processes, which involve trying to integrate two-dimensional, three-dimensional and time-based elements. The traditional approach to scene design, which involves graphic representation through sketching and then working physically in balsa wood and painted card, first requires the building of a model of the theatre, studio or site of performance as an empty space in which to locate the modelled scenography. The contemplation of this modelled empty space can, of course, form a very significant part of the process – the projection of the mind, as has been suggested in the work practice of Svoboda, into the as yet unarticulated scenic space.

This way of working may, of course, be transposed into the computer model. However, the fundamental lack of substance of the virtual model may also encourage the starting point of thought to be made anywhere within a potential combination of scenographic elements. A scenographer might choose to begin, for example, by conceiving of an interaction of a state of lighting accompanying some sounds within a dim, undefined quality of space that has no distinct physical parameters. This would be a perfectly reasonable sceno-graphic proposition, but one that would be practically impossible to create in advance in the design studio using traditional design prac-tice, in which an intuitive act of self-censorship by the scenographer might tend to reject such ideas or to leave them undeveloped. The computer, however, enables an advance simulation of precisely such scenographic interactions to be modelled, developed and previewed. Alongside this virtual modelling, and with a previously unachiev-able opportunity for artistic collaboration, the lighting designer can experiment and communicate ideas that traditionally had to wait until the lighting rehearsals a few days before performance, or to rely upon language and almost inevitably inadequate notes and sketches. The final effects of projected static or moving imagery, which have been notoriously difficult to predict, may be evaluated alongside all other aspects of the scenography. Within the computer also, costume designs may be digitally pasted onto photographs of the performer, and the effects and combinations considered as different swatches of fabrics and textures are similarly applied.

As the desire to utilize every conceivable aspect of the scenographic landscape has grown, and the concomitant technologies and work-shop skills became more complex and sophisticated, the twentieth century saw an enlargement and a gradual fragmentation of the scenographic team; from the work of one or two artists at the begin-ning to the large team of individual scenographers who would be credited for a production in a major theatre towards the close of the century. The controlling capabilities of the computer are providing the opportunity to re-integrate the work of this fragmented team, sharing ideas with other scenographers and, of course, directors and performers. In this way, new technologies offer significant opportunities for creating performance strategies that employ the entire vocabulary of theatrical resources within both dramatic and post-dramatic performance.

The computer-modelled, virtual environment and its images may extend beyond their important contribution within the preparatory and performance-planning process. The computer-generated image may, through its interface with the data projector, be projected onto stage surfaces with considerably more control and accuracy than by using a photographic diapositive or filmed imagery. Modulation, processing and movement may be added, and might create hitherto unattainable scenic effects. Three-dimensional, instantly changeable projected scenery and stereoscopic images may be modelled and, with live off-scene operators, may become dramatically involved and integrated in real time within the performance. Mark Reaney of the University of Kansas has pioneered the development of computer-created stereoscopic scenes in a range of performance – including the ass-like head of Bottom in *A Midsummer Night's Dream* that responded to the other performers as it literally floated over their heads.[12] The possibilities for the creation and manipulation of the stage image that the computer provides is becoming, essentially, a new source of spectacle that may well prove to be analogous to the Renaissance discovery of the perspective scene. The Renaissance framed its theatre within the proscenium arch, which multiplied its effects until the late nineteenth-century darkness of the theatre of Wagner in order, as Maaike Bleeker suggests, 'to support the illusion of detached spectatorship for which perspective is a conceptual metaphor'.[13] The contributions of computer-controlled technology and computer-created scenography offer metaphors of transience, instability, multiple framing and interactivity to a postdramatic world of performance.

But important though these recent technologies of light, sound and computing have been and are within a consideration of scenography, they do not, of course, exist within a self-sustaining continuum of development and change. As with the earlier historical consideration, these newer manifestations must be located alongside and within the context of the broader implications of postdramatic theatre, which suggest that fundamental and far-reaching cultural transitions are being reflected in the changes that are taking place throughout theatre and performance. Baz Kershaw argues:

Simultaneously, the mediatisation of society disperses the theatrical by inserting performance into everyday life – every time we tune into the media we are confronted by the representational styles of a performative world ... post-modernity signals an acute destabilisation of the cultural climate throughout the world: an end to all the human certainties of the modernist past.[14]

In *The Radical in Performance* (1999), Kershaw proposed the usefulness of locating contemporary theatre and performance on the cusp of what he called a 'paradigm shift': that is, a shift from the traditions of (modernist) building-based theatre production towards a pluralistic (post-modern) activity focused upon performance. The preceding chapters have primarily been concerned with the examination of an early twentieth-century rejection of past stage forms and aesthetics, and consequent attempts to build new theatres and to develop new scenographic forms. These attempts have generally been based upon redefinitions of the role and purpose of the scenographic machine, a more thorough integration of scenography and its technologies within the architecture of theatre, and an exploration of the opportunities provided by new technologies of stage lighting and sound reproduction. They have, at times, looked for inspiration to the past and to primitive anthropological understandings and models, and at other times they have pursued 'human certainties' in attempts to analyse and define essential qualities of human perception within which a new, more universally accepted art might be created. With few exceptions, they have all shared a humanistic and essentially modernist belief in the possibility of creating universal forms of theatre and performance, and moreover, scientific discovery and the new technologies of the century have been seen as available to achieve this.

The devastation of Europe by the First World War encouraged the modernist agenda of a 'clean sweep' with the past during the early 1920s, but the rapid spread of fascism and totalitarian politics throughout the late 1920s and 1930s, the subsequent Nazi Holocaust, the tragic absurdities of state totalitarianism in communist countries, the unthinkable enormity of nuclear conflict, and the more recent post-colonial nationalisms of the liberated and newly free have combined to unseat any future certainty to which the spirit of modernism might aspire. The final decades of the twentieth century certainly left little space for the aspiration to make art that could claim a rational basis within some potentially universal structure of human understanding. Perhaps only the commodification of the

Western musical-theatre spectacle might illustrate, ironically, that this modernist optimism has achieved some international fulfilment within the process of capitalist globalization.

The shifting of the paradigm from one of theatre to one of performance that occurred over the last twenty or so years of the twentieth century, has involved a movement away from a culture of theatre based within an architecture that was designed and called a 'theatre'. This paradigm is that of a building-based company of theatre artists who operated within an artistic hierarchy at whose pinnacle was a writer of plays, whose words were mediated through a director–interpreter of plays and on to a company of actors supported by a team of scenic and technical artists and artisans who realized a theatrical presentation of the play. It was a theatre that laid a claim to a universal audience, to making theatres and theatre companies that were representative of an entire city or town, to being a 'theatre for everyone'. It was, in fact, an image of theatre that had slowly developed ever since the theatre ceased to be primarily one of occasion and celebration during the medieval period, and became one of urban institution and commerce during the late sixteenth century. The dominance of this functioning of theatre has undergone a marked shift towards a paradigm that presents significant oppositions to this institutional model. The paradigm of 'performance' resists the clarity of rules, foundation and universality that modernism sought, and therefore it is a model that defies the attempt to articulate post-modern theatre and performance as a particular form. In practice the performed event has achieved a primacy of interest. But it is an event that may, or may not, achieve performance in a theatre building, or even clearly offer a bifurcated space for performers and spectators, and it may, or may not, be the result of the interpretation of a dramatic text; indeed, its 'text' may lie outside verbal language. Consequently the concern for the establishment of an ordered hierarchy (either in terms of artistic personnel, or in terms of the artistic role of individual component parts within a performance) no longer has the priority it once had. Performance may have no subject matter other than that of its status as an event; performance may arise from any source material – it may, or most likely will not employ dramatic literature – hence 'postdramatic' is in many ways a more useful term than 'post-modern'. The site of performance is no longer predicated upon a formal architecture that spatially determines the proper place for actors and for audience. The 'making of a performance' has become a significantly different activity from that of 'directing a play' and has required new practices, new technologies and a new stagecraft. Whilst the paradigm of performance does not reject or abandon the paradigm of theatre, the 'theatre' remains as just one kind, a sub-set, of performance. As Richard Schechner provocatively said in 1992:

> The fact is that theatre as we have known and practised it – the staging of written dramas – will be the string quartet of the twenty-first century: a beloved but extremely limited genre, a subdivision of performance.[15]

The re-location of theatre to this 'off-centre' position may well indicate that what I have called Craig's 1907 'agenda' from his 'Actor and the Über-Marionette' essay may be reflected in the shift of paradigm almost a century later: 'Today they *impersonate* and interpret; tomorrow they must *represent* and interpret; and the third day they must create. By this means style may return.'[16] In Hans-Thies Lehmann's account of postdramatic theatre, he considers the framing of the world that the earlier paradigm presented:

> The dramatic theatre, in which the scene stands for the world, can be compared to perspective: space here is both technically and mentally a window and a symbol, analogous to the reality 'behind'. Like the *finestra aperta* presented by Renaissance painting it offers what might be called an equivalent to the scale of the world, a metaphorical likeness obtained through abstraction and accentuation.[17]

As the paradigm shifts, so framing has been abandoned both literally, as proscenium, as single viewpoint and as theatre architecture, and metaphorically, as fixed spectatorial and authorial viewpoints that offer a 'scale' on the world beyond. This loss of the ordering and framing ability of perspective with its parallel and somewhat colonial conceit of providing the vantage point of a 'window on the world' that Loutherbourg sought, is being replaced by the quintessential relativism and ephemerality of contemporary performance. The dislocation and resistance to shared meaning that may be established within a specific place of performance and with particular audience reception, the vacillation 'between presence and absence, between displacement and reinstatement', as Nick Kaye argues,[18] suggest that the paradigm of theatrical performance may be structurally alien to *any* quest for certainty and stability. The consequent breaking down of the binary and the neat hierarchical relationships between page and stage, between producer/artist and consumer/audience, may be properly located alongside the parallel economic migration away from industrial manufacture with its focus on material product, to economies and industries that are predicated upon information and knowledge with a focus upon service and the customer experience. The technologies of computation that have had such significant effects upon the theory and practice of theatre, performance and scenography, and that have simultaneously both enabled and reflected the 'de-framing' and destabilization of the theatrical experience, have also been the technologies that have enabled internet access to knowledge and information and have generated an unprecedented ability to inter-relate with the world in ways that are similarly not 'framed' in colonial authority. The presentation and performance of self through the creation and 'up-loading' into the virtual theatre of a personal website, and the interaction of a performance website, have created significant alternatives to existing narrative modes, forms of representation, dramaturgies and physical places of performance. Within new dramaturgies and within these architectures of performance, the virtual actor, the avatar, may be brought into existence and may walk upon an entirely new space and within a completely re-visioned scenography of performance.

Notes

Notes to the Preface

1. Jacques Derrida, *Archive Fever* (1995), trans. Eric Prenowitz (Chicago: University of Chicago Press, 1998), p. 10. All quotations and references are from this edition.
2. Ibid., p. 55.
3. John Donne, 'A Valediction: of the booke' from *Songs and Sonnetts* (*c*.1593–1601), lines 53–4. *The Poems of John Donne*, ed. Herbert Grierson (London: Oxford University Press, 1933).
4. Derrida, *Archive Fever* (1998), p. 36.

Notes to the Introduction

1. Marvin Carlson, *Places of Performance: The Semiotics of Theatre Architecture* (Ithaca, NY: Cornell University Press, 1989), p. 38.
2. Madame (Lucia) Vestris ran the Olympic Theatre in London from 1831 until 1839. Her refinement and good taste created a considerable fashion for the extravaganzas, farces and burlesques that she produced.
3. For illustrations and discussion of these surviving theatres see Simon Tidworth, *Theatres: An Architectural and Cultural History* (New York: Praeger, 1973), and Richard and Helen Leacroft, *Theatre and Playhouse* (London: Methuen, 1984).
4. Anon., *The Case of the Stage in Ireland* (Dublin, 1758).
5. 'Even if the walls have to be of canvas, it is surely time to stop painting them with shelves and kitchen utensils. We have so many other stage conventions in which we are expected to believe that we may as well avoid overstraining our imagination by asking it to believe in painted saucepans.' August Strindberg, Preface to *Miss Julie*, trans. Michael Meyer (London: Eyre Methuen, 1976), pp. 101–2.
6. 'Every Tragedy, therefore, must have six parts, which parts determine its quality – namely, Plot, Character, Diction, Thought, Spectacle, Song.'

Francis Fergusson, *Aristotle's Poetics*, vi. 7 (New York: Hill & Wang, 1961), p. 62.

7. '[a]lmost every proper quality and convenience of a good theatre had been sacrificed, or neglected, to shew the spectator a vast triumphal piece of architecture! And that the best play ... could not but be under great disadvantages, and be less capable of delighting the auditor, here, than it could have been in the plain theatre they came from. ... This extraordinary and superfluous space occasion'd such an undulation, from the voice of every actor, that generally what they said sounded like the gabbling of so many people, in the lofty isles [sic] in a cathedral.' Colley Cibber, *An Apology for his Life* (1741) (London: J. M. Dent, 1914), p. 163.

8. 'Since the stages of Drury Lane and Covent Garden have been so enlarged in their dimensions as to be henceforward theatres for spectators rather than playhouses for hearers, it is hardly to be wondered at if managers and directors encourage those representations, to which their structure is best adapted. The splendour of the scenes, the ingenuity of the machinist and the rich display of dresses, aided by the captivating charms of music, now in a great degree supersede the labours of the poet.' Richard Cumberland, *Memoirs* (London, 1806), quoted in A. M. Nagler, *Sources of Theatrical History* (New York, 1952); reprinted as *A Source Book in Theatrical History* (New York: Dover Publications, 1959), p. 408.

9. Davy is known for his work on gases and especially for his study of nitrous oxide; Faraday is noted for his major contribution to the understanding of electromagnetism; and Maxwell for his theories that treat gases in terms of the motion of their constituent atoms and molecules and for the application of statistical mechanics to their behaviour. Their work had immediate and significant effects upon industrial development. For an account of the progressive and materialist science of the nineteenth century and its impact upon thought and philosophy, see John Gribbin, *Science, a History* (London: Allen Lane, Penguin Press, 2003).

Notes to Chapter 1: Performing Great Exhibitions

1. See Christopher Baugh, *Garrick and Loutherbourg* (Cambridge: Chadwyck-Healey, 1990).

2. See especially Edward Braun, *Meyerhold: A Revolution in Theatre*, 2nd edn (London: Methuen, 1995), pp. 27–44.

3. The Bibiena family members were probably the most influential theatre designers of the eighteenth century and included Ferdinando (1657–1743), Francesco (1659–1739), Giuseppe (1696–1757), Antonio (1700–74), and Carlo (1728–87). The Florentine painter Giovanni Battista Cipriani worked at Covent Garden Theatre in 1755, and Jean-Nicholas Servandoni (1695–1766), who spent most of his working life at the Paris

Opéra, worked in London on several occasions. For a general account of the employment of Italian artists on the London stage, see Sybil Rosenfeld, *Georgian Scene Painters and Scene Painting* (Cambridge: Cambridge University Press, 1981).

4. Undated letter by Loutherbourg to Garrick, c. March 1772, Harvard Theatre Collection, trans. by Christopher Baugh, in, ibid., pp. 123–4.

5. *The Works of Monsieur Noverre*, translated from the French (London, 1783), vol. 1, pp. 135ff. Noverre's statements on more general theatrical issues give a rarely cited source of eighteenth-century scenographic theory and serve as a significant parallel to Loutherbourg's practice in London:

How can it be expected that, so complicated a spectacle as that of the opera, will succeed if the chiefs of the various departments that constitute its very being, act without communicating their thoughts and intentions to each other?

The poet asserts his pretended superiority over the musician; the latter would think it derogatory to his dignity to consult the Ballet-master. The former will not stoop to enter into an explanation with the scene-painter who in turn only communicates to his inferiors: while the machinist whom he despises, rules despot-like over the journeymen of the opera. ...

The scene-painter, for want of being perfectly acquainted with the subjects of the drama, falls into the greatest error; never consulting with the author, he follows his own ideas; these often militate against the rules of probability which will have everything so disposed as to represent the scene of action. How can he be successful when he does not know the spot where it lies? Yet from such knowledge, and that of the subject, and from these alone, he should form his ideas, otherwise everything will be entirely out of character. ...

The person whose province it is to devise the dresses consults with no one; he often supplies the mode of dressing an ancient nation by one in the present fashion; and this only to please the whim of a female singer or dancer of some reputation ...

The business of the machinist is to place the painters' work in its proper light, according to the rules of perspective. His first care is to arrange the different parts of the decoration, in so nice an order, that they form together a complete ensemble. And his talent consists in being quick to bring forward and draw back the scenes. Now if he is not sufficiently intelligent to distribute the shades in proper order, the painters' work must lose its merit, and the effect of the decoration be destroyed. Such parts of the scenery which ought to be exposed in a strong light, look dark and black; whilst those which should be shaded and darkened are in full sight. It is not the great quantity of lamps, placed together as chance directs or even symmetry requires, that gives light to the stage and sets off the scenery. The talent consists in dividing those lights into unequal masses or parts in order to strengthen those places that want a great light, soften those that should have but little, and overlook those that require still less. ...

As the painter in order to preserve the rules of perspective, is obliged to introduce in his painting shades and lights gradually increasing and decreasing, the man whose business it is to shew them in a proper light, should, methinks, consult with the artist, that the same proportions may be preserved in the distribution of lights. Nothing can be more disagreeable to the eye than a whole scenery in one and the same colour: neither distance nor perspective can be observed. By the same rule, if the paintings, divided into parts, are placed in lights equally forcible, there will exist no distribution, no manner of proportion, and the whole scene will produce no sort of effect. (ibid., pp. 135ff)

See also Russell Thomas, 'Contemporary Taste in the Stage Decorations of London, 1770–1800', in *Modern Philology*, vol. XLII, 2 (1944).

6. There is a useful 'Directory of Victorian Scene Painters' by Hilary Norris in *Theatrephile*, vol. 1, no. 2 (March 1984), pp. 38–52. Their work is contextualized in Sybil Rosenfeld, *A Short History of Scene Design in Great Britain* (Oxford: Blackwell, 1973), pp. 103–10.

7. The Swiss chemist Aimé Argand (1755–1803) developed the principle of using a hollow circular wick surrounded by a glass chimney. The burning circumference of such a wick effectively more than trebled the output of light compared with a similarly sized flat ribbon wick. The glass chimney steadied the flame and provided an up-draft that further intensified the light.

8. William Henry Pyne, *Wine and Walnuts* (London, 1823), p. 296.

9. See Max Grube, *The Story of the Meininger*, ed. Wendell Cole (Coral Gables, FL: University of Miami Press, 1963).

10. For a general account of Charles Kean's management and production values at the Princess's Theatre, see Michael R. Booth, *Theatre in the Victorian Age*, Cambridge: Cambridge University Press, 1991, and his *Victorian Spectacular Theatre, 1850–1910* (London: Oxford University Press, 1981).

11. Belief in 'realization' is a dominant mode of the century. It is well examined in Martin Meisel, *Realizations: Narrative, Pictorial and Theatrical Arts in Nineteenth-Century England* (Princeton, NJ: Princeton University Press, 1983).

12. Michael Bell, 'The Metaphysics of Modernism', in *The Cambridge Companion to Modernism*, ed. Michael Levenson (Cambridge: Cambridge University Press, 1999), p. 11.

13. William Bodham Donne, *Essays on the Drama* (London, 1858), p. 206.

14. 'Herr Wagner's New Theatre at Bayreuth', in *The Practical Magazine*, July 1874, p. 8.

15. Geoffrey Skelton, *Wagner at Bayreuth* (London, 1965), p. 45.

16. Percy Fitzgerald, *The World Behind the Scenes* (London, 1881), pp. 20–1.

17. Ibid., p. 8.

18. Jean-Pierre Moynet, *L'Envers du théâtre: machines et décorations* (Paris, 1873), p. 147.

19. Fitzgerald, *World Behind the Scenes*, p. 6.
20. *Westminster Review*, February 1891, p. 279.
21. John Stokes, *Resistible Theatre: Enterprise and Experiment in the Late Nineteenth Century* (London: Paul Elek, 1972), pp. 115–16.
22. Emile Zola, *Le Naturalisme au théâtre* (1880), trans. Albert Bermel, in *Contradictory Characters: An Interpretation of the Modern Theatre* (London: University Press of America, 1984).

Notes to Chapter 2: Rejection of the Past

1. Christopher Innes, *Avant Garde Theatre, 1892–1992* (London: Routledge, 1993), p. 1.
2. Michael Levenson, 'Introduction', in *The Cambridge Companion to Modernism*, ed. Michael Bell, Michael Levenson (Cambridge: Cambridge University Press, 1999), p. 1.
3. 'The Metaphysics of Modernism', in Michael Levenson (ed.), *Cambridge Companion* (1999), p. 12.
4. Rückblick, Berlin, 1913, trans. William Seitz, in *Claude Monet: Seasons and Moments* (New York: Museum of Modern Art, 1960), p. 25.
5. J. J. Thomson, lecture to the Royal Institution, 30 April 1897, cited in John Gribbin, *Science: A History* (London: Allen Lane, Penguin Press, 2003), p. 491.
6. Notwithstanding the dominant mode of rejection during the twentieth century, it is only within the last two decades of the century that life-class has, generally, ceased to be compulsory within the academy.
7. During the period of the Boer War (1899–1902) most cities in Europe equipped themselves with electric tramways.
8. In Virginia Woolf, *Collected Essays*, vol. 1 (New York: Harcourt Brace and World, 1967), p. 320.
9. From Franz Marc, 'Two Pictures', cited in *Art in Theory, 1900–1990*, ed. Charles Harrison and Paul Wood (Oxford: Blackwell, 1992), pp. 99–100.
10. See his *Über das Geistige in der Kunst* (Concerning the Spiritual in Art) (Munich: Piper Verlag, 1912), cited in ibid., p. 88.
11. Denis Bablet, *Les révolutions scéniques du XXe Siècle* (Paris: Société Internationale d'Art XXe, 1975), p. 11.
12. Edward Gordon Craig, Foreword to the exhibition of his work by Manchester City Art Gallery, 1912.
13. Meyerhold claimed that 'meiningenitis' was a disease afflicting the entire established theatre.
14. V. E. Meyerhold, 'The Naturalistic Theatre and the Theatre of Mood', in *Teatr, kniga o novom teatre* (Theatre, a Book on the New Theatre) (St Petersburg: Shipovnik, 1908), reprinted in Meyerhold's

O teatre (Petersburg, 1913), cited in Edward Braun, *Meyerhold on Theatre* (London: Methuen, 1969), p. 23.

15. Konstantin Stanislavski, *My Life in Art* (New York, 1924; London: Folio Society, 2000), p. 326.

16. Baz Kershaw, *The Radical in Performance: Between Brecht and Baudrillard* (London: Routledge, 1999), p. 6.

Notes to Chapter 3: The Scene as Machine, Part 1

1. Edward Gordon Craig, *On the Art of the Theatre* (London: Heinemann, 1911; reprint, Mercury Books, 1962), p. viii.

2. Edward Gordon Craig, *Index to the Story of My Days* (London: Hulton Press, 1957), p. 297.

3. King's Patent Agency served as an approved interface between inventors and the Patent Office, providing legal and technical advice on the nature of submissions.

4. Edward Gordon Craig, *Scene* (London: Humphrey Milford and Oxford University Press, 1923), p. 1

5. Ibid., p. 25.

6. Edward Gordon Craig, 'The Actor and the Über-Marionette' (1907), in *On the Art of the Theatre* (1911) (London: Mercury Books, 1962), p. 61.

7. 'Cézanne', by Maurice Denis (1907), trans. Roger Fry, in *Burlington Magazine*, XVI, London (Jan.–Feb. 1910, cited in *Art in Theory, 1900–1990*, ed. Charles Harrison and Paul Wood (Oxford: Blackwell, 1992), p. 45.

8. Ibid., p. 75.

9. Edward Gordon Craig, *Daybook 1*, 3 February 1909, p. 77, Archive in the Humanities Research Center, University of Texas at Austin.

10. Konstantin Stanislavski, *My Life in Art* (London: Geoffrey Bles, 1924; 5th edn, 1948), p. 511.

11. Ibid., p. 519.

12. Ibid., pp. 523–4.

13. See the account in Laurence Senelick, *Gordon Craig's* Hamlet – *a Reconstruction* (Westport, CT; London: Greenwood Press, 1982).

14. Edward Gordon Craig, *Towards a New Theatre* (London: J. M. Dent, 1913), p. 6.

15. See especially Richard Schechner, *Performance Theory* (London: Routledge, 1988), and Richard Schechner and Willa Appel (eds), *By Means of Performance* (Cambridge: Cambridge University Press, 1990), and the overall approach of Erika Fischer-Lichte, *History of European Drama and Theatre*, trans. Jo Riley (London: Routledge, 2002).

16. Edward Gordon Craig, 'Proposals Old and New', in his *The Theatre Advancing* (London: Constable, 1921), pp. 93–4.

17. Simonson's chapter 'Day-Dreams: the Case of Gordon Craig', in *The Stage is Set* (New York: Harcourt Brace, 1932; reprint, Theatre Arts Books, 1975), pp. 309–50, typifies much of the passion and animosity that Craig has inspired in the more pragmatic theatre artist.
18. Adolphe Appia, 'Concerning the Costume for Eurhythmics', cited in Richard C. Beacham, *Adolphe Appia: Artist and Visionary of the Modern Theatre* (London: Harwood Academic Press, 1994), p. 133.

Notes to Chapter 4: The Scene as Machine, Part 2

1. Alexei Gvozdev, *Teatr imeni Vs Meyerholds* (1920–6) (Leningrad, 1927), p. 28, cited in Edward Braun, *Meyerhold on Theatre* (London: Methuen, 1969), p. 185.
2. 'The Actor of the Future and Biomechanics', report of Meyerhold's lecture, Moscow Conservatoire, 12 June 1922, in *Ermitazh*, Moscow, 1922, no. 6, cited in Braun, *Meyerhold on Theatre*, pp. 198–9.
3. Vsevelod Meyerhold, 'The Naturalistic Theatre and the Theatre of Mood', in *Teatr, kniga o novom teatre* (*Theatre: A Book on the New Theatre*) (St Petersburg: Shipovnik, 1908), reprinted in Meyerhold's *O teatre* (Petersburg, 1913), cited in Braun, *Meyerhold on Theatre*, p. 42.
4. Marjorie L. Hoover, *Meyerhold and his Set Designers* (New York: Peter Lang, 1988), p. 15, citing Meyerhold, *Zolotoe runo*, no. 5 (1907).
5. Ibid., p. 46.
6. Ibid., pp. 66–7.
7. Ibid., p. 23, citing Konstantin Rudnitsky, 'V teatre na Ofitserskoi', in *Tvorcheskoe nasledie V. E. Meierkhol'da*, ed. Vendrovskaia and A. V. Fevral'skii (Moscow: Vserossiiskoe teatral'noe obshchestvo, 1978), p. 149.
8. Jane Milling and Graham Ley, *Modern Theories of the Stage* (Basingstoke: Palgrave Macmillan, 2001), p. 63.
9. Letter from Meyerhold to Golovin, 30 May 1909, in *Alexander Yakov-levich Golovin* (Leningrad and Moscow, 1960), pp. 159–60, cited in Braun, *Meyerhold on Theatre*, p. 104.
10. Ibid., pp. 100–1.
11. Ibid., pp. 126–7.
12. *Vestnik teatra* (the *Theatre Herald*), no. 72–3 (1920), p. 10, in ibid., p. 173.
13. Cited and described in detail in Hoover, *Meyerhold and his Set Designers*, p. 126.
14. Braun, *Meyerhold on Theatre*, p. 233.
15. All three have worked, or work, as both director and designer. However, in the case of Robert Lepage the phrase 'maker of theatre works' would be more appropriate.

16. Christopher Baugh, 'Brecht and Stage Design, the *Bühnenbildner* and the *Bühnenbauer*', in Peter Thomson and Glendyr Sacks (eds), *The Cambridge Companion to Brecht* (Cambridge: Cambridge University Press, 1994), p. 235.

17. Neher to Brecht, *c*.1951, quoted in John Willett, *Caspar Neher, Brecht's Designer* (London: Methuen, 1986), p. 75. This is the only critical biography in English and although short, its catalogue format (Arts Council Touring Exhibition, 1986) permits it to offer a great deal of basic and reliable information about Neher's ideas and practice.

18. Bertolt Brecht, *Gesammelte Werke* (Frankfurt: Suhrkamp, 1967), vol. 15, pp. 442–3, translated by Juliette Prodhan and Christopher Baugh.

19. Ibid., pp. 443–4.

20. Cited in Willett, *Caspar Neher, Brecht's Designer*, pp. 109–11.

21. Bertolt Brecht, *Courage-Modell 1949* (Berlin: Henschel Verlag, 1958), trans. Eric Bentley and Hugo Schmidt, reprinted in *Encore*, vol. 12, no. 3 (May–June 1965), p. 5.

22. Kenneth Tynan, *Tynan on Theatre* (Harmondsworth: Pelican, 1964), p. 241.

Notes to Chapter 5: The Scene as Machine, Part 3

1. Rose-Marie Moudouès, 'Jacques Rouché et Edward Gordon Craig', *Revue de la Société de l'Histoire du Théâtre*, III (1958), pp. 313–19, cited in Denis Bablet, *The Theatre of Gordon Craig*, trans. Daphne Woodward (London: Eyre Methuen, 1966), p. 123.

2. Jarka M. Burian, 'Josef Svoboda's Scenography for the National Theatre's *Faust*: Postmodern or Merely Contemporary', in *Space and the Postmodern Stage*, ed. Irene Eynat-Confino and Eva Šormová (Prague: Regula Pragensis, 2000).

3. Ruggero Bianchi, 'Ob/scene vs Catastrophe', in Olga Chtiguel, 'Teorie a praxe postmodernismu', *Svět a Divadlo*, no. 3 (1990), p. 101.

4. In discussion with the author at Svoboda's home in Prague, November 1999, and referred to in Jarka M. Burian, *The Scenography of Josef Svoboda* (Middletown, CT: Wesleyan University Press, 1971), pp. 18–19.

5. See especially Otomar Krejča, *Zprávy Divadelního Ústava* (*News from the Theatre Institute* [Prague]), no. 8 (1967), p. 26.

6. Cited in Burian, *Scenography of Josef Svoboda*, p. 18.

Notes to Chapter 6: The Century of Light, Part 1

1. Gösta Bergman, *Lighting in the Theatre* (Stockholm: Almqvist & Wiksell, 1977), p. 297.

2. C. Reynaud, *Rapport sur la Mise en Scène (Machinerie et Eclairage) des Théâtres de Londres* (Paris: Bibl. de l'Opéra, 1893), p. 19.
3. Bergman, *Lighting in the Theatre*, p. 302.
4. Described in considerable detail in ibid., p. 292.
5. Ibid., p. 315.
6. Quoted in John Stokes, *Resistible Theatre: Enterprise and Experiment in the Late Nineteenth Century* (London: Paul Elek, 1972), pp. 94–5.
7. Adolphe Appia, *Music and the Art of the Theatre*, ed. Barnard Hewitt, trans. Robert W. Corrigan and Mary Douglas Dirks (Coral Gables, FL: University of Miami Press, 1962), p. 22.
8. Adolphe Appia, 'Theatrical Experiences and Personal Investigations', in Richard C. Beacham, *Adolphe Appia: Artist and Visionary of the Modern Theatre* (London: Harwood Academic Press, 1994), p. 7.
9. Appia, *Music and the Art of the Theatre* p. xi.
10. Richard C. Beacham, *Adolphe Appia: Artist and Visionary of the Modern Theatre* (London: Harwood Academic, 1994), p. 9.
11. Appia, *Music and the Art of the Theatre*, p. 118.
12. Ibid., p. 23.
13. Ibid., p. 62.
14. Ibid., p. 24.
15. Ibid., p. 17.
16. Ibid., p. 26.
17. Edward Gordon Craig, 'The Actor and the Über-Marionette', in *On the Art of the Theatre* (London: Heinemann, 1911; reprint Mercury Books, 1962), p. 61.
18. In *La Revue des Revues*, vol. 1, no. 9 (May 1904), cited in Richard Drain (ed.), *Twentieth-Century Theatre* (London: Routledge, 1995), p. 237.
19. Appia, *Music and the Art of the Theatre*, pp. 3–4.
20 Ibid., p. 74.
21 Ibid., p. 67.
22. There is no study of the theatre work of Mariano Fortuny in English. In Italian, two exhibition catalogues consider and illustrate a selection of Fortuny's theatre designs: *Immagini e Materiali del Laboratorio Fortuny* (Venice: Marsilio Editori, 1978), and *Mariano Fortuny* (Venice: Marsilio, 1999).
23. C. Harold Ridge, *Stage Lighting* (Cambridge: Heffer & Sons, 1928), pp. 109–10.
24. *Mariano Fortuny* (1999), pp. 230–3, illustrates the pages from Fortuny's *Théâtre Lumière* of c.1908 that clearly show the technologies that he proposed.
25. Cited in Beacham, *Adolphe Appia*, p. 93.
26 Ibid., p. 94.
27. Alan Dent, *Bernard Shaw and Mrs Patrick Campbell: Their Correspondence* (New York: 1952), pp. 137–9.

28. Kenneth MacGowan and Robert Edmund Jones, *Continental Stagecraft* (New York, 1922; London: Benn Bros, 1923), p. 68.
29. Ridge, *Stage Lighting*, pp. 80–1.
30. Fred Bentham, *Sixty Years of Light Work* (London: Strand Lighting, 1992), p. 55.
31. Ibid., p. 87.
32. Ibid., pp. 76–7.
33. John Rudlin, *Jacques Copeau* (Cambridge: Cambridge University Press, 1986), p. 68.
34. David Belasco, *The Theatre Through its Stage Door* (New York and London, 1919), p. 56.
35. Louis Hartmann, *Theatre Lighting* (New York and London, 1930), p. 26.

Notes to Chapter 7: The Century of Light, Part 2

1. Josef Svoboda, *The Secrets of Theatrical Space*, ed. and trans. Jarka Burian (Tonbridge: Applause, 1993), p. 6.
2. 'Notes sur la *mise en scène* de l'anneau du Nibeling', in *Revue d'histoire du Théâtre*, 1–11 (1954), p. 46ff, cited in Bergman, *Lighting in the Theatre* (Stockholm: Almquist & Wiksell, 1977), p. 326.
3. Wassily Kandinsky, 'Concerning the Spiritual in Art' (*Über das Geistige in der Kunst*) (Munich: Piper Verlag, 1912), extensively quoted in C. Harrison and P. Wood, *Art in Theory, 1900–1990* (Oxford: Blackwell, 1992), pp. 86–94. 'On Stage Compositions' (*Über Bühnenkomposition*) in *Der blaue Reiter Almanac* (Munich: Piper Verlag, 1912), cited in Bergman, *Lighting in the Theatre*, p. 319.
4. Cited in Bergman, *Lighting in the Theatre*, p. 320.
5. Walther Gropius, in *The Theater of the Bauhaus*, ed. Walther Gropius and Arthur S. Wensinger (Baltimore: Johns Hopkins University Press, 1961), p. 7.
6. Oskar Schlemmer, 'Man and Art Figure', in ibid., pp. 28–9.
7. It is important to remember the slippery nature of such terms and the habit they possess of 'locking' the significance of an artist's work within a historical chronology. See especially Melissa Trimingham's important re-evaluation in her 'Oskar Schlemmer's Research Practice at the Dessau Bauhaus', in *Theatre Research International*, vol. 29, no. 2 (2004), pp. 128–42.
8. László Moholy-Nagy, 'Theater, Circus, Variety – 5. The Means', in Gropius and Wensinger, *Theatre of the Bauhaus*, p. 67.
9. Sybil Moholy-Nagy, *László Moholy-Nagy, Ein Total-experiment* (Mainz-Berlin, 1972), p. 30, cited in Norbert M. Schmitz, 'László Moholy-Nagy', in *Bauhaus*, ed. Jeannine Fiedler and Peter Feierabend (Cologne: Könemann, 1999), p. 295.

10. Moholy-Nagy, 'Theater, Circus, Variety – 5. The Means', p. 67.
11. Ibid., p. 67.
12. 'Fotogram und Grenzgebeite' (Photogram and Related Areas), in *Die Form*, IV (1929), cited in Jeannine Fiedler and Peter Feierabend (eds), *Bauhaus* (Cologne: Konemann, 1999), p. 299.
13. Edward Gordon Craig, *Scene* (London: Humphrey Milford, Oxford University Press, 1923), p. 25.
14. Rose-Marie Moudouès, Mouduès, 'Jacques Rouché et Edward Gordon Craig', in *Revue de la Société de l'Histoire du Théâtre*, III (1958), p. 313.
15. Oskar Schlemmer, 'Theater (Bühne)', in Gropius and Wensinger, *Theatre of the Bauhaus*, p. 96.
16. Craig, *Scene* (1923), p. 20.
17. Bergman, *Lighting in the Theatre*, p. 338.
18. Svoboda, *Secrets of Theatrical Space*, p. 17.
19. Gropius and Wensinger, *Theatre of the Bauhaus*, p. 12.
20. C. Harold Ridge, *Stage Lighting* (Cambridge: Heffer & Sons, 1928), pp. 58–9.
21. Ibid., p. 60.
22. Walter René Fuerst and Samuel J. Hume, *Twentieth-Century Stage Decoration*, 2 vols (New York: Alfred A. Knopf, 1929; reprint, Dover Publications, 1967), vol. 1, p. 113.
23. Ibid., p. 114.
24. Ibid., p. 108.
25. Fred Bentham, *Sixty Years of Light Work* (London: Strand Lighting, 1992), p. 111.
26. Josef Svoboda, *The Secrets of Theatrical Space*, ed. and trans. Jarka Burian (Tonbridge: Applause, 1993), p. 52.
27. Ibid., p. 20.
28. Ibid., p. 18.
29. Ibid., p. 17.
30. Ibid., p. 57.
31. Ibid., p. 82.
32. In discussion with the author at Svoboda's home in Prague, November 1999.
33. Ibid., p. 20.

Notes to Chapter 8: The Scene as the Architecture of Performance

1. *Daybook I*, p. 77, 3 February 1909, p. 123, Humanities Research Center, University of Texas at Austin.
2. Gay McAuley, *Space in Performance* (Ann Arbor: University of Michigan Press, 1999), p. 5.

3. Andrew Todd and Jean-Guy Lecat, *The Open Circle: Peter Brook's Theatre Environments* (London: Faber & Faber, 2003), p. 52.
4. Edward Gordon Craig, *Scene* (London: Humphrey Milford, Oxford University Press, 1923), p. 3.
5. Ibid., pp. 4–5.
6. Edward Gordon Craig, *Index to the Story of my Days* (London: Hulton, 1957), pp. 298–9.
7. In the possession of the V&A Theatre Museum, London.
8. Cited in John Rudlin, *Jacques Copeau* (Cambridge: Cambridge University Press, 1986), p. 51.
9. Ibid., p. 55.
10. Richard Allen Cave, *Terence Gray and the Cambridge Festival Theatre* (Cambridge: Chadwyck-Healey, 1980), p. 12.
11. Ibid., p. 64.
12. Cited in Richard Schechner, 'Six Axioms for Environmental Theatre' (1968), in *The Drama Review: Thirty Years of the Avant-Garde*, ed. Brooks McNamara and Jill Dolan (Ann Arbor: University of Michigan Research Press, 1986), p. 169.
13. Cave, *Terence Gray*, p. 17.
14. Cited by Norman Marshall, in *The Other Theatre* (London: John Lehmann, 1947), p. 64.
15. Cited in ibid., p. 54.
16. K. MacGowan and R. Edmond Jones, *Continental Stagecraft* (New York, 1922; London, 1923), p. 142.
17. Cited in Marshall, *The Other Theatre*, p. 60.
18. Ibid., p. 66.
19. Cited in ibid., p. 68.
20. Walter Gropius and Arthur S. Wensinger, *The Theatre of the Bauhaus* (Baltimore: Johns Hopkins University Press, 1961), p. 1.
21. Ibid., p. 12.
22. Ibid., pp. 12–14.
23. Published in *Rekonstuktsia teatra* (Leningrad–Moscow, 1930), cited in Edward Braun, *Meyerhold on Theatre* (London: Methuen, 1969), p. 257.
24. *Shelter-Magazine*, May 1932, cited in Richard Schechner, 'Six Axioms for Environmental Theatre', p. 160.
25. *Architectural Record*, May 1930, in ibid., p. 160.
26. See especially, Iain Mackintosh, *Architecture, Actor and Audience* (London: Routledge, 1993).
27. This argument is persuasively presented by Mackintosh in his chapter 'Architects, Engineers and the Multi-purpose', in *Architecture, Actor and Audience*.
28. These most notably are the designs for Act 2 of Gluck's *Orpheus* for the eurhythmic performances staged during the festival at Hellerau in 1912.

29. Taken from the extensive extracts of Appia's writings in Richard C. Beacham, *Adolphe Appia: Artist and Visionary of the Modern Theatre* (London: Harwood Academic Press, 1994), pp. 272–3.
30. Ibid., p. 272.
31. Ibid., p. 274.
32. Richard Schechner, 'Six Axioms for Environmental Theatre', p. 151.
33. *Drama Review*, 15: 4 (Fall 1971), cited in David Williams (ed.), *Collaborative Theatre: The Théâtre du Soleil Sourcebook* (London: Routledge, 1999), p. 3.
34. 'Guy-Claude François: A chaque spectacle sa scénographie', in *Travail Théâtral – Différent: Le Théâtre du Soleil* (Lausanne: La Cité, 1976), cited in Williams, *Collaborative Theatre*, p. 36.
35. Quoted in Anne Tremblay, 'A French Director gives Shakespeare a New Look', in *New York Times*, 10 June 1984, cited in Williams, *Collaborative Theatre*, p. 36.
36. Jerzy Grotowski, *Towards a Poor Theatre* (London: Methuen, 1969), p. 99.
37. Ibid., p. 15.
38. Andrew Todd and Jean-Guy Lecat, *The Open Circle: Peter Brook's Theatre Environments* (London: Faber & Faber, 2003), p. 33.
39. Ibid., p. 27.
40. Most thoroughly in Andrew Todd and Jean-Guy Lecat, *The Open Circle*.
41. Ibid., p. 214.
42. Ibid., p. 87.
43. Ibid., p. 6.
44. Ibid., p. 153.
45. Ibid., p. 191.
46. Ibid., p. 79.
47. Johannes de Witt visited the Swan Theatre in 1594 and made a drawing of it. On his return to the Netherlands, his friend Arend van Buchell made a copy of de Witt's drawing and it is this which survives. Our own observation can testify to van Buchell's draftsmanship, but of course we have no evidence for that of de Witt.
48. Most usefully summarized in Andrew Gurr, 'Shakespeare's Globe: a History of Reconstructions and Some Reasons for Trying', and John Orrell, 'Designing the Globe: Reading the Documents', in Ronnie Mulryne and Margaret Shewring, *Shakespeare's Globe Rebuilt* (Cambridge: Cambridge University Press, 1997).
49. Bernard Beckerman, *Shakespeare at the Globe, 1599–1609* (New York: Macmillan, 1962), p. ix.
50. Mulryne and Shewring, *Shakespeare's Globe Rebuilt*, p. 17.
51. This remains a highly contested area. There is some textual evidence from the period that supports a highly painted stage and auditorium, whilst many would agree with designer William Dudley who said: 'Theatre is

about human activity, how people interact with each other. The architecture of the theatre ought not to inhibit that interaction. The sheer diversity of productions both then and now needs a bare bones structure only', in 'Designing for Spaces' in Ronnie Mulryne and Margaret Shewring, *Making Space for Theatre: British Architecture and Theatre Since 1958* (Stratford-upon-Avon: Mulryne & Shewring, 1995), p. 98.

52. The immediate ancestry of the present reconstruction is well described in Andrew Gurr, 'Shakespeare's Globe: a History of Reconstruction', in Mulryne and Shewring, *Shakespeare's Globe Rebuilt*, pp. 27–47.
53. There is discussion of Elizabethan scenography in Martin White, *Renaissance Drama in Action* (London: Routledge, 1998), pp. 124–33.
54. For illustration and comment on the Crucible Theatre, Sheffield, and the Swan Theatre, Stratford-upon-Avon, see Ronnie Mulryne and Margaret Shewring, *Making Space for Theatre.*

Notes to Chapter 9: Some Rejections of Technology in Theatre and Performance

1. An anecdotal but important account of Bruce Smith's scenography is to be found in Dennis Castle, *Sensation Smith of Drury Lane* (London: Charles Skilton, 1994).
2. 'The Stylised Theatre' (*Teatr, kniga o novom teatre*, Petersburg, 1908), reprinted in Meyerhold's *O teatre* (Petersburg, 1913), cited in Edward Braun, *Meyerhold on Theatre* (London: Methuen, 1969), p. 59.
3. Edward Gordon Craig, *Towards a New Theatre* (London: J. M. Dent, 1913), p. 6.
4. Richard Schechner, *Theatre Quarterly*, vol. 1, no. 2 (1971), p. 62.
5. W. J. Lawrence wrote a series of articles on 'The Pioneers of Modern English Stage Mounting', in *The Magazine of Art*, 1895.
6. Gilbert Murray's translations of Greek tragedy and comedy were very important and especially his translation of Euripides' *The Bacchae* (London, 1902), of which George Bernard Shaw said in his preface to *Major Barbara* (London, 1907): 'The Euripidean verses in the second act of *Major Barbara* are not by me, nor even directly by Euripides. They are by Professor Gilbert Murray, whose English version of *The Bacchae* came into our dramatic literature with all the impulsive power of an original work.' Of importance also were: J. Vogel, *Scenen Euripideischer Tragödien in griechischen Vasengemälden: Archäologische Beiträge zur Geschichte des griechischen Dramas* (Leipzig, 1886); Margaret Bieber, *Die Denkmäler zum Theaterwesen in Altertum* (Berlin–Leipzig, 1920), and as *The History of the Greek and Roman Theater* (Princeton, 1939); and Arthur W. Pickard-Cambridge, *Dithyramb, Tragedy and Comedy*

(Oxford, 1927), which led to his definitive *The Theatre of Dionysos in Athens* (Oxford, 1946).

7. See the discussion of this in John Fuegi, 'The Zelda Syndrome: Brecht and Elizabeth Hauptmann', in Peter Thomson and Glendyr Sacks (eds), *The Cambridge Companion to Brecht* (Cambridge: Cambridge University Press, 1994), pp. 112–13.

8. Antonin Artaud, *The Theatre and its Double*, trans. Mary Richards (New York, 1958), pp. 57–8.

9. Jerzy Grotowski, *Towards a Poor Theatre* (London: Methuen, 1969), pp. 88–9.

10. Zhurnal Doktora Dappertutto, 1914, no. 4–5, cited in Braun, *Meyerhold on Theatre*, p. 148.

11. Cited in Konstantin Rudnitsky, *Russian and Soviet Theatre: Tradition and the Avant-Garde*, trans. Roxane Permar (London: Thames & Hudson, 1988), p. 24.

12. Christopher Innes, *Avant Garde Theatre, 1892–1992* (London: Routledge, 1993), pp. 16–17.

13. See Dunbar H. Ogden (ed.), 'The International Theatre Exhibition: Amsterdam, 1922, Amsterdam: Tijdschrift voor Theaterwetenschap', *TTW, 30*, vol. 8, no. 2 (1992).

14. *Wendingen, maandblad voor bouwen en sieren*, 2: 3 (March 1919), p. 3, cited by Peter Eversmann in ibid., p. 30.

15. 'Het nieuws van den dag', 26 February 1922.

16. Peter Brook, *The Empty Space* (London: MacGibbon & Kee, 1968), p. 9.

17. Jerzy Grotowski, *Towards a Poor Theatre* (London: Methuen, 1969), p. 82.

18. The author was part of the technical crew and attended the subsequent performance of Grotowski's *The Constant Prince* in the Studio of Manchester University Drama Department, 3 October 1969.

19. Grotowski, *Towards a Poor Theatre*, p. 39.

20. Ibid., p. 37.

21. Anthony Smith, *Orghast at Persepolis* (London: Eyre Methuen, 1972), pp. 107–9.

22. Andrew Todd and Jean-Guy Lecat, *The Open Circle: Peter Brook's Theatre Environments* (London: Faber & Faber, 2003), p. 47.

23. Ibid., p. 52.

24. Ibid., pp. 50–1.

25. Marvin Carlson, *The Places of Performance: The Semiotics of Theatre Architecture* (Ithaca: Cornell University Press, 1989), p. 38.

26. Mikhail Bakhtin, *Rabelais and his World* (Cambridge MA: Yale University Press, 1968), p. 224.

27. Quoted in Braun, *Meyerhold on Theatre*, p. 124.

28. Ibid., p. 126.

29. The most thorough being Kenneth and Laura Richards, *The Commedia dell'Arte: A Documentary History* (Oxford: Blackwell, 1990).

Notes to Chapter 10: New Technologies and Shifting Paradigms

1. William Henry Pyne, *Wine and Walnuts* (London, 1823), pp. 296–9.
2. See Frank Napier, *Noises Off: A Handbook of Sound Effects* (London: Frederick Muller, 1936).
3. www.geocities.com/hairpages/hairhistory.html
4. Baz Kershaw, *The Radical in Performance: Between Brecht and Baudrillard* (London: Routledge, 1999), p. 5.
5. *Westminster Magazine*, 7–9 January 1779.
6. Erika Fischer-Lichte, *The Show and the Gaze of Theatre: A European Perspective* (Iowa City: University of Iowa Press, 1997), p. 115.
7. Hans-Thies Lehmann, *Postdramatisches Theater: Essay* (Frankfurt am Main: Verlag der Autoren, 1999), p. 11.
8. Michael Kirby, 'The New Theatre', cited in Brooks McNamara and Jill Dolan (eds), *The Drama Review: Thirty Years of the Avant-Garde* (Ann Arbor, MI: University of Michigan Research Press, 1986), pp. 63–4.
9. Christopher Balme, 'Editorial', *Theatre Research International*, vol. 29, no. 1 (March 2004), p. 1.
10. Ibid., p. 1.
11. See the web site at www.robertwilson.com for interesting examples of the integration of traditional graphic and new technologies.
12. In association with the Kent Interactive Digital Design Studio (KiDDS), at the University of Kent, July 2000, see www.kent.ac.uk/sdfva/msnd/design/storyboard/index.htm
13. Maaike Bleeker, 'Look who's Looking! Perspective and the Paradox of Postdramatic Subjectivity', in *Theatre Research International*, vol. 29: 1 (March 2004), p. 40.
14. Baz Kershaw, *The Radical in Performance*, p. 6.
15. Richard Schechner, 'A New Paradigm for Theatre in the Academy', in *Drama Review*, 36: 4 (1992), p. 8.
16. Edward Gordon Craig, 'The Actor and the Über-Marionette' (1907) in *On the Art of the Theatre* (1911) (London: Mercury Books, 1962), p. 61.
17. Lehmann, *Postdramatisches Theater*, p. 288, cited in Bleeker, 'Look who's Looking!' p. 31.
18. Nick Kaye, *Postmodernism and Performance* (London: Macmillan, 1994), p. 23.

Further Reading

The role of scenography and the impact of technology within theatrical production are referred to in many general histories of the theatre – although they are usually considered with a view, primarily, to gaining a better understanding of the theatre's contemporary dramatic literature. In addition, there are a few general histories of scenography, and a number of detailed studies of theatre architecture. There are a few books of technical description and instruction that provide important historical information, but there are very few books that consider the application of specific technologies within theatre and performance. The Selective Bibliography provides details of these, and specifically includes works that have been useful to me in writing this book; and it offers some guidance for those who wish to pursue further study of individual artists and theatre practitioners. In the Selective Bibliography I have indicated with an asterisk those books to which readers may refer should they wish to pursue the basic theme of this book – the fundamental synergy that lies between theatre, scenography, technology and performance.

A Selective Bibliography

Appia, Adolphe, *Music and the Art of the Theatre*, ed. Barnard Hewitt, trans. Robert W. Corrigan and Mary Douglas Dirks (Coral Gables, FL: University of Miami Press, 1962).

Aronson, Arnold, *The History and Theory of Environmental Scenography* (Ann Arbor, MI: UMI Research Press, 1981).

Bablet, Denis, *The Theatre of Gordon Craig*, trans. Daphne Woodward (London: Eyre Methuen, 1966).

——, *Les Révolutions scéniques du XXe siècle* (Paris: Société Internationale d'Art XXe Siècle, 1975).

——, *Revolutions in Stage Design of the XXth Century* (Paris: Léon Amiel, 1977).

——, *Les Voies de la création théâtrale: Mises en scènes, années 20 et 30* (Paris: CNRS Editions, 1979).

——, *Josef Svoboda (1969–70)*, ed. D. Monmarte (Lausanne: Editions L'Age d'Homme, 2004).

Barberis, Maurizio *et al.*, *Mariano Fortuny* (Venezia: Marsilio, 2000).

Bakhtin, Mikhail, *Rabelais and his World*, trans. Helene Iswolsky (Cambridge, MA: Yale University Press, 1968).

Baugh, Christopher, *Garrick and Loutherbourg* (Cambridge: Chadwyck-Healey, 1990).

——, 'Brecht and Stage Design, the *Bühnenbildner* and the *Bühnenbauer*', in Peter Thomson and Sacks Glendyr (eds), *The Cambridge Companion to Brecht* (Cambridge: Cambridge University Press, 1994).

——, 'Stage Design from Loutherbourg to Poel', in Joseph Donohue (ed.), *The Cambridge History of British Theatre*, vol. 2: *1660–1895* (Cambridge: Cambridge University Press, 2004).

Beacham, Richard C., *Adolphe Appia: Texts on Theatre* (London: Routledge, 1993).

——, *Adolphe Appia: Artist and Visionary of the Modern Theatre* (Amsterdam: Harwood Academic, 1994).

Bel Geddes, Norman, *Horizons* (London: Bodley Head, 1934).

Bentham, Fred, *Sixty Years of Light Work* (London: Strand Lighting, 1992).

Bergman, Gösta, *Lighting in the Theatre* (Stockholm: Almqvist & Wiksell, 1977).*

Brandt, George W., *Modern Theories of Drama* (Oxford: Oxford University Press, 1998).

Braun, Edward, *Meyerhold on Theatre* (London: Methuen, 1969).

——, *Meyerhold: A Revolution in Theatre* (London: Methuen, 1995).

Brewster, Ben and Jacobs, Lea, *Theatre to Cinema: Stage Pictorialism and the Early Feature Film* (Oxford: Oxford University Press, 1997).

Brockett, Oscar G. and Findlay, Robert R., *Century of Innovation: A History of European and American Theatre and Drama since 1870* (Englewood Cliffs, NJ: Prentice-Hall, 1973).*

Brook, Peter, *The Empty Space* (London: MacGibbon & Kee, 1968).

——, *The Shifting Point* (London: Methuen, 1988).*

Burian, Jarka, *The Scenography of Joseph Svoboda* (Middletown, CT: Wesleyan University Press, 1971).

——, *Leading Creators of Twentieth-Century Czech Theatre* (London: Routledge, 2002).

Carlson, Marvin, *Places of Performance: The Semiotics of Theatre Architecture* (Ithaca, NY: Cornell University Press, 1989).*

Cave, Richard Allen, *Terence Gray and the Cambridge Festival Theatre* (Cambridge: Chadwyck-Healey, 1980).

Chaudhuri, Una and Fuchs, Elinor (eds), *Land/Scape/Theater* (Ann Arbor, MI: University of Michigan Press, 2002).

Craig, Edward Gordon, *On the Art of the Theatre* (London: Heinemann, 1911; reprint, Mercury Books, 1962).

——, *Towards a New Theatre* (London: J. M. Dent, 1913).

——, *The Theatre Advancing* (London: Constable, 1921).

——, *Scene* (London: Humphrey Milford, Oxford University Press, 1923).

Derrida, Jacques, *Archive Fever*, trans. Eric Prenowitz (Chicago: University of Chicago Press, 1998).

Drain, Richard (ed.), *Twentieth-Century Theatre* (London: Routledge, 1995).

——, *Drama Review: Russian Issue*, vol. 17, no. 1, T57 (New York, 1973).

Fuerst, Walter René and Hume, Samuel J., *Twentieth-Century Stage Decoration*, 2 vols (New York: Alfred A. Knopf, 1929; reprint, Dover Publications, 1967).

Fülöp-Miller, René and Joseph Gregor, *The Russian Theatre, its Character and History*, trans. Paul England (London: Harrap, 1930).

Goodwin, J. (ed.), *British Theatre Design: The Modern Age* (London: Weidenfeld & Nicolson, 1989).

Gray, Camilla, *The Great Experiment: Russian Art, 1863–1922* (London: Thames & Hudson, 1962).

Gropius, Walter and Wensinger, Arthur S. (eds), *The Theater of the Bauhaus* (Baltimore: Johns Hopkins University Press, 1961).

Grotowski, Jerzy, *Towards a Poor Theatre* (London: Methuen, 1969).

Grube, Max, *The Story of the Meininger*, ed. Wendell Cole, trans. Ann Marie Koller (Coral Gables, FL: University of Miami Press, 1963).

Harold Ridge, C., *Stage Lighting* (Cambridge: Heffer & Sons, 1928).

Harrison, Charles and Wood, Paul, *Art in Theory, 1900–1990* (Oxford: Blackwell, 1992).

Hoover, Marjorie L., *Meyerhold and His Set Designers* (New York: Peter Lang, 1988).

Howard, Pamela, *What is Scenography?* (London: Routledge, 2002).

Innes, Christopher, *Avant Garde Theatre, 1892–1992* (London: Routledge, 1993).*

——, *Edward Gordon Craig: A Vision of the Theatre* (Amsterdam: Harwood Academic, 1998).

Innes, Christopher (ed.), *A Sourcebook on Naturalist Theatre* (London: Routledge, 2000).

Kaye, Nick, *Postmodernism and Performance* (London: Macmillan, 1994).

Kershaw, Baz, *The Radical in Performance: Between Brecht and Baudrillard* (London: Routledge, 1999).

Law, Alma, 'Meyerhold's *The Magnanimous Cuckold*', *Drama Review*, T93 (Spring 1982), pp. 61–86.

Leach, Robert and Borovsky, Victor (eds), *A History of Russian Theatre* (Cambridge: Cambridge University Press, 1999).

Leacroft, Richard, *The Development of the English Playhouse* (London: Methuen, 1973).

Leacroft, Richard and Helen, *Theatres and Playhouse* (London: Methuen, 1984).

Levenson, Michael (ed.), *The Cambridge Companion to Modernism* (Cambridge: Cambridge University Press, 1999).

Littlewood, Joan, *Joan's Book: The Autobiography of Joan Littlewood* (London: Methuen, 1994).

Mackintosh, Iain, *Architecture, Actor and Audience* (London: Routledge, 1993).*

Marshall, Norman, *The Other Theatre* (London: John Lehman, 1947).

McAuley, Gay, *Space in Performance* (Ann Arbor, MI: University of Michigan Press, 1999).

McCandless, Stanley, *A Method of Lighting the Stage* (New York, 1932; 4th edn, Theatre Arts Books, 1958).

——, *A Syllabus of Stage Lighting* (New Haven, CT: Drama Books, 1964).

Morgan, Nigel H., *Stage Lighting for Theatre Designers* (London: Herbert Press, 1995).

Mulryne, J. R. and Shewring, Margaret (eds), *Making Space for Theatre: British Architecture and Theatre since 1958* (Stratford-upon-Avon: Mulryne and Shewring, 1995).

——, *Shakespeare's Globe Rebuilt* (Cambridge: Cambridge University Press: 1997).

Napier, Frank, *Noises Off: A Handbook of Sound Effects* (London: Frederick Muller, 1936).

Ogden, Dunbar H., *The International Theatre Exhibition: Amsterdam, 1922* (Amsterdam: Tijdschrift voor Theaterwetenschap), *TTW*, 30, vol. 8, no. 2 (1991).

Pavis, Patrice, *Theatre at the Crossroads of Culture* (London: Routledge, 1992).

Pugliese, Orazio (ed.), *Immagini e Materiali del Laboratorio Fortuny* (Venezia: Marsilio, 1978).

Rees, Terence, *Theatre Lighting in the Age of Gas* (London: Society for Theatre Research, 1978).

Rees, Terence and Wilmore, David (eds), *British Theatrical Patents, 1801–1900* (London: Society for Theatre Research, 1996).

Ried Payne, Darwin, *The Scenographic Imagination* (Carbondale, IL: Southern Illinois University Press, 1981).

Rosenfeld, Sybil, *A Short History of Scene Design in Great Britain* (Oxford: Blackwell, 1973).*

Rudlin, John, *Jacques Copeau* (Cambridge: Cambridge University Press, 1986).

Rudnitsky, Konstantin, *Russian and Soviet Theatre: Tradition and the Avant-Garde*, trans. Roxane Permar (London: Thames & Hudson, 1988).

Rudnitsky, Konstantin, *Meyerhold the Director*, ed. S. Shultze, trans. George Petrov (Ann Arbor, MI: Ardis, 1981).

Russell, D. A., *Theatrical Style: A Visual Approach to Theatre* (Palo Alto, CA: Mayfield, 1976).

Schechner, Richard, 'Six Axioms for Environmental Theatre' (1968), in Brooks McNamara and Jill Dolan (eds), *The Drama Review: Thirty Years of the Avant-Garde* (Ann Arbor, MI: University of Michigan Research Press, 1986), pp. 151–71.

Schmidt, Paul (ed.), *Meyerhold at Work* (Manchester: Carcanet New Press, 1981).

Slonim, Marc, *Russian Theatre from the Empire to the Soviets* (London: Methuen, 1963).

Smith, Anthony, *Orghast at Persepolis* (London: Eyre Methuen, 1972).

Stanislavski, Konstantin, *My Life in Art* (London: Geoffrey Bles, 1924).

Stanislavski, Konstantin, *Stanislavsky on the Art of the Stage*, ed. David Magarshack (London: Faber & Faber, 1950).

Stokes, J., *Resistible Theatres: Enterprise and Experiment in the Late Nineteenth Century* (London: Paul Elek, 1972).

Svoboda, Josef, *The Secrets of Theatrical Space*, ed. and trans. Jarka Burian (New York: Applause Theatre Books, 1993).*

Tidworth, Simon, *Theatres: An Architectural and Cultural History* (New York: Praeger, 1973).*

Todd, Andrew and Lecat, Jean-Guy, *The Open Circle: Peter Brook's Theatre Environments* (London: Faber & Faber, 2003).

Trimingham, Melissa, 'Oskar Schlemmer's Research Practice at the Dessau Bauhaus', in *Theatre Research International*, vol. 29, no. 2 (2004), pp. 128–42.

Van Gyseghem, André, *Theatre in Soviet Russia* (London: Faber & Faber, 1943).

Van Norman Baer, Nancy (ed.), *Theatre in Revolution: Russian Avant-Garde Stage Design, 1913–1935* (New York: Thames & Hudson and the Fine Arts Museums of San Francisco, 1991).

Volbach, Walther, *Adolphe Appia: The Prophet of the Modern Theatre* (Middletown, CT: Wesleyan University Press, 1968).

Wiles, David, *A Short History of Western Performance Space* (Cambridge: Cambridge University Press, 2003).*

Willett, John, *The Theatre of Erwin Piscator: Half a Century of Politics in the Theatre* (London: Eyre Methuen, 1978).

——, *Caspar Neher: Brecht's Designer* (London: Methuen, 1986).

Williams, David (ed.), *Collaborative Theatre: The Théâtre du Soleil Sourcebook* (London: Routledge, 1999).

Worrall, Nick, 'Meyerhold Directs Gogol's *Government Inspector*', in *Theatre Quarterly*, vol. 2, no. 7 (1972), pp. 75–95.

Index

Page numbers in **bold** denote illustrations; page numbers in *italics* denote notes.